VIDEOBLOGGING
BEFORE
YOUTUBE

TRINE BJØRKMANN BERRY

Theory on Demand #27
Videoblogging Before YouTube
Trine Bjørkmann Berry

Cover design: Katja van Stiphout
Design and EPUB development: Rosie Underwood

Published by the Institute of Network Cultures, Amsterdam, 2018

ISBN: 978-94-92302-22-9

Contact
Institute of Network Cultures
Phone: +3120 5951865
Email: info@networkcultures.org
Web: http://www.networkcultures.org

This publication is available through various print on demand services and freely downloadable from http://networkcultures.org/publications

Trine Bjørkman Berry has given us a rich and illuminating narrative of the communities, aesthetics and technologies of videoblogging before YouTube - revealing it to be a site of mundane expression, cultural innovation and social hope. At a moment when the digital media imagination seems to have been captured by corporate behemoths, we need more stories like this.

Jean Burgess, Professor of Digital Media and Director of Digital Media Research Centre, Queensland University of Technology, Australia

Trine Bjørkmann Berry's compellingly written and highly original study of the historically located and embodied, medium-specific and cultural-technical practices of the early-adopter video blogging community eloquently fills a significant gap in previous studies of online video. Through her painstaking ethnographic, historical, aesthetic and media-archeological research she successfully argues that, in order to maintain critical understandings of the media practices and theories we observe around us today, it is essential to remember and understand the media practices of the past, even or perhaps especially those that led to 'dead-ends' and 'failed' media forms. This is an essential study that will change the ways in which we think about past, present and future online creative communities and digital platforms.

Catherine Grant Professor of Digital Media and Screen Studies, Birkbeck, University of London

Bjørkmann Berry's sharp, timely and endlessly fascinating book explodes a common assumption that the world of YouTube celebrities, online memes and 'haul videos' is horribly banal and ephemeral. At its heart is a revealing ethnographic analysis of the practices of videobloggers. This is an ambitious, richly-layered and resonant study: alive to broader aesthetic, technical, political, and cultural questions, it reveals the complexities and significance of online video cultures more generally. By charting the emergence of these media 'hybrids' and immersing us in their fast-mutating subcultures, Bjørkmann Berry forces us to look well beyond the obvious example of YouTube - and requires us to think afresh about the 'newness' of all so-called 'new media'. Such historical sensibility is a rare commodity and should make her Videoblogging Before YouTube vital reading for anyone with an interest in contemporary media.

David Hendy, Professor of Media and Cultural History, University of Sussex.

This critical history of the present, and disruptive intervention into the progress narratives of new media technologies, is crucial reading for anyone in media studies. Trine Bjørkmann Berry's Videoblogging Before Youtube is a fascinating, in depth and meticulous cultural history of an important moment in the history of digital media. It examines the use of video in its vernacular, everyday and experimental formats in a moment of transition. The book brings together richly ethnographic material in relation to media practices of videoblogging and interrogates this authoritatively and beautifully, in relation to film and digital media theory. It shows us the value of thinking about media futures in relation to their histories, and the moments of practice, disruption and appropriation that are so important in understanding the current media landscape.

Kate O'Riordan, Professor of Digital Culture, University of Sussex, UK.

For my parents and for my children.

The film of tomorrow appears to me as even more personal than an individual and autobiographical novel, like a confession, or a diary. The young filmmakers will express themselves in the first person and will relate what has happened to them. It may be the story of their first love or their most recent; of their political awakening; the story of a trip, a sickness, their military service, their marriage, their last vacation...and it will be enjoyable because it will be true and new... The film of tomorrow will resemble the person who made it, and the number of spectators will be proportional to the number of friends the director has. The film of tomorrow will be an act of love.

– Francois Truffaut, 1957.

ACKNOWLEDGEMENTS

Writing a book is never a solo expedition; it enrols other people, some voluntary, some through need and others by accident. This book reflects a project that has been running since 2005, and owes a debt of gratitude to many generous, inspiring and thoughtful friends, associates and networks who by good fortune I was able to meet, bounce ideas off, discuss and argue with along the way. During the course of this research I had to manage the pressures of my own everyday life experiences from pregnancy to relocation, from sickness to health. To all who made time for me I would like to give my deepest thanks.

Specifically, I would like to thank Geert Lovink for his generous help, support and patience while I finished the final drafts of this book. I would also like to thank him for pushing me to write this book in the first place; to Miriam Rasch and everyone else at the Institute for Network Cultures for all the help and support along the way; to my copyeditors, Rosie Underwood and David M. Berry; to Marcus Leis Allion for designing the diagram in chapter 4. A number of people have helped me in a number of ways at different stages of writing this book and in particular I would like to mention Arne Andreassen, Nils August Andresen, Thomas Austin, Caroline Bassett, Sarah Baumber, Matthew Beetar, David M. Berry, Rikke Bjørkmann, Tullen Bjørkmann, Michael Bull, Jean Burgess, Hanne Castberg Tresselt, Cécile Chevalier, Gemma Cobb, Amelia Culliford, Soraya Cotwald-Ray, Anders Fagerjord, M. Beatrice Fazi, Natalie Flynn, David Gauntlet, Alison Gibb, Claudia Ginsburg, Catherine Grant, Lucy Haynes, Hegel, David Hendy, Tanya Kant, Raquel Leis Allion, Tine Levin Granlund, Adrian Miles, Gemma Quinton-Moulds, Caroline Nikiforov-Clarke, The Pelham Arms, Jane Perry, Kate O'Riordan, Elizabeth Reed, Laura Reynolds, Sara Russet, Hedda Rønnevig, Shirley Tang, Rachel Tavenor, Daniela Tepe and Cecilia Virlombier. I would also like to thank Dr Adam MacDermaid-Gordon and everyone at the Royal Sussex County Hospital for looking after me. I would also like to thank the wonderful institution that is the British NHS.

This book would not be possible without the very generous members of the videoblogging community, who not only welcomed me into their lives when I signed up for the videoblogging email list in August 2005, but who have helpfully shared their insight and experiences with me over the course of many years. In particular I would like to thank Richard BF, Cheryl Colan, Roxanne Darling, Jay Dedman, Loiez Deniel, Zadi Diaz, Juan Falla, Steve Garfield, Jen Gouvea, Gena Hackett, Richard Hall, Bekah Havens, Ryanne Hodson, Rupert Howe, David Howell, Raymond M. Kristiansen, Daniel Liss, Casey McKinnon Jan Mcloughlin, Paris Marashi, Mary Matthews, Erin Nealey, Erik Nelson, Gromik Nicholas, Andreas Haugstrup Pedersen, Susan Pitman, Jennifer Proctor, Adam Quirk, Sam Reinsew, Charlene Rule, Markus Sandy, Mica Scalin, Brittany Shoot, Enric Teller and Michael Verdi.

Through what has been a rather tough year, my family have been patient and understanding, and I would like to thank my husband David for being there through all of it. Lastly, no words can describe the love and joy I get from my three wonderful children, Helene, Henrik Isak and Hedda Emilie Davidsdatter. This is for them.

T.B.B.

Lewes, 2018.

CONTENTS

1. SITUATING VIDEOBLOGGING

This book is about a particular moment in media history when the internet switched dramatically from a mostly textual medium to a fully multimedia one. At first the revolutionary potential of this digital transformation took place under the surface, indeed most people were oblivious to the changes taking place. Today, we take for granted the delivery of different media forms streaming seamlessly across the web, just as much as we take for granted the seemingly unlimited storage aspects for photo and video. However, back in the early 2000s standards were weak and complicated, bandwidth was slow and erratic, and storage was miniscule compared to today's internet. One could say that we lived in a different media universe, and in important respects this would be true. Throughout this book I revisit this often forgotten world that was pre-social media, pre-YouTube and most importantly, refreshingly amateur in its experimentation and aesthetic. My focus is on what was known as 'online video' and what soon became known as *videoblogging*. I want to demonstrate the ways in which this practice which was mostly small-scale, self-funded and bottom-up, a truly experimental media form, was an important predecessor to, and anticipated, our current media ecology.

The story of online video is usually said to begin at 8:27 pm on Saturday, April 23, 2005, when a 19 second long video clip entitled *Me at the Zoo* was uploaded to YouTube, making it the first video published online through the YouTube platform and shared around the world through the website.[1] This video featured a short recording of one of the YouTube founders, Jawed Karim, on a visit to a local zoo. The video was notable for its mundane sense of the everyday. As the New York Times noted, 'the video has a certain pleasing obviousness. "Here we are in front of the, uh, elephants," Karim says. "They have really, really, really long" — suspense, but no double entendre — "trunks". Karim turns to face the elephants as if to confirm his observation. "And that's pretty much all there is to say."'[2] Nonetheless, as of January 2018, the video has received over 44 million views and nearly four hundred thousand comments from viewers.[3] This video represents a key moment in media history, however it was not the first, and perhaps not the most important video to be posted online.

In the years since, online video has been transformed from an expensive to distribute media-form to one which can be networked, shared, downloaded and re-used with ease. Digital videos, a kind of 'vernacular avant-garde', can now be found in a variety of short-form genres, from family videos to haul videos (documenting things people have bought) to unboxing videos (people opening the wrapper from their new purchases) and from a new type of YouTube

---

1   The banality of the title and content pointed in some ways to early video on the internet was predominantly documentary/biographical or self-consciously aesthetic. As *The New York Times* observed in 2009, 'this founding clip makes and repeats a larger point, too, with every pixel: Video — trivial or important — can now quickly and at no cost be published, broadcast and shared 'Me at the Zoo' also sets a style standard for the classic YouTube video: visually surprising, narratively opaque, forthrightly poetic' Virginia Heffernan, 'Uploading the Avant-Garde', *The New York Times*, 3 September 2009, http://www.nytimes.com/2009/09/06/magazine/06FOB-medium- t.html?_r=0.

2   Heffernan, 'Uploading the Avant-Garde'.

3   Including the very first, by the user Tim Leister, a friend of Karim who used the username COBALTGRUV, and who ironically described this founding video as 'Interesting…'.

celebrity to amusing 'meme' videos. Indeed, one of the most watched videos on YouTube is an amateur family video titled *Charlie bit my finger* which has had more than 857 million views as of January 2018. Between 2009 and 2010, it became a viral hit and temporarily became the most viewed video on YouTube. It has since been overtaken by a host of music videos like Psy's *Gangham Style* (3 billion views), Wiz Khalifa's *See You Again* (3.3 billion views) and Luis Fonsi's *Despacito* (4.6 billion views). Today, music videos occupy at least the top 5 most viewed videos on YouTube, signaling a shift in digital video consumption from amateur to professional, often corporate sponsored, content. This further highlights the ways in which the internet continues to move in a more commercial direction. Video is now generating serious income for a number of different participants but also, and importantly, for YouTube itself.

Rewind to 2005, however, and YouTube was losing money. Despite being nearly exhausted by the massive costs of infrastructure, bandwidth and storage, YouTube nonetheless grew at a furious pace from 2005 to 2006, until it was bought by Google, a then seemingly puzzling purchase for a search engine giant. The cost was an outrageous figure of $1.65 billion (£2.2 billion in 2017), which made its founders instant millionaires. By 2010 YouTube hosted more than 120 million videos and 300 million accounts, creating new viral videos and must-watch clips daily which would be circulated by email and other media.[4] As *The Economist* noted, by 2014 'viewers are spoiled for premium-quality choice… and remarkably [spend] close to an hour watching videos online'[5] per day, in comparison to the 4.5 hours spent watching television. In 2016, online-video advertising in the US was forecast to rise to $10 billion, and Forbes forecasts that the US digital marketing spend will close in on $120 billion by 2021. This demonstrates the prescience of Google's move into streaming media and highlights the way in which audiences have adapted to online video and transformed the possibilities for its monetization. From start-up, to incorporation into an internet giant, this narrative about the story of digital video is the dominant way in which we understand video becoming part of the internet.[6]

In contrast, in this book I argue that one of the key moments in the development of the practices of online video actually begins *before* the founding of YouTube, as indeed do many of the practices and aesthetics that YouTube's founders made use of in their early video work. In order to examine the often forgotten pre-history to YouTube's later dominance of online video, I examine the earlier moment of community practice and video-making. In some ways my approach can be understood as complementary to a media archaeology, in as much as it seeks to uncover what we might call the 'failed' project of videoblogging, and is certainly informed by some of the insights of that method. Not only in seeking to uncover past technologies and old media forms but also using such media to think about contemporary digital culture. Indeed, I share a 'discontent with "canonized" narratives of media culture and history… that widely endorsed accounts of contemporary media culture and media histories alike often tell only selected part of the story, and not necessarily correct and relevant parts.'[7] As

4   Hermione Hoby and Tom Lamont, 'How YouTube made superstars out of everyday people', *The Guardian*, 11 April 2010, http://www.theguardian.com/technology/2010/apr/11/youtube-web-video-stars.
5   The Economist 'New Tube', *The Economist*, May 3-9 (2014).
6   Indeed, GAFA (Google, Amazon, Facebook and Apple) and related platforms now dominate the web and our experience of the Internet.
7   Erkki Huhtamo and Jussi Parikka, *Media Archaeology: Approaches, Applications, and Implications*,

such, I want to add that this book is *a* history of videoblogging, and by no means *the* history of videoblogging, just as it aims to position itself in *a* history of some media, not *the* history of all media. It aims to highlight the continuities and ruptures and 'construct alternative histories of suppressed, neglected, and forgotten media that do not point teleologically to the present media-cultural condition as their "perfection".'[8] Hence, this book uses non-institutionally archived historical resources, collected as part of the project, and focuses on different facets of online moving-image culture and its technological conditions of possibility to present a corrective to the overly YouTube oriented histories.[9]

Nonetheless, the research materials on which this book draws form an archive of sorts – a distributed network of texts (interviews, emails, websites), memory (the videobloggers and others, materialised in texts but also through the affective re-experience of the films), and a large collection of videos. The videos are more dispersed than they were in 2005, particularly after Blip.tv, one of the main sites for hosting videoblogs, closed its doors in November 2013, but they are still mostly locatable, although not always straightforward to find. YouTube, which was considered such a poor platform by the videobloggers back in 2005, has ironically remained more stable as a site for storing, finding and re-discovering videoblogs – some videobloggers have even retrospectively uploaded their old films to YouTube.[10]

I explore this early online video history and seek to understand it within its historical context as a creative and experimental community of video-makers that has been largely forgotten. The research project itself was originally conceived of in those early days, from around 2001, when the internet was rife with the ideological promise of creative freedom for rugged individuals (usually gendered as a man), entrepreneurial figures soon to become dominant on the web. A cyberlibertarian ideal, given to neoliberal ideas and venture capital funding, was soon to be seen making money on the 'information superhighway'. These individuals knew how to take advantage of the wild west of the internet as it turned into what Tim O'Reilly called Web 2.0 – using what Barbrook and Cameron had previously described as the Californian Ideology; Information technologies are claimed to 'empower the individual, enhance personal freedom, and radically reduce the power of the nation-state. Existing social, political and legal power structures will wither away to be replaced by unfettered interactions between autonomous individuals and their software.'[11]

London: University of California Press, 2011: 3.

8   Huhtamo and Parikka, *Media Archaeology: Approaches, Applications, and Implications*.

9   The lack of a historical archive is a major handicap to undertaking this kind of research project with early online video, relying in large part on the personal collection amassed by the researcher, and in some repositories, such the Internet Archive, or personal collections of the video-bloggers. A large cultural history has already potentially been lost due to the difficulty of persuading traditional archiving bodies to take internet culture seriously, and also to understand that it is more than a textual and still-image medium, requiring a complex set of technologies to be taken into consideration, such as the multiplicity of video codecs that were used for early work.

10   For a similar exploration of groups and communities of video makers who actively avoided YouTube as their main platform for distribution, see John Hondros, *Ecologies of Internet Video: Beyond YouTube*. New York: Routledge, 2018.

11   Richard Barbrook and Andy Cameron, 'The Californian Ideology', 1996, http://www.hrc.wmin.ac.uk/theory-californianideology-main.html.

This was the idea of seeing the internet as a marketplace, populated by self-actualising rational actors in a competitive free market. For example, John Perry Barlow famously argued
in his influential article *A Declaration of the Independence of Cyberspace* that cyberspace,
immaterial in form and thus a 'civilisation of the Mind' should not – could not – succumb to
the rules and regulations of the world of 'flesh and steel'.[12] The notion of the rational, individual actor, an entrepreneur, was further popularised through the work of a number of writers,
for example Eric Raymond and Lawrence Lessig.[13] It became an influential way to conceive
of the political economic structures of the internet, and as Lanier later argued, the internet
'needs entrepreneurs to come up with the products that are competing in the first place. In
other words, clever individuals, the heroes of the marketplace, ask the questions which are
answered by collective behaviour.'[14] But of course, in reality,

> The Net's development was almost completely dependent on the much reviled Amer-
> ican federal government…. large amounts of tax payers' dollars went into building the
> [internet] infrastructure and subsidising the cost of using its services. At the same time,
> many of the key [internet] programs and applications were invented either by hobby-
> ists or by professionals working in their spare-time.[15]

But we should also remember that the early internet was also populated by cyborgs, cyber-god-
desses, feminists and queer bodies.[16] And for others, the internet and the web offered something more than a digital market, a place of contact, communion and community – and this
is where the videoblogging story really starts.

Indeed, videoblogging was also hugely reliant on the collective resources that produced the
internet and its technologies. It was created through volunteerism and the contributions
of videobloggers' work towards a notion of community. Which is not to say there were not
aspects of capitalism inherent in the development of these cultural practices and artifacts,
in fact, some of the early pioneers were keen to create standalone possible 'products' that
might be later sold or licensed in the creative economy. However, there remained an early
commitment to free software, open source, community-oriented values and the excitement
of building not only the technical infrastructure for videoblogging, but also a new aesthetic
and grammar of video culture. These are the issues that fuelled videoblogging in its early
days and drive the focus in this book.

We should remember, however, that the claims of technological and creative freedom often
mask the gendered reality of an internet political economy that favoured the already wealthy,

12   John Perry Barlow, A Cyberspace Independence Declaration, 1996, http://w2.eff.org/Censorship/
     Internet_censorship_bills/barlow_0296.declaration.
13   Eric S. Raymond, *The Cathedral & the Bazaar*, Beijing: O'Reilly Media, 2001, Lawrence Lessig, *Free
     Culture*, London: Penguin Press, 2003.
14   Jaron Lanier, DIGITAL MAOISM: The Hazards of the New Online Collectivism, *Edge*, 2006, http://edge.
     org/conversation/digital-maoism- the-hazards-of-the-new-online-collectivism.
15   Barbrook and Cameron, 'The Californian Ideology'.
16   Donna Haraway, 'A cyborg manifesto: Science, technology, and socialist-feminism in the late 20th
     century.' *The international handbook of virtual learning environments* (2006).

connected, or famous – indeed, the practices that emerged were sometimes less about creative freedom, and more about power, technical skill and know-how. The emergent practices that developed on the internet after 2000 were reliant on existing knowledge of how the technologies worked and could be applied, a gendered technological environment and political economy. Although this book does not formally adopt a political economic approach, it is clear that wealth and capital were hugely influential and technological know-how was unevenly distributed between the participants.[17]

There are a few key issues I wish to highlight in relation to this. These are important, and underlie and inform this work. Firstly, many of the videobloggers I will go on to discuss self-identify as amateur. By amateur I gesture towards the idea that one does something without getting paid, that instead of monetary recompense, the personal satisfaction of having created (or achieved) something is assumed to be sufficient reward. In the digital age, the definition of being an amateur includes being someone who pursues a passion for personal, rather than professional, pleasure; someone who lacks either the knowledge or means to produce professional–quality work; or someone who labours without expecting to be paid.[18] The definition of a media amateur can also describe 'technically interested private individuals who acquire and develop technology before commercial use of the technology is even recognisable'.[19] In other words, being an amateur may not be purely about doing something you love, for free, but is also linked to the access to and knowledge of a practice and is usually contrasted with professional work. It also refers in some sense to the notion of the 'early adopter'. The definition of amateur also needs to be contextualised and historicised, and in her seminal study, Patricia Zimmerman shows how the concept of the amateur has shifted historically. She locates the origins of amateur film within a particular, historically specific romanticized vision of the bourgeois nuclear family, 'thereby amputating its more resistant economic and political potential for critique'. For Zimmermann, amateur film 'occupies one of the central contradictions of communications in the twentieth century: on the one hand, domination and consumption; on the other, resistance and hope'.[20] This is a crucial starting point for thinking about the interplay of amateur media forms and new digital media.

Secondly, understanding of how early adopters of videoblogging practices engaged with the nascent technologies available to them is central to this book. This contributes to an understanding of how their practices developed and were conceptualised, alongside new kinds of visual tropes and styles that emerged from their practices and experimentations.[21]

---

17   Geography might play a part here too, as observed by Rupert Howe: 'Even though I was a geek, I was
      one of those people that used to think that people who spent time talking to other people on the internet
      were sad. That attitude prevailed among the general population until Facebook blew it away. I'd say it
      was much more prevalent in the UK than in the US. Later when we met in person, Jay Dedman and
      I spoke about this. I said that people in the UK were suspicious of technology and geeks. He said,
      'Americans think that technology is the only thing that's going to save us'.
18   Michael Z. Newman, 'Ze Frank and the poetics of Web video', *First Monday,* 13.5. 2008.
19   Brigit Richard, 'Media Masters and Grassroots Art 2.0 on YouTube', in Geert Lovink and Sabine
      Niederer (eds) , Amsterdam: The Institute for Network Cultures, 2008: 142.
20   Patricia Zimmerman, *Reel Families: A social history of Amateur Film*, Indiana University Press, 1995: ix-x.
21   Videoblogging as practice is not uniquely limited to the videoblogging community explored in this book,
      and one could argue that videoblogging has multiple of definitions and uses, however, in this book the

New, often custom-written digital technologies and the emergence of new forms of amateur online communication, sharing and culture, crystallised in the practice of what they began to call videoblogging. A videoblogger was defined as someone who produces and maintains a videoblog, and is also likely to self-identify as a 'videoblogger'. One of the main distinctions drawn between someone posting videos to YouTube (here referred to as 'vloggers') and a videoblogger, is that the videoblogger maintains her own blog. This was usually individually designed, with custom blog-rolls (or vlog-rolls), archives and about pages, where they post videos weekly or monthly.[22]

Thirdly, the terms videoblogger and videoblogging share their history with terms such as life-casting, video-streaming, video-podcasting and vlogging. It has become common to use the term videoblogging within academia when referring to the practice of posting home-made videos to video sharing sites such as Dailymotion, Vimeo or YouTube, but there are variations of the terms in use. Adrian Miles first referred to 'vogs' in his early writings and experiments with online video though he also refers to 'desktop video'. Lange consistently refers to 'vlogging' and 'vloggers' in her work. Burgess and Green use both 'videoblogging' (and 'videobloggers') and 'vlogging' (and 'vloggers') to describe the practice of posting videos to YouTube, Vend-erbeeken refers to 'Web Video', Willett to 'moblogs' and Treske defines 'the time and space that we as human beings share with 'video'... a video sphere'.[23] Despite these differences, there is a certain agreement in definition of the term(s) as videoblogging emerged as the social practice of posting videos on an internet blog, originally a form of online journal called a web-log. Thus, a videoblog is a blog that uses video as its main form of expression. This definition is complicated by the emergence of vlogs on YouTube, where vlogging would grow to include anyone posting a video of themselves online but also encompassed other kinds of user-generated content in video form. To distinguish between posting video on YouTube and within the videoblogging community, and following the practice of the videobloggers them-selves, I refer to videos posted to YouTube as vlogging and vloggers, and in the videoblogging community as videoblogging and videobloggers.

Fourthly, videoblogging practices drew on blogging, on audio podcasting, and the sharing of photos which had emerged on sites such as Flickr. By the mid-2000s, the hype surround-

---

terms 'videoblogging' and 'videoblogger' are used to specifically to denote the members of the early-adopter community under examination, in the period 2004-2009.

22   Today videoblogging has come to be strongly associated with posting video to YouTube, and a much easier process than all the technical know-how required in the early days.

23   Jean Burgess and Joshua Green, YouTube, Digital Media and Society Series, London: Polity, 2009; Rebekah Willett, 'Always on: Camera Phones, Video Production and Identity', in David Buckingham and Rebekah Willett (eds) Video cultures, London: Palgrave McMillan, 2009; Andreas Treske The Inner Lives of Video Spheres, Amsterdam: Institute for Network Cultures, 2013; Adrian Miles, Vogma, a Manifesto, http://hypertext.rmit.edu.au/vog/manifesto/, 2000; Adrian Miles, Softvideography: Digital Video as Postliterate Practice, in Byron Hawk, David M. Rieder and Ollie Oviedo (eds) Small Tech: The Culture of Digital Tools, Minneapolis: University of Minnesota Press, 2008; Patricia Lange, The Vulnerable Video Blogger: Promoting Social Change through Intimacy, The Scholar and Feminist Online, volume 5, no. 2, www.barnard.edu/sfonline, 2007; Robrecht Vanderbeeken, Web Video and the Screen as a Mediator and Generator of Reality, in Geert Lovink and Rachel Somers Miles (eds) Video Vortex Reader II: Moving Images Beyond YouTube, Amsterdam: Institute for Networked Cultures, 2011.

ing the concept of Web 2.0 was starting to make its way from tech journalism and into the mainstream media, and the 'participatory turn' in media was heralded as the next big thing.[24] In this fervent environment, early videobloggers sought to create new art, documentary, film, technology and, in some cases, a hint of micro-celebrity.

By bringing these issues together, this book contributes to our understanding of the early practices surrounding online video production through a cultural history. By developing a critical understanding of how the practices developed and were used by the early adopters of videoblogging it outlines a new cultural-technical hybrid. It outlines an historical ethnography of the sociotechnical practices between 2004 and 2009. A running thread throughout concerns the challenges of studying a history such as the one I am analysing here, complicated by the fact that the empirical data is historically very recent. The book is also a reflection on the digital present, touching, as it does on many practices that were absorbed into 'new' technologies (these will no doubt be out of date within a few years too) such as Instagram stories and Snapchat.

I also want to challenge the claim that technology, especially internet technology, is 'participatory', this is a form of technological determinism. I want to restate that people make their own culture, but not always in the media ecologies of their own choosing. Although it is important to uncover the way in which hype and excitement about these possibilities served to actually inspire individuals and collectives seeking to build new technologies, we need to remain firmly focussed on the way in which people make their own history, their own culture and their own communities. By contesting fairly common descriptions of cultural practice on the internet, and providing a cultural history that creates dominant narratives, particularly the smooth corporate tales of mass market success and profitability, I hope to offer an alternative to, and corrective for, these celebratory descriptions. Today, with the success of massive socio-technical platforms such as YouTube, Blogger and Soundcloud, many of the smaller communities of practice across the internet, some of which were part of creating many of the practices around them that we now take for granted, have either been forgotten, disbanded or co-opted into corporate platforms. This highlights the importance of documenting these early cultural practices and communities. For example, the upset caused by Yahoo's decision to shut down the social community GeoCities in 2009 led internet archivist Jason Scoll to pose the following question: 'is user content a right, a treasure, a heritage, a meaningful part of the human condition?'.[25] This question also lies at the heart of this book, preoccupied as it is with a history of a part of digital culture that is at risk of being forgotten, and which is becoming harder and harder to uncover due to the decisions by hosting companies to mass-delete large volumes of data from their servers and by contemporary accounts to overstate the contribution of corporate platforms at the expense of grassroots organising and creativity.[26]

---

24   Henry Jenkins, *Convergence Culture. Where Old and New Media Collide*, New York: New York University Press, 2006.

25   Laura E. Hall, 'What Happens When Digital Cities Are Abandoned?', *The Atlantic*, 2014, http://www.theatlantic.com/technology/archive/2014/07/what-happens-when-digital-cities-are-abandoned/373941/.

26   This highlights the importance of current work on web archives, see for instance Niels Brügger 'Web history and social media', in *The SAGE Handbook of Social Media*, Jean Burgess, Alice Marwick and Thomas Poell (eds) London : Sage Publications, Incorporated, 2018, pp. 196-212, but also the work of Olia Lialina, 'A Vernacular Web, The Indigenous and The Barbarians', talk at the Decade of Web

Despite a large volume of writing on YouTube, the use of online video in political campaigns and so forth, little has been written about the everyday practices of vernacular online video production at the turn of the millennium. These practitioners and artists avoided the emerging dominant platforms of YouTube and Vimeo, indeed they offered a direct critique to these giant aggregating systems. Videoblogging was the result of the rapid growth in digital technologies and the relative cheapness of new digital equipment for recording, storing and sharing data. This increased availability of digital media technologies, recording and editing software, networking platforms and distribution tools ignited a flourishing of creativity amongst amateur and semi-professional media creators, much of which converged (at the time) under the umbrella of either 'citizen journalism' or 'the creative consumer'.[27]

In 2004, a group of videobloggers came together to form a community of practice originally based primarily around individual websites and an email group. In subsequent chapters, I explore the contours of this community through interviews with a group of users (33 individuals in total, self-identified as 16 men and 17 women), and close reading of the technologies available to, utilised by and sometimes created by them.[28] I also critically engage with the discourses surrounding these technologies and their practices and artifacts. I look at not just the material underpinnings of the video practices, but the practices themselves and the aesthetic these practices manifested.

Briefly, as a quick background to the book, I want to highlight the main empirical resources that were drawn on in the development of the argument. Firstly, I undertook semi-structured interviews to explore the interplay between the technologies used in videoblogging as moving-image culture, and the co-production of identity, community and critical technical practice that developed unique short-form narratives, aesthetics and meanings.[29] Secondly, I use historical data specific to videoblogging, such as archived email lists, articles and books

Design Conference in Amsterdam, January 2005, http://art.teleportacia.org/observation/vernacular/ . It is also worth mentioning the Internet Archive (http://arhive.org), founded in 1996 by Brewster Kahle, which is one of the earliest video archive or storage websites for video. Kahle has been committed to building a full archive of the internet, storing every webpage and providing a history of the internet through the Way-Back Machine. Referred to only as 'The Archive', this has the potential to be perhaps the most lasting of all the video archiving sites. It is still possible to find videoblogs from this period in these archives. Many videobloggers used the archive to host their earliest videos (before the founding of Blip.tv, another video-hosting site) and many continued to cross-post their films there for many years, as a backup. However, the majority did not, which means much of the early videoblogging archive is already lost. Cross-posting was an important videoblogger practice of uploading the same video to a number of different repositories and hosting sites in order to spread the risk of one of the sites going bankrupt or merely disappearing without notice from the web. It was also practiced as a way of spreading content to wider audiences.

27   Luke Goode 'Social news, citizen journalism and democracy', *New Media & Society,* 11.8 (2009): pp. 1287-1305; Jean Burgess, *Vernacular Creativity and New Media,* PhD Diss. Creative Industries Faculty, University of Technology, Queensland, 2007: 11.

28   User is here used to refer to 'active internet contributors, who put in a 'certain amount of creative effort' which is 'created outside of professional routines and platforms'', cited in José van Dijck, 'Users like you? Theorizing agency in user-generated content', *Media, Culture & Society,* 31.1 (2009) p. 41.

29   Phil Agre, 'Toward a critical technical practice: Lessons learned in trying to reform AI', *Bridging the Great Divide: Social Science, Technical Systems, and Cooperative Work, Mahwah, NJ: Erlbaum,* (1997): pp. 131-157.

(written at and around the time by the videobloggers themselves) to develop a critical technical and cultural understanding of how the cultural-technical practice of videoblogging emerged and developed. Lastly, I combine this historical material with rich ethnographic data gathered from interviews and participant observation of the videoblogging community, and apply this knowledge to a selection of videoblogs to gain a deeper understanding of the aesthetic of what I call the short-form digital film. To this end, I asked the following questions; how did early communities of practice and related cultural forms crystallise around digital video on the internet between 2004-2009?; why did the technical-cultural assemblage of the videoblog emerge as a specific instance of short-form digital film, and how was the community around this media-form sustained?; and how did the videobloggers understand and conceptualise their own practice and the co-construction necessary in creating the conditions of possibility for videoblog work, sharing and community building? These questions inform my work and act as a heuristic for the discussions in the book.

The concept of 'community' used here probably requires some explanation. Benedict Anderson argued that all communities are in some sense 'imagined' and that throughout history various forms of communication media have played an important role in determining the different styles these communities have taken.[30] I argue that the videoblogging community can be understood similarly, although my meaning of community is defined in terms of the weak ties made possible by the internet, rather than the nation-state community that Anderson was interested in. Similarly, in early discourses surrounding the internet, the term 'virtual community' – first coined by Howard Rheingold – was often liberally applied to any group of people convening online around shared topics of interest. It follows, therefore, that the concept of 'virtual community' is open to a variety of interpretations at a variety of moments. That technologies affect social relations is also not a new idea. Already in 1990, Ursula Franklin announced herself 'overawed by the way in which technology has acted to reorder and restructure social relations, not only affecting the relations between social groups, but also the relations between nations and individuals'.[31] The term virtual community may seem somewhat out-dated today, as we now tend to think of groups of people who meet and socialise online as operating across social networks, yet to historically position videoblogging requires the utilization of certain concepts that were used at the time, such as 'community', 'cross-post', 'meet-up', and so forth. Social networking sites such as Facebook, Twitter and Instagram either did not exist or were in a very early development in the period I am looking at.[32] Although the videoblog community did gradually migrate over to these platforms, the early history of the community was organised in a very different way with very different technologies.

---

30   Maria Bakardjieva and Andrew Feenberg, 'Involving the Virtual Subject: Conceptual, Methodological and Ethical Dimensions', *Journal of Ethics and Information Technology*, 2.4 (2004): pp. 233-240. See also Benedict Anderson, *Imagined communities: Reflections on the origin and spread of nationalism*. London: Verso Books, 2006.

31   Ursula Franklin, *The Real World of Technology*, Ontario: Anansi, 1990, p.13. See also Sherry Turkle, *Life on the Screen*, London: Simon and Schuster, 2011; Sherry Turkle, *Alone together: Why we expect more from technology and less from each other*, London: Hachette UK, 2017.

32   For instance, Facebook was founded in February 2004, but didn't open registration to other universities until October 2005, and to the wider public in September 2006. Twitter launched in March 2006. Instagram was first released on the iTunes app store in October 2010.

In many ways, this book started by attempting to engage with and capture a rapidly changing "digital present" in which new technologies were announced glorified and abandoned on a yearly, if not monthly basis. Many articles, papers and books published at the time shared a certain naïve optimism about the potential of new digital technologies, seen for instance in Jenkins exploration of participatory culture which lauded digital technologies for their ability to bring people together and empower them to produce and consume content in completely new ways. As he later put it, 'a participatory culture is one which not only lowers the barriers to participation but also creates strong social incentives to produce and share when one produces with others'.[33] In some ways, today we are less likely to reproduce these overly optimistic observations, in a time when the reality of participation looks a lot more like surveillance than freedom.

When I started planning this study in 2005, the mainstream media, as well as media studies itself, was charged with anticipation about the new participatory turn in online culture, as well as excitement about 'being digital', 'life on the screen', online communities, etc.[34] The promise of cheaper technologies, smoother learning curves and easier access to both digital technologies and the internet itself, spurred an excitement about a condition of possibility within digital culture that would somehow aid creativity and increase participation among users. Linked to this was the importance of digital literacy, with writers such as Livingstone arguing that digital literacy was 'crucial to the democratic agenda' because users of new media were not merely consumers, but citizens.[35]

I mention these debates because they strongly shaped the original project that formed the basis of this book. In a sense, I am here attempting to historicise my own experience of early videoblogging because so many of the debates have since moved on to other questions – notably debates around automation, surveillance and the emergent political time-bomb that is fake news. This book, however, came out of another almost gentler moment in digital culture, a period in which questions of creativity, identity and community were very much at the forefront of culture. Within this small video sub-culture on the internet, was a relatively small group of artists and video-makers who enthusiastically spent their time producing short digital films that they shared with the world through their blogs. YouTube was still in its infancy, social media did not exist and, to use a common internet meme, Pluto was still a planet.[36] And yet, this tiny community was ambitiously trying to create a new grammar, a fresh aesthetic and a genuinely sharing community of practice around the idea of 'videoblogging'.

---

33 Henry Jenkins, 'What happened before YouTube?', in Jean Burgess, Joshua Green, (eds) *YouTube. Digital Media and Society Series,* Cambridge: Polity, 2009, p. 116.

34 My initial thoughts on this were heavily influenced by the work of writers such as Nicholas Negroponte, *Being Digital,* New York: Vintage, 1996, Sherry Turkle's *Life On the Screen* and Howard Rheingold, *The virtual community: Homesteading on the electronic frontier.* Harvard: MIT press, 2000.

35 Sonia Livingstone, 'Media literacy and the challenge of new information and communication technologies'. *Communication Review*, 7.3-14 (2004): p. 11.

36 BWPWAP, or Back When Pluto Was a Planet, is "an expression used whenever one wants to talk about things in our recent past that have changed quickly"– for a more detailed discussion of this term, see the full curatorial statement from Transmediale 2013 in Kristoffer Gansing et al 'BWPWAP CURATIORIAL STATEMENT', *Transmediale 2013*, Amsterdam, http://www.transmediale.de/content/bwpwap-curatiorial-statement.

I conducted interviews with the videoblogging community in the period between June and September 2007. Around the time, the term 'Web 2.0' suddenly became a hotly debated topic on the internet. Tim O'Reilly's paper on the social web seemed to encapsulate the very essence of what I saw was happening in the videoblogging community. The ideas and concepts in Web 2.0 were not so much new technological standards, as the articulation of the web as a platform, where 'real-time streams'[37] of live data could be accessed at any time and from anywhere via RSS and syndication, and where the individual device from which you accessed this data was rendered irrelevant because the software used to display that data was 'written above the level of a single device'.[38] Web 2.0 was always a contested term, for example Trebor Scholz argues that the ideology of Web 2.0 is merely a 'framing device of professional elites that define what enters the public discourse about the impact of the Internet on society'.[39] Nevertheless, its articulation still represented an important moment for the development of the social web and the starting point of many Web 2.0 companies, like YouTube and Twitter. It is also an important discursive moment in the history of videoblogging, particularly with regard to framing the practice within a wider discourse of participatory media.

Lev Manovich goes a long way to describe the 'emergent conventions, the recurrent design patterns, and the key forms of new media'[40] which he sees as the new dominant cultural form of the 21st century. Manovich highlights numerical representation, modularity, automation, variability and transcoding as the main principles of new media, although he is perhaps more famous for his theorisation of the database as narrative form. In any case, the softwarization of media, and further, the softwarization of cultural artifacts and the rise of what has come to be known as a digital aesthetic or digital art, has contributed to a 'new' typology of sorts of what constitutes a digital cultural artifact.[41] In terms of the commercial aspects and the wider questions of monetizing the Web 2.0 technologies, and knowing the amount of free labour that goes into the creation of both successful Web 2.0 businesses and the plethora of not-so-successful and failed businesses, it seems pertinent to reiterate that in this book, there are obvious political economic considerations related to the exploitation of free labour and the enclosure of what has been called the digital commons.[42] Chanan discusses this

37   David M. Berry, *The Philosophy of Software: Code and Mediation in the Digital Age*, London: Palgrave, 2011, p 143-171.
38   Tim O'Reilly, 'What is Web 2.0. Design Patterns and Business Models for the Next Generation of Software', 2005, from http://oreilly.com/web2/archive/what-is-web-20.html.
39   Trebor Scholz, The Participatory Turn in Social Life Online, 2007, http://www.slideshare.net/trebor/the-participatory-turn; see also Evgeny Morozov, 'The Meme Hustler', *The Baffler*, 2013, http://www.thebaffler.com/salvos/the-meme-hustler; and Caroline Bassett, Maren Hartmann, Kathleen O'Riordan, 'After convergence: what connects?', *The Fiberculture Journal*, 2008, http://thirteen.fibreculturejournal.org, who who were 'wary and aware' of the 'discourse circulating around these innovations; one that proclaims their importance, underscoring and perhaps overplaying their radical novelty.'
40   Lev Manovich, *The Language of New Media*, London: MIT Press, 2001: 38. Manovich rejected the term 'aesthetics' in favour of 'language' – arguing that it 'implies a set of oppositions which I would like to avoid— between art and mass culture, between the beautiful and the ugly, between the valuable and the unimportant'. However, as a field, digital aesthetics has been established as a useful concept in describing the collection of stylistic elements and tropes that encompass the digital and so it is used in this book to denote this enclave of practices, styles and techniques.
41   Lev Manovich, *Software Takes Command*, London: Bloomsbury Academic, 2013a.
42   Tiziana Terranova, 'Free Labour: Producing Culture in the Digital Economy', *Social Text,* 18.2 (2000):

in relation to videoblogging where, drawing on Marx, he conceptualises the work done by videobloggers as 'free aesthetic labour'.[43] However, whilst this is an important critique, this book seeks to do other work, more related to the socio-technical and cultural unfolding of a new aesthetic-technical project. As such, and for reasons of conceptual clarity and space, I largely bracket out the political economic issues. This is not to say that there are not important questions to be asked in relation to free labour and videoblogging itself, but that the focus in this book is the material cultural formations which relate to the condition of the web from 2004-2009[44] under which videoblogging emerged and flourished as a cultural and material practice. This enables me to explore the way in which the technical, the social, narrative and imaginaries surrounding videoblogging are constructed in particular ways before the platform was commodified and co-opted into the larger digital economy.

The theoretical framework of this book draws on emerging theories surrounding materiality and digitalisation within the field of media studies, particularly drawing links with German media theory and its emphasis on the materiality of media, which makes explicit certain characteristics in relation to undertaking a media history that I find useful. I argue for a material understanding of the digital, seeing videoblogs as material artifacts. Indeed, videoblogs depend entirely on physical technology both during production, distribution and consumption. At no point does a videoblog escape from this materiality. Matthew Kirschenbaum's analysis of the hard drive is a wonderful example of thinking about materiality. Storing a video for editing requires a hard drive. A hard drive is a non-volatile storage device made of rotating platters with magnetic surfaces, and a video file (as with all digital files) rests on this physical layer, without which it would not exist. In other words, although 'as a written trace digital inscription [may be] invisible to the eye, […] it is not instrumentally undetectable or physically immaterial'.[45] What this means is that, despite having little or no technical knowledge of the underlying structures of the computer, and particularly the hard drive, the videoblogger depends on its materiality, and it's stability, for her work. The irony here, as Kirchenbaum points out, is that 'since hard disks, in most users' experience, either work flawlessly or else crash spectacularly, the notion of the device as a binary black box with no capacity for error short of global failure is perhaps inevitable. But these functional extremes are precisely what reinforce the

---

pp. 33–58; Michael Hardt and Antonio Negri, *Multitude*, London: Hamish Hamilton, 2005; Eben Moglen, 'The DotCommunist Manifesto: How Culture Became Property and What We're Going to Do About It', 2001, http://moglen.law.columbia.edu.

43 Michael Chanan, Tales of a Video Blogger, *Reframe*, 2012, http://reframe.sussex.ac.uk/activistmedia/2013/03/free-e-book-tales-of-a-video- blogger-by-michael-chanan/.

44 A note on dates; I define the period of the early videoblogging community as falling between 2004 (when the email list was started) and 2009 (by which time the community had more or less disbanded). However, at some points in this book, I refer to earlier instances of video-in-a-blog, notably Kontras and Miles as significant moments in the history of videoblogging. These moments are included to highlight the difficulty of pinpointing exactly when an historical period begins and when it ends, and further, the importance of keeping an open mind about the fluidity of periods of medial change. It is perhaps also worth noting that although I draw on archival material from 2004 onwards, my initial interviews were conducted in 2007, thus reflecting the historical specificity of that time (ie the videobloggers had already had a few years to reflect on their practices).

45 Matthew Kirschenbaum, 'Extreme Inscription: The Grammatology of the Hard Drive', *Text Technology*, 13. 2 (2004): pp. 91-125.

dominant perception of immateriality'.[46] It is also notable that exemplary as Kirschenbaum's forensic approach to the hard disk is, we must also note the historical nature of hard disks, which are themselves increasingly being replaced by a new material storage medium, namely solid-state drives (SSD). It is ironic that the very immateriality that hard disks made possible to experience, when looked back upon, were actually noisy mechanical, and actually quite fragile constituent parts of a computer. It is clear then that 'immateriality' is an historically constructed and technically created form of experience in relation to the digital, much like the dial-up modem, floppy disc or CD Roms.

Equally, the early instability of the videoblogging practice begs the question of how to study it. Following a long tradition of scholars questioning how to study the media,[47] N. Katherine Hayles argues for what she calls a media-specific analysis of media, an approach to critical enquiry which acknowledges that texts are always embodied entities and that the form of embodiment of a given text matters to its interpretative meaning. However, like McLuhan, Hayles does not call for media to be 'considered in isolation from one another', rather, following Bolter and Grusin, she argues that 'media constantly engage in a recursive dynamic of imitating each other, incorporating aspects of competing media into themselves while simultaneously flaunting the advantages that their own forms of mediation offer'.[48] This book, then, considers videoblogging a media-specific practice, meaning that its material and symbolic properties are both important. These properties are in constant interplay, and can be seen to co-construct each other. As Hayles argues, 'in emphasizing materiality, I do not mean to imply that all aspects of a medium's apparatus will be equally important. Rather, materiality should be understood as existing in complex dynamic interplay with content, coming into focus or fading into the background, depending on what performances the work enacts.'[49] In this sense, some aspects of the videoblogging practice may be given more importance than others. For example, certain kinds of videoblogs require closer attention to the embodied use of the camera to convey certain messages, whereas others might place a stronger emphasis on narrative, editing or effects. The aim, then, is to highlight the dynamic interplay between the technology and the content, the medium and the performance, through which the videoblog is constructed.

Although questions of identity and community remain crucial in understandings digital culture, particularly with regard to a new generation of users, it is crucial to look at the symbolic and the material. For example, some of the early cyber-feminism literature argued that 'the virtual and material are intertwined and superimposed on every aspect of cyberspace'. It is also interesting to note the growing influence of New Materialisms, for instance in the work of Iris van der Tuin and Rosi Braidotti.[50] At universities, studying the digital is no longer

---

46   Kirschenbaum, 'Extreme Inscription: The Grammatology of the Hard Drive', p. 95.
47   Raymond Williams, *Television: technology and cultural form*, London: Routledge, 1990 (1974); Roger Silverstone, *Why Study The Media?*, London: Sage, 1999; Christian Metz, *Film Language: A Semiotics of the Cinema*, University Of Chicago Press, 1990.
48   N. Katherine Hayles, 'Print is flat, code is deep: The importance of media-specific analysis', *Poetics Today*, 25.1, (2004): p. 69.
49   Hayles, 'Print is flat, code is deep: The importance of media-specific analysis', 2004: 71.
50   Margaret Morse, 'Virtually Female: Body and Code', in Jennifer Terry and Melodie Calvert (eds)

confined to a single strand within media studies, tagged on at the end of the course, but is being adopted across the humanities and the university more generally. Today we are faced with 'computational media' and 'computational culture'.[51] We might note that Ursula Franklin argued that 'everyone's vernacular reality has changed' and that 'there are genuinely new activities that are possible now that could not have been done without the new technologies and their infrastructure'. In particular, she refers to the ability of these new technologies to more easily transfer, store and reconstruct information and the fact that 'some of these affect our approaches to and perceptions of the future, that is, the projected realities'.[52]

To understand this I have found Nick Couldry's work on media as practice very helpful for developing my conceptualisation of videoblogging as a practice. Couldry makes it clear that he doesn't want to reject other forms of media research, like studies of audiences or texts, altogether. However, he argues that by reorienting the study of media towards practice, one is allowed to answer questions about media in 'more precise ways… based in the details of everyday practice and its organisation'. To Couldry, his approach is 'alarmingly simple; it treats media as the open set of practices relating to, or oriented around, media'. In other words, he aims 'to decentre media research from the study of media texts or production structures (important though these are) and to redirect it onto the study of the open-ended range of practices focused directly or indirectly on media'.[53] In this book, then, practice is defined both as the way in which the videobloggers engage with the technologies available to them, the way in which these ways of engaging became adopted by the community as a whole, and how a sense of what videoblogging was became adopted as a kind of standard.

Equally, Roger Silverstone's writing on media and everyday life has been very influential on my own research on videoblogging. In his work on technology and the everyday, Silverstone attempts to formulate an approach to studying media that takes into account both the material approaches associated with a political economic and structural side of media production, and the symbolic content of media, i.e. audience research, textual analysis etc. This book uses Silverstone's argument that media are doubly articulated as its methodological starting point. Although referring to television, he could easily be talking about the digital when he argues, it is 'through its double articulation into culture its significance is extended beyond its status "simply" as object or medium, for in its status as medium, and through the provision of information and entertainment, television provides the basis for an "education", a competence, in all aspects of contemporary culture.'[54] Silverstone's work is situated in a long history of writings attempting to bridge the gap between the material analysis of media and the cultural signification of the media content. For example, Raymond Williams argued, 'the social history and the social analysis needed to be directly related to critical and analytical

Processed Lives; Gender and Technology in Everyday Life, London: Routledge, 1997, p. 28.

51   David M. Berry, *Understanding Digital Humanities*, London: Palgrave Macmillan, 2012; Manovich, *Software Takes Command*.

52   Franklin, *The Real World of Technology*, p. 47.

53   Nick Couldry, 'Theorising Media as Practice', *Social Semiotics*, 14. 2 (2004): pp. 117; see also Nick Couldry, *Media, society, world: Social theory and digital media practice*. London: Polity, 2012.

54   Roger Silverstone, *Television and Everyday Life,* London: Routledge, 1994: 123.

examination of the materials *and* processes of the specific communication',[55] in contrast to Marshall McLuhan, who famously proclaimed that the medium is the message, emphasising the importance of studying medium-based analyses of media as 'it is only too typical that the 'content' of any medium blinds us to the character of the medium'.[56] In his attempt to reconcile these positions, Silverstone argues that media is not either-or, but both material and symbolic – hence his notion of the media as doubly articulated. This book follows in this tradition by emphasising not just the content of videoblogs, but their materiality. This is done in three stages; firstly, by tracing the technical constellation around videoblogging we start to see the outline of the videoblogging platform articulated by competing and often normative ideas of how the platform 'should be' – and eventually the emergence of a hegemonic platform imaginary. Secondly, through a formal analysis of a number of video blogs, a particular aesthetic emerges; a medium-specific aesthetic which is both influenced by and works in conjunction with the technical restrictions of the platform. Finally, by conceptualising videoblogging as a media practice, materially performed through embodied experiences and discursively reflected upon by the participants themselves, we see the emergence of a videoblogger identity. I now want to turn to situating videoblogging historically in the next chapter to broaden and deepen these discussions in terms of specific case of videoblogs and the practices of videoblogging.

---

55   Williams, *Television: technology and cultural form*, p. vi (emphasis mine).
56   Marshall McLuhan, *Understandig media. The Extensions of Man.* New York: Routledge, 1964: 9-11.

2. THE EARLY HISTORY OF VIDEOBLOGGING

Video on the web has had a number of false starts with a variety of companies attempting to be the first to solve the delivery of online video. However, the technical issues were difficult, not only in terms of raw download bandwidth, which was miniscule in comparison with today, but also in terms of the lack of a universal video standard that could be used on the internet. The previous standards developed with physical products in mind, such as DVDs, were unsuitable, being large in size and not easily reconstituted for packet switching delivery. MPEG1 and MPEG2, for example, required the entire file to be downloaded before playback could start, and even then the file sizes tended to be gigantic. Whilst standards bodies sought to develop more suitable protocols, companies such as Apple began experimenting with a number of new formats, and the underground pirate-film networks began to gravitate towards the DivX format. But even on the 'player' side, users would often find that their existing software could not cope with an esoteric video codec (Code Decode video plugin) or even a strange set of video format requirements – size, scan, colours and interlace were just a few of the multiple settings on early video coding software.[57]

For example, on January 2nd 2000, Adam Kontras, a radio host travelling to Los Angeles from his hometown Columbus, Ohio, posted what is now widely considered to have been the first video-in-a-blog to his website. Kontras was on a mission to break into Hollywood, and for the following years chronicled his attempts to break into show business. The first video, however, was just 11 seconds of compressed footage (he had compressed it down to a remarkable 222 KB) of Kontras smuggling his cat J-Dog into a hotel (0:11min, 160x112). The video featured Kontras and his fiancée Jessica carrying their cat through a hotel lobby. Kontras continued to post these little videos almost every day throughout the year 2000. Kontras' site (accessed today through the Internet Wayback machine), was a personal website with text and links, and thus not what I define or the videobloggers themselves define, as a 'videoblog', however, it was possibly the first known instance of someone linking to a video file from their website. Whether many people were actually able to view it at the time, is more difficult to ascertain. Certainly, viewing audiences would have been relatively small.

Another example was on the 27th of November 2000, when Adrian Miles posted his first video on his blog. Miles was an academic based at RMIT University in Melbourne, Australia, where his research interests included hypertext, networked interactive video, and interactive documentary. In the winter of 2000 he was granted a fellowship in Norway and left the warm beaches of Australia for the wet and windy streets of Bergen. Miles had long been interested in the intersection of video and the digital and on this uncharacteristically sunny Wednesday morning in Bergen, he decided to give it a try himself. Miles' video (QuickTime, 2:10, 194x144, figure 1) was accompanied by a short text, which can be seen as Miles' first attempt to articulate his thoughts on videoblogs, or *vogs*, as he called them, writing 'welcome. This is a video blog. Don't know if there are lots around, or what they should be called. But if its ok

---

57   This complexity of encoding and decoding can still be seen in the French VLC project, https://www.
      videolan.org/vlc/.

to call a web log a blog then this can be a vog'. Miles' work is interesting because as well as being a practitioner, he was one of the first people to start theorising online video as part of his practice. A few days later, on December 6th 2000, Miles posted his first iteration of what was to be known as the 'Vogma manifesto'. In it, Miles called for a set of principles (nine to be exact) for posting video to the internet. Over the years, Miles expanded on his manifesto, turning it into a full article, which has been widely cited.[58] The initial video, however, would have had a limited audience, but the bringing together of a project ('Vogma'), hypertext and video as an online cultural challenge was inspiring to a number of people who were also developing an interest in online video.

Figure 1: *Welcome* (Miles, 2000).[59]

Miles set out a simple set of rules for videoblogs. Coming out of a hypertext tradition and with years of practical experience with film and video, in *The Vogma Manifesto*, Miles wrote that a 'vog';

> respects bandwidth
> is not streaming video (this is not the reinvention of television)
> uses performative video and/or audio
> is personal uses available technology experiments with writerly video and audio
> lies between writing and the televisual explores the proximate distance of words and moving media
> is Dziga Vertov with a mac and a modem.[60]

Miles' definition is useful for a number of reasons. Firstly, it was one of the first attempts at theorising online video, written at a time when posting a video on the internet was incredibly difficult, hence the first rule; respecting bandwidth. It is also interesting in that it distances online video from the televisual through the rejection of streaming technologies. Thus, Miles' definition has already defined the online video as a discrete, limited format, one which has a clearly defined beginning, middle and end, and stands alone in a potential sea of other

---

58   Miles, 'Vogma, a Manifesto', 2000, http://vogmae.net.au/ludicvideo/commentary/vogmamanifesto.html.
59   A quick note on my method in relation to the images of videoblogs included in the book may help with their understanding. Essentially these images are made up of three frames, one from the beginning, one from the middle and one from the end of the videos. The idea is to give a sense of the arc of narrative, visual movement and aesthetic of the video in a simple visual form. I call these images *time-images*, after the Deleuzian idea in relation to cinema, although in this sense they are very much meant to be static representations of time-based media.
60   Adrian Miles, 'Vogma, a Manifesto'.

online videos. It also sets the videoblog apart from live streaming technologies that were to flood the internet a few years later, Justin.tv being a notable example. Miles also defined the online video as 'personal', a definition that may have excluded a number of practitioners who considered themselves 'videobloggers' but who did not make inherently personal content (see for instance *Galacticast*, *Epic Fu* and *Chasing Windmills* – these shows were videoblogs but not 'personal'). Lastly, Miles' definition nods to the filmmaker Dziga Vertov in an attempt to provide historical antecedents for online video.

In between these early experiments, most people accepted that the combination of low band-width and dispersed video standards meant that online video would have to mature sufficiently before becoming useful. Despite these early instances of video-in-a-blog, the practice of videoblogging as we think of it today didn't really begin until 2004. In a seven second long videoblog posted to his site on the first of January 2004, Steve Garfield declared 2004 'the year of the videoblog'.[61] Garfield, a video producer and editor, had started blogging in 2000, and being convinced the internet had more to offer, he had started tinkering with video in 2002. From his home in Boston, Massachusetts, he was determined to make videoblogging the next new big thing. This was also the year Jay Dedman and Peter van Dijck got together to start the Videoblogging Yahoo Group, an email list that would act as the central hub for videoblogging activity and community, from its inception till the community more or less disbanded in 2009. Dedman and van Dijck met in 2002. Van Dijck, originally from Belgium, had relocated to New York for work and had a small place in Harlem. He and Dedman got on well, and would spend a lot of time walking around the parks of New York discussing the future of robots. They were both technically literate. Van Dijck moved to Hoboken soon after-wards, but the two stayed in touch. A couple of years later, on one of their walks, they started talking about video. Dedman, a video-editor, was working for the Manhattan Neighbourhood Network (MNN) at the time, and was getting frustrated with the community television model. They used to hang out, bounce ideas off each other and put the world to rights. After a long walk in Central Park one evening, they hit upon the idea of posting video to the internet. They both got very excited. Soon after, in May 2004, they discovered Steve Garfield's videoblog and figured the best way to get people to work together was to create a space they could meet. Distance was an issue though, so the space would have to be virtual. On the evening of May 31st they created the videoblogging mailing list.

The email list was an interesting choice. Not only did it connect people who lived in geo-graphically disparate places and bring them to a shared space online in which they could communicate, it also gave them the opportunity to reach all the members by sending just one email. Slowly, the users began to treat the email list as a form of membership list. This emphasised a sense of inclusion and shared ownership of the videoblogging project. As more people joined, older members would greet new members, and the group would mostly self-regulate in terms of community behaviour and expectations. The email list also had an automatic archiving function which was important in that it gave the fledgling community a sense of how it was growing and developing shared traditions and norms.

---

61 Steve Garfield, *Year of the Videoblog*, 2004, https://web.archive.org/web/20041231011613/http://homepage.mac.com/stevegarfield/videoblog/year_of.html.

Peter Van Dijck posted the first message to the Yahoo videoblogging email list (hereafter referred to as 'the email list') on June 1st 2004. His main focus was providing technical support, but Dedman insisted that they needed a community of users. This idea of building a 'community' around a new technical medium product or technology was not new, of course. However, rather than being generated by a large corporation seeking to sell a product, such as Apple who actively used community-building early in their history, these individuals were first and foremost excited by the potential of new forms of expression on the internet. To Dedman, it wasn't enough to discuss this amazing new ability to put video on the web, they needed to bring more people into the conversation. The pair were quickly joined by others, including Garfield, Adrian Miles, Anders Haugstrup Pedersen, an MA student based in Copenhagen, and Mica Scalin, an artist who saw online video as allowing the medium of web content to 'truly come into its own and begin establishing its unique language'. It attracted her, she said, 'because of this unique combination of traits in a visual medium. What is most interesting to me is that it provides a way to tell a story that could eliminate worn-out narrative forms.'[62]

The first flurry of messages on the email list was mostly technical, but there were also discussions, and theorisations about the medium and its potential. For the first 4 months there were less than 50 members on the list, with an average of 300 messages sent each month. In December 2004 this jumped to over 1000 messages, which led the way into one of the most active years in the history of the community.[63] On July 9th 2005, Adam Quirk, initiated and hosted the first ever Vloggercue (videoblogger BBQ) on his roof-top in Hoboken, New York. Quirk had started videoblogging in 2004 when there were only a handful of people on the videoblogging list. An introvert, Quirk had found it difficult to get to know people after he'd moved to the city with just his girlfriend and his cat, and videoblogging afforded him the chance to 'have conversations with these other people online and experience some kind of socializing without having to resort to going to bars and meeting strangers face to face'. Vloggercue 2004 was attended by a small group of videobloggers, among them Jay Dedman, Steve Garfield, Bre Pettis (who started the website *We are the Media* and would go on to found MakerBot), the founders of Blip.tv, Josh Leo (one of the youngest videobloggers at the time, and later host of the web show *Daily Kawaii*) and Chris Weagel (who found success with the daily – and slightly absurd – videoblog production company *Human Dog*). This was the first time many of the videobloggers had met in person.[64] Also present was Joshua Kinberg, who would go on to make FireAnt, and Ryanne Hodson, co-creator of freevlog.org, both of which I explore more fully later. The event was a huge success, both in terms of getting together to discuss technical issues with videoblogging, but also in terms of forging bonds between the members of the group. The night even inspired some romance, with Hodson and Dedman soon after becoming a couple.

---

62   Mica Scalin, Email to Videoblogging list, 1 June 2004, https://groups.yahoo.com/neo/groups/
      videoblogging/conversations/topics/3.
63   I discuss the email list and the group activities there in more detail in chapter 3.
64   For Steve Garfield's photos from the evening, see https://www.flickr.com/photos/stevegarfield/
      sets/570690. Ryanne Hodson also documented the event with a few videos, see for example, https://
      ryanedit.blogspot.co.uk/2005/07/vloggercue-weekend-begins.html and http://ryanedit.blogspot.
      co.uk/2006/01/vloggercue-flashback.html?m=0.

Despite the increasingly activity on the email list and occasional events within the community, videoblogging remained a niche activity, limited to a small group of people who mainly hung out online and thrived on the process of sharing their experiences and learning from each other. This all changed on the 21st July 2005 when Rupert Howe – a website designer and amateur film maker living and working in London, UK – posted a short video, *Should I Stay or Should I Go* (figure 2) on his blog, *Fat Girl In Ohio*. Despite never formally studying film (he read classics at Oxford and hated it), Howe's great passion had always been the cinema, so it made sense for him to name his blog after the famous quote by filmmaker Francis Ford Coppola, who once said that his

> Great hope is that now that [we have] these little 8mm video recorder people who normally wouldn't make movies are going to be making them. And, you know, suddenly one day some little fat girl in Ohio is going to be the new Mozart, and you know, and make a beautiful film with her father's little camera-corder and for once this whole professionalism about movies will be destroyed forever and it will become an art form.[65]

Fat Girl In Ohio was Howe's second videoblog. In the spring of 2005 he had been working for his father, but he was bored and spent his days making short videos which he posted to a blog,[66] and messing around on the internet. Without a distribution network, Howe had been emailing the videos to his friends and his blog had little or no traffic. Again, this was all about to change.

Although individuals had created personal webpages (home pages) for years, Pyra Lab's launch of Blogger in 1999 contributed to changing how people interacted on the internet. Blogger was a publishing platform that allowed individuals without any previous skill to run their own blogs easily and free of charge. The term weblog was coined by John Barger in December 1997 whereas the more popular term 'blog' was coined by Peter Merholz in April/ May 1999. The terms were used to signify a personal homepage that was distinctly different from a personal home page. Instead of a static web page with text, links and images, blogs are 'web-based journals in which entries are displayed in reverse chronological sequence'.[67] As early adopter and early weblogger Rebecca Blood points out, there have been personal websites that have subsequently been identified as 'blogs' since 1998. Initially, there were very few of these weblogs, which meant that – similarly to the early videoblogging community – the bloggers were all reading each others posts. With the launch of Blogger and what she calls the 'post-Blogger explosion' the nature of blogs changed. Whereas the early community of bloggers had been concerned with the 'web at large', the new bloggers treated their sites more like a diary and these blogs, which were often updated several times during the day, were 'a record of the blogger's thoughts: something noticed on the way to work, notes about the weekend, a quick reflection on some subject or another.'[68]

---

65   Francis Ford Coppola, *Hearts of Darkness: A Filmmaker's Apocalypse, Fax* Barh, George Hickenlooper and Eleanor Coppola (Dir) USA: Paramount, 1991.
66   http://workingformydad.blogspot.com.
67   Susan C. Herring, Lois Ann Scheidt, Sabrina Bonus and Elijah Wright, 'Bridging the Gap: A Genre Analysis of Weblogs', *System Sciences*, 2004, pp. 11.
68   Rebecca Blood, 'Weblogs: A History and Perspective', *Rebecca's Pocket*, 7 September 2000, www.rebeccablood.net/essays/weblog_history.html, accessed 5 March 2014.

Similarly, danah boyd traces the development of the early blogging platforms, including Type-pad, Diaryland and Live Journal as well as the evolution of the definition of blogging. Whereas most early theorisation of blogs attempted to define it as a genre of writing, boyd finds it more helpful to 'reframe blogs as a culture-driven medium upon which the practice of blogging can occur'. She argues that within the context of communication, 'a medium is the channel through which people can communicate or extend their expressions to others' in a similar way that paper is the medium of writing. Drawing on McLuhan, boyd contends that a medium allows people to express themselves and asserts that 'blogs are precisely this; they allow people to extend themselves into a networked digital environment that is often thought to be disembodying. The blog becomes both the digital body as well as the medium through which bloggers express themselves.'[69] This is a useful way of thinking about blogs and is relevant for the way in which videoblogging later developed. Through blogs, wikis and message boards, the idea was that previously passive readers became active writers and producers of knowledge. Through aggregation and syndication, the individual user could create her own media stream.

Figure 2: *Should I Stay or Should I Go* (Howe, 2005)

In his video *Should I Stay or Should I Go*, Howe moves around in his London home, talking, more or less coherently, directly into his handheld camera, a Kodak dx7440, about his reactions to a terrorist attack. Rupert told me he was recommended that particular camera by Andreas Haugstrup Pedersen, another videoblogger on the email list, because he 'liked the colour in his videos.' This is interesting in relation to an already evident aesthetic con-sideration of videoblogging practice. At one point, the camera cuts to a map, trailing Howe's finger to show how close he lives to the location of the attacks. The cuts are fast, and longer sequences have been trimmed to make the video snappier and flow better. After a sharply edited section in which he discusses his feelings about the attacks, Howe moves into the garden. Flooded in natural sunlight (he was shooting on this small, handheld camera, with no additional 'production values' such as lighting, sound or crew), he makes a short, but bold statement about how he will not leave London – instead he will take his sister and nephew to the park and spend a normal afternoon with them. As he puts it, 'I guess… we're not afraid'. *Should I Stay or Should I Go*, (QuickTime, 2:47, 320×240) was shot, edited and produced in Howe's home in Shepherds Bush in 2005, and showed him talking directly to the camera about his reactions. The video footage had been shot on the day of the explosions.[70]

---

69   danah boyd, 'A Blogger's Blog: Exploring the Definition of a Medium', *Reconstruction*, 6. 4 (2006).
70   Howe had originally posted a shorter, less polished version of the video, which he took down because
      he felt it was too personal. The version I am referring to here is the later video which was picked up by
      the news media.

Like Kontras, Miles and Garfield before him, Howe posted his video on his small, relatively unknown videoblog, but the video was picked up and featured on the online edition of the *New York Times*. Howe was not a journalist, nor a filmmaker, nor a public person. He was an amateur video-maker with a camera and an internet connection, talking about an event that was lacking a personal video side to the story. This was a format that was new and fresh and seemed to speak from the heart – giving it a personal, on-the-spot situational quality, which was magnified by the technical limitations of the medium of video. Howe was one of the first to experience the world of new and old media feeding off each other in challenging ways.

I highlight *Should I Stay or Should I Go* for three reasons. The first is personal. Although it was by no means the first video posted online, the video marked my own discovery of the use of video, as opposed to text, within the blog format. Despite having read (and written) blogs for a while, I had never before seen anyone use video to communicate through their website, and my reaction to Howe's video was a mix of fascination and excitement. The intimacy channelled through the video (mostly close-ups of Howe's face, with his home always in the background) seemed different to me to the mainly text-based blogs I was used to reading. I was inspired to watch other videos on his blog, and later, to follow the links in his sidebar to other videoblogs. From there, I discovered an entire community of videobloggers, and I was fascinated by the many videos, genres and topics covered, from the political to the personal, videos about families, children and cats, videos captured whilst the videoblogger was at work, walking down the street, or just rolling out of bed. It seemed to me to raise a number of interesting questions in terms of artistic expression, identity and community. On one level, therefore, *Should I Stay or Should I Go,* marks one of my personal starting points for not only videoblogging and the community of users, but also my interest in the practice and – eventually – this book.

Secondly, the story arc of Howe's videoblog (initially small in scope and entirely personal, followed by massive attention from mainstream media, and eventual disappearance) is an example of the instabilities of videoblogging as media-form, especially in its early days. In this case, the cause was partially economic. Howe had to take the video offline because he could no longer afford to keep it online. This instability, in Howe's case, wasn't altogether positive, however. As a result of the feature in the *New York Times* the traffic to his site grew exponentially, eventually resulting in him having to take his entire website down. This is because bandwidth has a political economy that has been hidden by the rise of YouTube. Essentially, the website owner pays for bandwidth and when that usage is exceeded the website is disconnected.[71] His mention in the *New York Times* meant hundreds of thousands (or even millions) of visitors from across the world visited his site, and watched his videos. Before the days of free online video hosting, Howe was paying for his own traffic, and suddenly found himself in a situation where he owed his Internet Service Provider (ISP) large sums of money. As he told me, 'The rate was something like £10 per additional 1GB, and the files would have been around 5-6mb per minute (at 750mbps) and around 3 mins - so say 18mb each. That

---

71   Slashdot, a technology website, became famous for 'Slashdotting' websites by sending millions of users to a site. This has since developed into what's called Distributed Denial of Service (DDoS) attacks, where a network resource or website is made unavailable to users after multiple attacks from a variety of sources.

means I would have maxed out my allowance with 555 views. And then had to pay £18 for every 1,000 views after that. So 10,000 would have been £180 and so on with no realistic proposition of getting anything back from advertising or [merchandise]. That was much more than I had to spend.' I should also add that the bandwidth costs weren't Howe's only reason for removing his blog. As he explained to me after he 'got profiled in the *New York Times*, and I got a lot of hits, [I] got afraid of being found out by people I worked with. So I took my site down. I really really really regret this. I got freaked out by it and walked away.'[72]

My third reason for mentioning *Should I Stay or Should I Go* is that it can be seen as an example of the practices that emerged in the early 2000s that contributed to the increased number of users with little or no previous technical knowledge who entered and started partic-ipating in a global media landscape.[73] And it is an early example of how this could be achieved through the medium of film. *Should I Stay or Should I Go* thus represents a meeting point between citizen media (Howe was engaging in debate with other citizens about terrorism), citizen journalism (Howe was reporting on where the attacks took place, what some of the early news and reactions were), personal media (Howe was talking from a subjective position, about the concerns of his own family and doing so from within his own home. Howe also used his own private equipment and initially shared his video mainly to a small community of friends, i.e. other videobloggers) and user-generated content (Howe's video was featured on the New York Times website alongside works by their own journalists).

Howe felt he was left with no option but to remove the entire site. However, videoblogs were unstable in other ways too. There was, for instance, no standard format that was used by all videobloggers. Whereas some preferred to encode their videos using Apple's QuickTime, others relied on Windows' media player or one of many Flash players available across the internet. Sites such as YouTube, Blip.tv, Vimeo and others all had different players, which would display videos in slightly different ways. For example, some players, like the Blip-embedded plug-in, allowed the viewer to navigate within the video being shown (by pausing, fast forwarding or stopping) but also browse through the entire archive of videos by the artist they were watching. In contrast, at the time, if a videoblogger used YouTube, the viewer could only access other videos at the end of the current one. Digital formats (or codecs) could easily change and/or became obsolete, sites were moved and links broken, and some formats (such as Flash) might play nicely on the web, but not on mobile devices (such as the video compatible iPod, and, later, the iPhone).[74] Technologically, therefore,

---

72 Personal correspondence with Howe.
73 Jenkins, *Convergence Culture. Where Old and New Media Collide*.
74 Steve Jobs' letter from April 2010 expands on Apple's reasoning behind choosing to disallow Flash on the iPhone. Jobs explains that Apple is committed to open standards on the web, and that Flash is 100% a propriatory product owned by Adobe. Further, he points out that despite Adobe's claims that because they refuse to use Flash, Apple customers cannot access what he calls the 'full web,' there are 'over 50,000 games and entertainment titles on the App Store' and 'are more games and entertainment titles available for iPhone, iPod and iPad than for any other platform in the world.' Jobs goes on to highlight the issues with reliability, security and performance associated with Flash and the lack of ability to use touch screen technology, before presenting a damning account of the way in which Flash drains the battery life of a device ('The difference is striking: on an iPhone, for example, H.264 videos play for up to 10 hours, while videos decoded in software play for less than 5 hours before the

videoblogs were susceptible to vanishing due to their instabilities and shifting versioning of the underlying technical a priori.

From a social or cultural point of view, and particularly within the community of these early videobloggers, there were intense debates about what videoblogging *was*. Some contributors refused to define it, while others insisted on making strong links with, for instance, televisual techniques and aesthetics, blogging, or amateur film. Some videobloggers also wrote or created manifestos for videoblogging, causing large disagreements and debates. For instance, the video manifesto *Vlog Anarchy* by Michael Verdi, Haugstrup and Shoot's *The Lumiere Manifesto* and Adrian Miles' already referred to *Vogma Manifesto*; the latter two both reminiscent of the Dogma 95 manifesto written by filmmakers Lars von Trier and Thomas Vinterberg back in 1995, with strict principles of digital 'austerity'. These debates from both within the community and in the more general arena, were coupled with the question of what videoblogging was *for*.

Some people, like the creators of *Galacticast* (galacticast.com), *Epic FU* (epicfu.com) and *Ryan Is Hungry* (ryanishungry.com) would later attempt to monetise their videoblogging activities, relying on advertising, sponsorships and corporate investment to generate income. There was also awareness within the community of the inherent problems with attempting to make money, as Howe commented on the email list. 'I would never pay $3 for a video to my phone,' he asserted, 'But then I watch all these people's videos for free on my iPod every day.' Most practitioners treated their videoblog as a personal diary, a visual archive of their lives, and argued that they would never dream of trying to make money from videos they saw as highly personal. After a particularly unpleasant exchange between a new member and the 'core' community around the buying and selling of domain names, Steve Watkins, an active member who would often write long, considered replies to issues, stated bluntly that 'business and money often get a bit of a rough ride here, as they do elsewhere on the net. Some people have ideals about the net and what is happening with vlogging which doesn't really have much to do with profiteering.'[75]

So, for example, Jen Gouvea, who lived in San Francisco with her boyfriend Kent Bye, ran a website exploring the 'internal and external approaches to social change and how the two are reciprocal.' The pair had started videoblogging as a way to communicate, they made videos about 'spiritual activism' and used their online presence to promote spirituality and well-being. Gouvea had no previous camera experience, so she kept her videos simple with few edits. Having grown up without a lot of technology in her life and considering herself a 'bit of an introvert', Gouvea never posted videos about her everyday life, yet told me her videos were 'sometimes almost too personal, to a point where it might only make sense to me and a few

---

battery is fully drained'). Lastly, and most importantly to Jobs, Apple's decision to disallow Flash on the iPhone relates to the company's refusal to allow what Jobs calls 'a third-party layer of software'. As he argues, 'If developers grow dependent on third party development libraries and tools, they can only take advantage of platform enhancements if and when the third party chooses to adopt the new features. We cannot be at the mercy of a third party deciding if and when they will make our enhancements available to our developers' Apple, Thoughts on Flash, 2010, http://www.apple.com/hotnews/thoughts-on-flash/.

75   Steve Watkins, Email to Videoblogging list, 6 December 2006, https://groups.yahoo.com/neo/groups/videoblogging/conversations/messages/53080.

select initiated'. Some tried to find ways to use their videoblogging skills to generate income in tangential ways. Another videoblogger, Adam Quirk, told me 'I don't think videoblogging itself will ever pay the bills, but I think I can find ways to make money through other projects related to it, such as creating video ads for other companies, or selling products through our video blog'. These different approaches to videoblogging as a practice, as a medium, as a distribution network and through various moments of contestation and debate, were reflected in the debates over lack of a coherent and stable definition of videoblogs, especially in its early days.

As mentioned in the last chapter, in September 2005, Tim O'Reilly, entrepreneur and publisher, announced the contours of what he called the 'Design Patterns and Business Models for the Next Generation of Software', thus launching what became known as Web 2.0. In computing, a 2.0 upgrade (from a 1.x version of a program) indicates significant changes and improvements. Likewise, Web 2.0 indicates a significant upgrade, or shift in the how the web works. Examples of Web 2.0 technologies include the move from static to dynamic webpages, the increase in user-generated content and the growth of social networks. Andrew Keen argued that Web 2.0 is 'Socrates's nightmare: technology that arms every citizen with the means to be an opinionated artist or writer'.[76] Keen despaired at the 'cult of the amateur', a culture that merges the ideology of the 1960s counterculture with the techno fetishism of Silicon Valley to produce 'an ideology [that] worships the creative amateur: the self-taught filmmaker, the dorm-room musician, the unpublished writer. It suggests that everyone – even the most poorly educated and inarticulate amongst us – can and should use digital media to express and realize themselves.'[77]

Within the contours of this book, however, Web 2.0 was an important concept for three reasons. Firstly, the discourses and 'hype' surrounding the term were very important to the videoblogging community, and its sense of emerging identity and practice. The promise of dynamism and widened participation was important to the videoblogging project. The growth of YouTube meant more people started to understand and appreciate the work the videobloggers had been championing. Secondly, the technical advantages that the Web 2.0 technologies offered (such as seamless RSS syndication for instance) had an effect on the development of the videoblogging platform. Thirdly, Web 2.0 ironically heralded the beginning of the end for the videoblogging community. As the big Web 2.0 companies, such as YouTube, started to attract users, and Twitter and Facebook became the key social networks for communication, video and photo-sharing on the web, the videoblogging community began to breakdown. So, Web 2.0 is important as a symptom for understanding the problems videoblogging was facing at the time, whilst simultaneously signalling the beginning of its transformation from craft practice to being co-opted into industrialised global media systems.

---

76   Although it seems highly likely that Socrates would not have had this nightmare, he theorized that we all have the capacity to 'remember' complex ideas.

77   Andrew Keen, *The Cult of the Amateur: How blogs, MySpace, YouTube, and the rest of today's user-generated media are destroying our economy, our culture, and our values.*

As mentioned in the last chapter, in February 2005, Chad Hurley, Steve Chen and Jawed Karim founded YouTube.com, at that point a rather small Web 2.0 platform, allowing anyone with a video camera, computer, a mobile device and internet access to watch and publish video content online. The contribution of YouTube was to simplify the technical process of videoblogging, leading to a transformation of online video culture. This was a shift from the idea of the website as a personal storage facility for video content to a platform for public self-expression. It was also the beginning of a shift to a new political economy for video online, although few at the time realised this.

We might think of the mass-media distribution model of the twentieth century as a 'one-way, hub-and-spoke structure, with unidirectional links to its ends, running from the centre to the periphery'.[78] These structures facilitated the control of a small number of big media corporations, whether private (commercial) or public (national), over the media landscape. In contrast, the underlying internet protocols have affordances towards networked and decentralised ways of transferring information. Early commentators on the internet lauded it as an alternative distribution model, without the gatekeepers of 'big media', allowing anyone with access to it, the possibility of becoming an active member of the public sphere. However, as the debates around net neutrality show us, although the 'old' gatekeepers of the media are losing some of their power, there are new gatekeepers emerging that control both access to, and interactions within the web itself, be it Google, Amazon, Apple or Facebook.

Until YouTube was sold to Google in October 2006, one of the fiercest competitors in the video platform market was Google's own Google Video.[79] The purchase of YouTube by Google is significant as it was a deliberate attempt to bet on video as a key cultural force online. Google's acquisition was not just about 'bringing innovative technology into the home, as its own GoogleVideo was already running on superior software; it was about bringing in communities of users'.[80] YouTube had the largest number of users of any Web 2.0 platform at this time, and securing access to this user-group was clearly one of Google's aims with the acquisition. This strategy was similar to Facebook's later purchase of Instagram in April 2012 and News Corp's less fortunate purchase of MySpace in 2005.

Signifying this shift towards user-generated content in 2006, Time Magazine designated person of the year as 'you' – the everyday person uploading, sharing and disseminating content across the internet. In the issue, 'the editors paid tribute to the millions of anonymous web users who dedicate their creative energy to a booming web culture'[81]. In contrast to Thomas Carlyle who argued that 'the history of the world is but the biography of great men', Time highlighted that alongside stories of war and conflict (in Iraq, Israel and Lebanon), 2006 offered an alternative story, one in which participatory culture and the global media landscape began to merge.

---

78   Yochai Benkler, *The Wealth of Networks: How Social Production Transforms Markets and Freedom*, London: Yale, 2006, p. 179.
79   Google Video was launched in January 2005 and was officially closed in August 2012.
80   José van Dijck, 'Television 2.0: YouTube and the emergence of homecasting' *Creativity, Ownership and Collaboration in the Digital Age*, Cambridge, Massachusetts Institute of Technology (2007): p. 27-29.
81   van Dijck, 'Television 2.0: YouTube and the emergence of homecasting'.

The shift from the individual, personal website as the main source for video content, to plat-form-based sharable media, was a perfect fit for the ideas about a user-led revolution that characterizes rhetoric around Web 2.0. As the Time article argued, 2006 was

> A story about community and collaboration on a scale never seen before. It's about the cosmic compendium of knowledge Wikipedia and the million-channel people's net-work YouTube and the online metropolis MySpace. It's about the many wresting power from the few and helping one another for nothing and how that will not only change the world, but also change the way the world changes.[82]

It is an interesting footnote to these larger media tectonic shifts that, at a more prosaic level, by December 2006 the videoblogging email list membership had risen to 1000 members.

As YouTube began to fight a number of copyright claims from the large media conglomerates because of users uploading clips from movies and television, videoblogging also began to encounter legal issues. If there was a breach of copyright law, a video hosting site (such as YouTube or Vimeo) must remove a video immediately to avoid itself becoming embroiled in a copyright claim. There were debates around issues of copyright, with writers such as Lessig arguing that the US copyright laws had begun to place substantial limits on creativity.[83] These factors were in danger of encouraging a 'precautionary' environment in relation to online video in particular. If users began to be worried about possible expensive legal issues from uploading a video with a snippet of background music or video, this would have chilled the growth of video usage in social media. The worry was not just that casual users might be caught up in dragnet copyright suits – but also political movements, activists and others might have copyright used to silence them. Indeed, new and innovative music, artists and video experimentation might also be inhibited. The use of the notion of a 'safe harbour' was crucial to these developments, but a side effect was that media sharing sites became (over) zealous in the removal of any content that could be considered to be copyright infringing.[84]

These ideas and others were picked up and developed in 2007, when Geert Lovink and the Institute for Network Cultures in Amsterdam organised the first *Video Vortex* conference. The conference, which ran seven workshops over five years and produced two books, attempted to contextualise the developments in the emerging field of video-based media on the inter-net and critically engage with questions surrounding 'art online, visual art, innovative art, participatory culture, social networking, political economy, collaboration and new production models, censorship...YouTube, collective memory, cinematic and online aesthetics'. Over the years, some videobloggers were invited to the *Video Vortext* conferences, including Andreas

---

82   Lev Grossman, 'You — Yes, You — Are TIME's Person of the Year, *Time Magazine*', 2006 http://content. time.com/time/magazine/article/0,9171,1570810,00.html , accessed 15 June 2014.

83   Lessig, *Free Culture*; see also David M. Berry, *Copy, Rip, Burn: The Politics of Copyleft and Open Source*, London: Pluto Press, 2008.

84   More recent years have also seen the rising importance of social media and videoblogging, in particular in relation to social movements such as the Arab Spring, which echoes what Geert Lovink once called 'tactical media', which utilises digital technologies such as Twitter and Facebook, to post violent videos directly from political protests in potentially violent conflict zones.

H. Pedersen and Brittany Shoot (who wrote *The Lumiere Manifesto*),[85] Michael Verdi, Adrian Miles and Jay Dedman. Within the videoblogging community, these invites were seen as indications that videoblogging was being recognised within academia and a further legitimation of their practices.

It is important to keep in mind that the internet today is very different from the internet in 2004. Although many of the issues that were raised and discussed in 2004 remain relevant today, the way in which they were debated and the concerns they prompted were experienced in a different milieu. This historical dimension is crucial for understanding media as I believe a comparative approach can be very powerful in relation to understanding the kind of media disjunction that videoblogging signified. Consequently, at this point I want to take a historical detour to think about previous iterations of film and video technology, and also how artists, filmmakers and theorists thought about these changes. The aim is to broaden the connections and to start to make links to the continuities and often explicit references videobloggers made to this previous history.

For example, we might recall that in 1929, Dziga Vertov released *Man with a Movie Camera* which, in his words, was 'an experiment in the cinematic communication of visible events without the aid of intertitles, without the aid of a scenario, without the aid of theatre'. The film followed Soviet citizens as they went about their everyday lives, working, playing, and interacting. Yet the movie was not shot as a narrative story, rather, Vertov shot the movie over four years, and the footage was later edited together from what we might now call a vast database.[86] The film is lauded for its experimentation with a range of different cinematic techniques, yet it's greatest contribution is perhaps its message that the camera can travel anywhere, and capture anything from any angle, position or placement. Vertov's influence on later film and video movements stems from his concept of the camera as an eye (the *kino-eye*);

> An enhanced eye, beyond human perception, that catches life unawares, understood as "that which the eye does not see," as the microscope and telescope of time, as the negative of time, as the possibility of seeing without limits and distances, as the remote control of movie cameras, as tele-eye, as X-ray, as "life caught unawares". Kino-eye as the possibility of making the invisible visible.[87]

The kino-eye, however, is not transparent, in that it also foregrounds its own construction as formal intervention, as mediation, and hence adds artistic value to whatever is being created. As Dawson argues, Vertov proclaimed 'primacy of the camera itself (the 'kino-eye') over

---

85   *The Lumiere Manifesto* called for videoblogging to embrace the simplicity of the 'natural limits of the original Lumieres' by encouraging the creation of videos of no more than 60 seconds that featured no edits, no audio, no effects, no zoom and a steady, a fixed camera. The collection of Lumiere videos archived on http://videoblogging.info/lumiere/ currently stands at 1665 videos by 110 participants.

86   Seth Feldman, 'Vertov after Manovich', *Canadian Journal of Film Studies*, 16.1, (2007).
     Interestingly, an early example of convergence between amateur and professional/mainstream culture, the movie *Tarnation* (dir: Caouette 2003) was created from a large database of sorts of archived home move footage, including answer phone messages, photographs, Super 8 footage and VHS videotape.

87   Lev Manovich, 'Visualizing Vertov', *Russian Journal of Communication*, 5. 1, (2013) pp. 44-55.

the human eye [...] He clearly saw it as some kind of innocent machine that could record without bias or superfluous aesthetic considerations (as would, say, its human operator) the world as it really was'.[88]

Vertov's influence on film has been widely discussed and remarked upon, but interestingly his work also consciously or unconsciously inspired the practice of videoblogging. Videobloggers followed one or more of Vertov's elements in their work. Whether they explored everyday life, interactions with other videobloggers, stories with clear conventional narratives or more experimental videos, their cameras – like the kino-eye – acted as an extension of their own eyes looking out on the world, catching life candidly and often blind to traditional cinematic conventions. Like Vertov, the videobloggers didn't try to hide the camera, technology and tools they used as part of their practice. Instead, by making these elements part of the aesthetic itself, they added a specific Vertovian vernacular aesthetic to their work that has subsequently become recognisable.

It would be fair to say that the history of moving images presents a series of cyclical phenomena, or repeating commonplaces[89] – which, when placed side by side, might induce in the media historian a sense of *déjà vu*. Erkki Huhtamo uses as an example the similar reactions from the audience watching Étienne Gaspard Robertson's *Fantasmagorie* shows in Paris towards the end of the 18th century, and the first presentation of the *Cinématographe* by the Lumiére brothers, famously showing a train arriving at a train station (*L'Arrivée d'un train à La Ciotat*, 1895). Huhtamo also draws similarities to a more recent display of such immersive performances, the 'stereoscopic movie spectacle *Captain EO*, the 'onslaughting' aspect of which has been enhanced – in addition to the customary 3-D effects – by laser beams, which are released as if from the screen world to the audience space'. What connects these seemingly different experiences, is what Huhtamo calls *topoi*, what he refers to as commonplace formulas that act as 'building blocks of cultural tradition'.[90]

I think it is helpful to use these ideas to consider the way that 'topics of media culture... are recurring, cyclical phenomena and discourses that circulate'. This allows one to think of moments in media history as 'motifs that are recurring – whether as more general cultural phenomena... or in more tactical use'. I also want to link to Zielinski's work and the notion of an archaeology of videoblogging that 'does not follow a divine plan' but instead acknowledges 'an interest in and a need for new ways of understanding media cultures outside the mainstream'.[91] In other words, I am interested in tracing the development of certain *motifs* that can be seen as recurring in the history of film, video and digital media. These often fall into the following forms; (i) *significant technological advances*, in this case small, handheld cameras, making portability and mobility not only possible, but desired; (ii) *the relationship between technical change and aesthetic change*, for instance the employment/development

---

88   Jonathan Dawson, 'Dziga Vertov', *Senses of Cinema*, issue 23 (2003).
89   Jussi Parikka, *What is Media Archaeology?* Cambridge: Polity, 2012.
90   Erkki Huhtamo, 'From Kaleidoscomaniac to Cybernerd. Towards an Archeology of the Media' 19
      June 2014, 1997, from http://www.stanford.edu/class/history34q/readings/MediaArchaeology/
      HuhtamoArchaeologyOfMedia.html.
91   Zielinski, in Parikka, *What is Media Archaeology?*: 11-14.

of certain narrative techniques, such as talking directly to the camera, as opposed to the more traditional voice-of-god-style of narrative; (iii) *community*, the coming together of individuals to form communities of practice, experimentation and technical expertise. Indeed, the videobloggers might have seen themselves as pioneers in a new visual medium, but these motifs appear in many previous instantiations of amateur video production, both past and present, and by reflecting on the similarities and differences we can learn a lot about the motivations, trajectories and inspirations for the subsequent development of videoblogging. Nonetheless, it is helpful to follow the call to start in the middle, 'from the entanglement of past and present' and explore 'the part-futures and future-pasts, as well as parallel side-lines of media archaeology.'[92] This should not distract from seeing what is distinctive in particular historical constellations around media-forms. That is, that although there may be similarities and continuities, there are also discontinuities and disjunctions.

To illustrate the way in which videoblogging sought continuities as well as contrasts with previous media forms, take the example of a discussion on the videoblogging email list in November 2009. Here, Rupert Howe made a point that a video he had watched that morning 'however pretentious you may think this sounds... really [is] carrying forward and reinventing the tradition of observational documentary filmmaking that can be traced back through Direct Cinema, Cinema Verité and Kino Pravda all the way to the Lumiére brothers' first films'. This was not the only comment of its kind to be made on the email list. The other members often brought up cinematic styles or theories – drawing comparisons with videoblogging or recognising the debt their practice owed to video and film pioneers of the past. For instance, as commented by Adrian Miles on the email list in February 2005, there were clear attempts made to position videoblogging in a wider history of film and cinema. As he argued;

> There's Astruc's famous camera stylo... Chris Marker's experiments with video (he has whole series of two and three minute works that to a contemporary eye are vogs), and of course Vertov's numerous manifestos and dreams in the 1920s where he explicitly called for filmmakers to be distributed everywhere contributing from everywhere and the work being collated and shown nationally. What he was describing of course we would recognise as CNN.[93]

In many ways, then, there was certainly a knowledge of early forms of cinema amongst the videobloggers, and some of the early videoblogger practices could be mapped onto Vertov's checklist, including 'rapid means of transport, highly sensitive film stock, light handheld film cameras, equally light lighting equipment and a crew of super-swift cinema reporters'.[94]

I believe it is crucial to position videoblogging within the context of this history of early cinema. As others argued, 'most so-called new media have been imagined from a cinematic

---

92 Parikka, *What is Media Archaeology?* p 5.
93 Adrian Miles, Email to Videoblogging email list, 26th May 2005, accessed 09/09/2014 from https://groups.yahoo.com/neo/groups/videoblogging/conversations/messages/12 165.
94 Vertov, quoted in Dawson, 'Dziga Vertov'.

metaphor'.[95] Indeed, cinema itself exists in what Rodowick calls an 'expanded field' – which means that entertainment was not necessarily cinema's intended function, rather, 'there have been very distinct uses of the cinematograph and the moving image, as well as of the recording and reproducing technologies associated with them, other than in the entertainment industries'. Elsaesser gives the example of cinema's medical and scientific use, military and surveillance use, censoring, monitoring as well as 'the sensory-motor coordination of the human body in classical cinema.'[96] Renov further reflects on cinema's 'potential for the observation and investigation of people and of social/historical phenomena'.[97] Tom Gunning argues along similar lines, pointing out that a 'full understanding of film's relation to technology demands more than a longer span of diachronic history' and that, instead, the history of film needs to be read alongside a 'wider system of interlocking technologies which compose the terrain of modern experience'.[98] These observations apply equally to the development of videoblogging, which has become more important as a cultural practice in recent years.

Here it is worth mentioning Steve Neale's approach to cinema, which is important for the way he bridges two separate schools of thought in cinema history; the first in which film technology is treated as 'a self-contained sphere with a self-contained history', a chronological account in which 'each new feature or process either displaces those already in existence or else simply adds to them, increasing the stock of technical resources available'; the second being completely engrossed with the concept of realism and the indexical which 'works from the premise that the sounds and images comprising films are linked ontologically to the objects that the microphone and camera record'. Neale draws on the theories of Bazin and Kracauer, which explore a contradictory and troubled relationship with technology. Here, the advances in technology allow for more realistic cinema, yet this increased use of technology leads to it's complete disappearance, with representation and technology being repressed, along with the film industry itself. Neale develops a 'counter-approach' by locating technological innovation within aesthetic, ideological and economic, scientific and technical contexts, all of which exist within the broad umbrella of the film industry.[99]

Of course, the invention of the movie camera and the subsequent development of film have had far reaching effects on what we now call the cultural industries, but also on the growth

95   David N. Rodowick, *The virtual life of film*, Cambridge, MA: Harvard University Press, 2007, p. viii, see also Manovich, *The Language of New Media*, p. 78-79, who argues that 'a hundred years after cinema's birth, cinematic ways of seeing the world, of structuring time, of narrating a story, of linking one experience to the next, have become the basic means by which computer users access and interact with all cultural data'.

96   Thomas Elsaesser, 'Early Film History and Multi-Media: An Archaeology of Possible Futures?' in Wendy H. K. Chun and Thomas Keenan, (eds) *New media, old media: a history and theory reader*, London: Routledge, 2006, p. 20-21.

97   Michael Renov, *The Subject of Documentary*, London: University of Minneapolis Press, 2004: p. 171-172.

98   Tom Gunning, 'Systematizing the Electric Message', in Charlie Keil and Shelley Stamp (eds) *American Cinema's Transitional Era: Audiences, Institutions, Practices*, Berkeley: University of California Press, 2004: p. 19.

99   Steve Neale *Cinema and Technology: Image, Sound, Colour*, London: Macmillan Education, 1985, pp 159-160. See also André Bazin. *What is cinema?*. Vol. 2. University of California Press, 2004, Siegfried Kracauer, *Theory of film: The redemption of physical reality*. Princeton University Press, 1960.

and reach of amateur cultural production. In this context, the movie camera and – later – the video camera allowed ordinary people the opportunity to create moving images, whether within the context of the home, or in a wider societal context. As mentioned above, Vertov's 'checklist' for *Man With A Movie Camera* has inspired many subsequent manifestos for filmmaking and film-makers. Vertov's distinctive kind of self-reflective cinema, in which the viewer identifies themselves with the filmmaking process, doesn't reappear until the end of the 1950s, most notably in the work of filmmakers like Chris Marker or Jean-Luc Godard, described the 1972 translation of Vertov's writings as the 'cinematic equivalent of Chairman Mao's 'Little Red Book.'[100] Vertov's influence can also be seen reflected in the *Dogme manifesto* (written by Lars von Trier and Thomas Vinterberg in 1995) and the '10 Golden Rules of Lomography', which encourages a similar method for capturing photography, based on 10 'anti-rules', 'clearly intended to offer resistance to the ways in which the rules of "professional photography" repress "ordinary" creativity and continually redraw the boundaries between amateur and professional'.[101] Vertov also continues to inspire film and photography movements in the digital age.[102] Here though, I want to draw attention to its use as an inspiration directly for videoblogging, particularly, Adrian Miles' *Vogma Manifesto*, a list of 'commandments' for early videoblogs, and Pedersen and Shoot's *Lumiere Manifesto*. The videobloggers drew on this cinematic history and made a point of connecting lineage to it. Miles even went as far as proclaiming that videoblogging, or vogs as he called them, were 'Dziga Vertov with a mac and a modem.'[103]

Where Vertov concentrated on the visual power of cinema, with the camera as an enhanced eye through which the world could be captured, the French critic and film director Alexandre Astruc conceived of the camera in a more literary tradition, as a pen, which he called the *caméra-styló*, another cinematic metaphor frequently referred to on the videoblogging

---

100 Jeremy Hicks, *Dziga Vertov: defining documentary film*, London: IB Tauris, 2006, p. 134. It is worth mentioning here that Godard, too, held some influence over a section of the videoblogging community. Although I don't have much space to discuss his work in much detail here, some of the mentions on the list included this thought experiment from Adrian Miles; 'there is no art without constraint. Bandwidth, screen size, user time and network stutter are constraints (Thought experiment, if Godard started his career as videoblogger, what do you think he'd be doing?)'. Robert Croma, who made short artistic pieces pushing digital effects to their limits, invoked Godard in a debate about the whether videoblogging should follow cinematic conventions; 'To me there's a large element of YAWN to the strictures and suggestions being proffered here… How very very dull it all becomes when you tell people this is how you should do it if it's to be done 'correctly'. So terribly boring. 'Watch those eyelines.' 'Don't shoot from below.' And definitely no jump cuts. Godard must be vomiting as we speak... Free your mind, tell your stories in whatever way feels good to you. Life's too short.' Two of my informants also listed Godard as one of the filmmakers influencing their work (Sam Reinsew, Brittany Shoot). One also cited Vertov as influential on his work (Sam Reinsew).

101 Jean Burgess, 'Re-mediating Vernacular Creativity: Digital Storytelling', Paper Presented at *First Person: International Digital Storytelling Conference*, Australian Centre for the Moving Image, Melbourne, Australia, February 2006, 15 June 2014, from http://eprints.qut.edu.au/3776/1/3376.pdf.

102 I would also like to draw attention to the Norwegian amateur photographer Carl Størmer, who when he was a student in the 1890s, would walk around Oslo, Norway with a spy camera fastened in his buttonhole and secretly take everyday pictures of people he encountered. This shows how these amateur everyday practices have been around for far longer than the digital camera. For more, see https://www.boredpanda.com/spy-camera-secret-street-photography-carl-stormer-norway/.

103 Adrian Miles, 'The Vogmae Manifesto', 2000.

email list. Miles, for instance, remarked that 'a camera in your phone is pretty much Astruc's Camera Stylo isn't it?' For Astruc, the camera follows the tradition of the literary, where 'the idea of the camera as a tool to write with – indeed twice over, first when you shoot and then when you write the film on the timeline' is in focus.[104] He argued that cinema developed a language, much like the essay or novel had done previously. As Astruc argued, 'new age of the cinema [is] the age of caméra-styló (camera-pen)… the cinema will gradually break free from the tyranny of what is visual, from the image for its own sake, from the immediate and concrete demands of the narrative, to become a means of writing just as flexible and subtle as written language.'[105]

Astruc imagined that the breakthrough for film and cinema as an art form would not come through the entertainment industry, where it had been treated as a mere 'fairground attraction', but as 'a fundamental tool for human communication'. Astruc further argued that 'with the development of 16mm and television, the day is not far off when everyone will possess a projector, will go to the local bookstore and hire films written on any subject, of any form, from literary criticism and novels to mathematics, history, and general science.'[106] Although there is no denying how important Astruc's remark became to the pioneers of the French new wave cinema of the late 1950s and 60s, his thoughts just as well apply to video and the rise of videoblogs.[107]

Although Atruc was correct when he suggested that these developments within film and television would revolutionise media, it is also the case that with film, cultural production was itself democratised in new and unforeseen ways. For example, in the 1930s, as part of the consciousness-raising propaganda machine in socialist Soviet Union, Alexandre Medvedkin travelled across the Soviet Union on a *kino-poezd*, or ciné-train, consisting of 'three train carriages transformed into a film-production studio complete with projection room and living quarters'.[108] Medvedkin's ciné-train is interesting here because of the production processes that were used.[109] Medvedkin and his team would stay in one place for a few days, make a film and screen it in that same location. This meant that the feedback loop from conception to completion was very tight and that the intended audience were also the subjects of the

---

104 Chanan, 'Tales of a Video Blogger'.

105 Alexander Astruc, 'The Birth of a New Avant-Garde: La Caméra-Styló', in Timothy Corrigan (ed) *Film and Literature: An Introduction and Reader*, NJ: Prentice-Hall, 1999 (1948): p. 160. This emphasis on narrative writing through video has been explored through the work of Laura Rascaroli, 'The essay film: Problems, definitions, textual commitments.' *Framework: The Journal of Cinema and Media* 49, no. 2 (2008): 24-47; Timothy Corrigan, *The Essay Film: From Montaigne, After Marker*, New York: Oxford University Press, 2011; and Catherine Grant. 'The audiovisual essay as performative research', NECSUS: European Journal of Media Studies, Autumn 2016, http://www.necsus-ejms.org/the-audiovisual-essay-as-performative-research/.

106 Alexander Astruc, 'The Birth of a New Avant-Garde', p. 161.

107 Marsha Kinder, 'The Conceptual Power of On-Line Video: 5 Easy Piece', in Geert Lovink and Sabine Niederer, (eds) *Video Vortex Reader: Responses to YouTube*, Amsterdam: The Institute for Network Cultures, 2008.

108 Interestingly, Marker both celebrated and criticized Medvedkin in his film *The Last Bolshevik* (1993)

109 The moving train is an interesting *topoi* in media history, from the Lumière Brothers' *L'Arrivée d'un train en gare de La Ciotat* (1895), via Medvedkin to numerous digital video.

films. The group's motto was 'film today and show it tomorrow,' an idea that is echoed in later film and video work. This fast production-line system of capturing, producing and displaying film was revolutionary, and, years later would inspire French film maker Chris Marker to experiment with a similar process, when he worked with the factory workers in Besançon. The ultimate aim of Medvedkin and his contemporaries was to 'hold up a transformative and coercive mirror to the people, to show them the facts of their daily existence, which, once reflected back to them, would provoke them to take their lives into their own hands and change'.[110] In other words, to break false consciousness by making people aware of their own subjective position in a larger objective movement of history. That is, to help people become aware of their own place within society, culture and politics, and hence become reflexive and critical actors.

This 'film today – show tomorrow' approach to film making can be seen reflected in videoblogging work from everyday life, to conventions and conferences. For instance, at Vloggercon 2005 – the first videoblogging conference to move beyond the videobloggers own homes and incorporate representatives from various start-ups and community groups – the organisers would film panels all day and spend the nights editing and uploading video so that those unable to attend would be able to take part in the conversations as soon as possible. The fast turn-around of videoblogging – most people I talked to would publish their videos within a week of shooting – echoes Medvedkin's attempt to close the loop between filming and viewing, and is something that digital filming and editing made easier.

We might also consider another history of amateur/documentary film making known as 'Militant Film', or 'experiments in *autogestion*',[111] in which a group of workers at Rhodiaceta textile factory in Besançon, known as *Groupe Medvedkine*, 'emerged from a sustained *recontre* with the French film maker Chris Marker'.[112] Marker spent a period of time in the factory, interviewing and filming the workers (not always with the permission of the factory owners) and produced a film, *A bientot j'espere* (*Be seeing you*, 1968), which explored life in the factory, with focus on the factory occupation in 1967, following one worker in particular, a young militant, Georges Maurivard. The aim, in Marker's own words, was 'to give the power of speech to people who don't have it, and, when it's possible, to help them find their own means of expression'.[113] What was important about this example is that although the workers demanded better working conditions and increased pay, the originality of the Rhodiaceta strike, and what places it as one of the main influences of the protest movement that engulfed Europe in the spring of 1968, was the workers' demand for access to culture. Marker's work thus emerges out of a particular social and political context. Videoblogging was equally emergent at a time of relative political and cultural change, for example the 7/7 terrorist attack in London.[114]

---

110 Trevor Stark, 'Cinema in the Hands of the People': Chris Marker, the Medvedkin Group, and the Potential of Militant Film, *October Magazine*, 139 (2010): p 131.
111 Trevor Stark, 'Cinema in the Hands of the People': Chris Marker, the Medvedkin Group, and the Potential of Militant Film, p. 118.
112 Chris Marker, 'Marker Direct', *Film Comment,* 39.3 (2003): p. 119.
113 Marker, 'Marker Direct': 39.
114 Similar technologies are now being used in the Black Lives Matter movement in America. Black Lives Matter are utilising personal media technologies, social media and video technology to engage citizens

Personal video accounts of citizen engagement with political issues, with video broadcast and shared on social media, contributed to debates in the mainstream media, academia and beyond and led ultimately to a growing recognition of the importance of vernacular video.

In 1968, when screening *A bientot j'espere*, Marker was strongly criticized by a large proportion of the workers for romanticising their struggle, exploiting the workers and misrepresenting the women in the film; making them appear merely as wives, 'rather than as workers and militants in their own right'.[115] In response, Marker supplied those of the workers who were interested with filming and editing equipment, as well as training in film production, and helped setting up a second, parallel film company, which became the Besançon Medvedkin Group. Intended to be more open and collaborative than Marker's own work, 'this militant cinema would follow a collective and non-hierarchical model of production, seeking to abolish the separating between expert and amateur, between producer and consumer'. There were also parallels between the Medvedkin group and the contemporary work of another French film maker, Jean-Luc Goddard, who established the *Groupe Dziga Vertov* 'with its parallel but ultimately irreconcilable claims for self-reflexivity, collectivity, and class consciousness'.[116] Indeed, these fed into videoblogging in addition to Vertov's notion of the *kino-eye* and Astruc's concept of the *camera-stylo* and have proven hugely influential on both theories and practices of digital film and videoblogging itself.

There were also videobloggers who used their practice as a way to both engage with political issues, and indeed take political action. In particular, the videoblogger Josh Wolf, who was arrested, and later sentenced to prison, for refusing to testify before a U.S. grand jury. When arrested, Wolf also failed to hand over unpublished video footage he shot during a raucous clash on the streets between San Francisco police officers and anti-G8 protesters in July 2005. The incident was interesting because it challenged the relationship between the videobloggers and the media. Like many a videoblogger at the time, Wolf employed a discourse that was often scornful of corporate-controlled media. He was freed on April 3rd 2007, after seven and a half months in prison, when his lawyers reached a compromise with the federal prosecutors. He eventually handed over the tapes, but was excused from identifying any of the individuals that featured on the video. He famously appeared on *The Colbert Report* on June 12th 2007 where he discussed with Stephen Colbert whether or not bloggers should be classified as journalists, arguing that bloggers' practices and subject matter meant that they should be considered journalists even if they lack official recognition.

I now want to zoom in on another important background for thinking about videoblogging, namely the creation of home-movies. This is a practice that can be traced back to the end of the 1890s. As an aesthetic, it highlighted domesticity situated within particular cultural contexts, allowing people to curate mediated versions of their own lives that encouraged new ways of seeing the present and shaping their collective memory. Through this form, peo-

on a grass root level. This is also seen in the campaign #metoo.

115 Stark, 'Cinema in the Hands of the People': p. 126-127.

116 Stark, 'Cinema in the Hands of the People': p. 119.

ple 'negotiated their relationship with their surroundings and sense of self'.[117] The practice developed in a period in which 'amateur film was defined in economic and technological terms rather than within social, aesthetic, or political relations'.[118] Zimmermann provides perhaps the most extensive overview of amateur film in her exploration of the development and conceptualisation of home movies from the early days of cinema (from 1897 onwards) until the late twentieth century. Her work shows how the early developments of film cameras, film stock and projection equipment had great influence on artists, entrepreneurs, workers and hobbyists.[119] What her account shows is that, given access to equipment and technical knowledge of filmmaking, individuals were allowed to play and experiment with the making of films, exemplified by Stan Brakhage's experimentation with splitting the lens and non-camera-based film making. In a limited sense, then, home filmmaking was potentially 'democratised' from the very beginning.[120] However, it actually remained a mostly private practice, especially in terms of projection and viewership, for reasons of distribution and medium affordances.[121]

Zimmermann argues that amateur film from the 1950s can be seen in parallel with the social, political and economic conditions in post-war America. Zimmermann traces the development of what has been known as a 'Do-It-Yourself' (DIY) ideology - where the 'domestication of amateur filmmaking as a leisure-time commodity erased any of its social, political, or economic possibilities'.[122] It is interesting that Zimmermann also makes links between gender, patriarchy and power, although these issues are not at the centre of her study. Instead, she traces the material conditions for amateur filmmaking,[123] the standardization of the 8mm equipment (over 16mm, first made commercially available in 1923[124] which became standard for semi- and professional film making) and the development of what she calls 'aesthetic control' whereby many stylistic traits from Hollywood were incorporated into amateur film-making in the domestic sphere. Among the avant-garde, on the other hand, filmmakers were encouraged to break with aesthetic conventions and 'exploit their minimal budgets through exploration, experimentation, and risk taking'.[125] Here, we see a divergence between amateur-domestic filmmaking, on the one hand, and avant-garde experimentation on the other. This desire to break with conventions, and push the aesthetic boundaries of the medium can

117   Heather Norris Nicholson, 'In amateur hands: framing time and space in home-movies', *History Workshop Journal*, 43 (1997): p. 203.

118   Zimmerman, *Reel Families: A social history of Amateur Film*, p. 12.

119   Zimmerman, *Reel Families: A social history of Amateur Film*: p. 12-13. See also Broderick Fox, 'Rethinking the Amateur, Acts of Media Production in the Digital Age', *Spectator*, 24:1 (2004): 5-16 and Alan Kattelle, 'A Brief History of Amateur Film Gauges and Related Equipment, 1899-2001', 17 July 2014, http://oldfilm.org/content/brief-history- amateur-film-gauges-and-related-equipment-1899-2001 for an overview of amateur film gauges from 1898 – 1973.

120   Again, as has been argued with regards to the internet, questions of class, gender, and race problematize any notion of 'democratized' media access, technological expertise, and practice.

121   For an interesting moment of public use of amateur film footage on the film footage of the assassination of John F. Kennedy, see Alex Pasternack, 'The Other Shooter: The Saddest and Most Expensive 26 Seconds of Amateur Film Ever Made', *Motherboard*, 15 July 2014, http://motherboard.vice.com/en_uk/blog/the-other-shooter-the-saddest-and- most-expensive-26-seconds-of-amateur-film-ever-made.

122   Zimmerman, *Reel Families: A social history of Amateur Film*, p. 113.

123   Zimmerman, *Reel Families: A social history of Amateur Film*, p. 113-121.

124   Norris Nicholson, 'In amateur hands: framing time and space in home-movies', p. 202.

125   Zimmerman, *Reel Families: A social history of Amateur Film*, p. 130.

be seen echoed in the discourses of the videoblogging community. It is interesting to note that those identifying as personal or everyday life videobloggers were more likely to adopt more 'traditional' narrative structures.[126]

According to Zimmermann, the rise in amateur filmmaking was assisted by a number of factors, including increased free time for the middle classes, a general increase in knowledge about technical equipment and filming technique. This was due partially to publications such as *Amateur Movie Maker* and *America Cinematographer*, which encouraged 'technique and technical mastery as the first phase on the road to achieving cinematic "perfection"'.[127] However, despite being constructed discursively as a private hobby, amateur film contributed to the democratisation of media production, and digital affordances may in the future 'liberate it as a more accessible and meaningful form of personal expression and social and political intervention'.[128]

The political potential of moving images was brought one step closer to fruition with the invention of video. Whereas Marker, and Medvedkin, Vertov and Astruc had worked hard to utilise film in their art for political critique and change, the emergence of video gave rise to a new set of practices made possible by the more flexible medium of videotape. Ina Blom persuasively argues that video 'propels artists to take media power in their own hands, using televisual techniques for the non-instrumentalist purposes of art'.[129] From the start, video was always conceptualized as a personal, intimate medium. From the first versions of the Portapaks to the miniature digital camcorders of the late 1990s and early 2000s, video has always been 'low to the ground and potentially private, and intimate in use.'[130] Indeed, in the 1960's Sony introduced the new category of the 'industrial standard' video-recorders and as Garcia explains, 'these machines were the first relatively affordable and easy to use video standard. What had been until then the exclusive domain of the TV industry suddenly became more widely available'.[131] It is interesting how, throughout history, we see a return to the same discourse regarding the potential for 'ordinary people' to take control of their own media production and consumption. One of the early movements to articulate these ideas was the Guerrilla television movement.

In the 1971 Guerrilla Television Manifesto, Michael Shamberg outlined a technological radicalism attacking commercial television, arguing that it was 'a conditioning agent rather than a source of enlightenment' for the masses.[132] Video was seen as a decentralising force that had the potential to bring forth a 'Whitmanesque democracy of ideas, opinions, and cultural

---

126   Norris Nicholson, 'In amateur hands: framing time and space in home-movies', p. 202.

127   Zimmerman, *Reel Families: A social history of Amateur Film*, p. 68.

128   Zimmerman, *Reel Families: A social history of Amateur Film*: 157.

129   Ina Blom, 'The Autobiography of Video: Outline for a Revisionist Account of Early Video Art', *Critical Inquiry*, 39. 2, 2013: 277.

130   Tom Sherman, 'The Nine Lives of Video Art: Technological evolution, the repeated near-death of video art, and the life force of vernacular video...' Lecture held during the conference 'Video Vortex - Responses to YouTube', Amsterdam, 18 January 2008.

131   David Garcia, '(Un)Real-Time Media: 'Got Live if you Want It'', in Geert Lovink and Sabine Niederer, (eds) *Video Vortex Reader: Responses to YouTube*, Amsterdam: The Institute for Network Cultures, 2008: p. 294.

132   Deidre Boyle, 'Subject to Change', *Art Journal*, 1985: 229-230, 10 April 2013, http://www. experimentaltvcenter.org/sites/default/files/history/pdf/boylesubjecttochange_182.pdf.

expressions'. Integral to this was the idea that this new form of video would be made by and for ordinary people. The ideas behind Guerrilla television were articulated in Shamberg's work, as well as in the magazine *Radical Software* (published by the collective Raindance, made up of, among others, Shamberg, Frank Gillette, Paul Ryan and Ira Schneider). Shamberg was strongly influenced by Marshall McLuhan[133] and argued that the significance of the medium of video was 'much greater than that of a mere improvement of an old medium, that videotape could be a powerful cultural tool'.[134] He provides a theoretical context for Guerrilla television, and this is also where his influences are most strongly seen; arguing that 'Americans are information junkies'. He was also influenced by the cybernetics of Norbert Wiener and Buckminster Fuller, with his theoretical exploration resting on four elements; 'a philosophy of media ecology, a critique of 'Media-America' and broadcasting, a belief in video as a remedy to this system, and a tentative understanding of how computers might influence the future of video.'[135] Central to the movement was Shamberg's belief that 'guerrilla television gets cameras to the people to let them do it themselves', heralding a new age of media production by the people, for the people.

Shamberg saw enormous potential for citizen journalism in the work of the video-makers at the time, and it is tempting to draw parallels between video collectives such as TVTV and Videofreex on the one hand, and the early videoblogging community on the other. Shamberg wanted to disrupt the media ecology of 'Media America', to empower individuals to actively take part in their own media environment, because, following McLuhan, he believed that 'media and man evolve together', and that video represented the most important cultural technology of our time, as it 'frees film to become an art form'.[136] Interestingly, in the early days of the videoblogging community, individual members would often volunteer at their local Apple store, teaching people simple video editing techniques and how to start a videoblog. For example, Susan Pitman, a single mother of two who videoblogged about her kids and went under the moniker 'kitykity', told me she had given her first video presentation at an Apple store in December 2005. The response from the store indicated that there was a real interest in videoblogs and editing skills, with Pitman telling me, 'before I ever gave the presentation, the lead instructor at the store told me that he wanted me to present once a month, and to pick dates for the next couple months.'

Ryanne Hodson also volunteered teaching videoblogging at her local Apple store, and Steve Garfield even set up the collective Boston Media Makers, a small but regular media training

---

133 The videobloggers were certainly aware of the work of McLuhan, as a few quotes off the email list show, 'I just stumbled on this superb quote from Marshal McLuhan. 'The old medium is always the content of the new medium. As movies tend to be the content of TV and as books tend to be the content of movies.' It pretty much perfectly sums up the web. It started by gobbling up TV, radio, movies, music etc., but since some of these media companies wholesale boycotted it a black market of goods spring up as well as leaving a tremendous opportunity for innovative media makers... i.e. the world of videoblogging and YouTube among others.

134 Michael Shamberg, *Guerilla Television,* New York, NY: Holt, Rinehart and Winston, 1971: 32.

135 William Merrin, 'Still fighting 'the Beast': Guerrilla television and the limits of YouTube.' *Cultural Politics* 8.1, 2012: 97-119.

136 Shamberg, *Guerilla Television*, p. 7-8.

workshop in Boston that still continues to run. This volunteerism – and the enthusiasm and excitement about videoblogging it reflected – was common in the early days of videoblogging. It was also a reflection of how different and specialized the practice was. We sometimes forget that most internet users had never posted - or even watched – a video online at this point. This can be seen reflected in a comment on the videoblog email list by Clint Sharp who argued that;

> We're doing something different that's going to change things. I have no visions of being on a sitcom. I do have visions of someday professionally creating niche content or in some way doing video, audio and text related to technology. I do have visions of people being able to find content of interest to them that Television wouldn't produce because 99% of people aren't interested in it... There's nothing wrong with the old media system... it's just that we're doing something different. Old Media has served us well for 50 years, but we're changing things.[137]

As with earlier forms of amateur and semi-professional media production, the Guerrilla television movement would not have been possible had it not been for the changes in the technologies available to them. The new video equipment was compact, lightweight and affordable, and the hand-held video recorders and accessories allowed individuals to record and edit film and video on the go. This technological basis made for an aesthetic that is reflected in the content of the films/videos, featuring interviews, close-ups, point of view shots and 'smaller' visual vistas than those utilised in cinematic productions. These portable technologies contributed to the emerging *style* of these kinds of films and videos, a style that initially disrupted the viewers' ideas of what film and television should be like, and which, eventually, formed part of what has subsequently become known as the DIY aesthetic. Today, this way of seeing has been adopted into mainstream film and broadcast television programs, such as *The Office, The Blair Witch Project, Grizzly Man* and others.[138]

The style and content of Guerrilla television was largely determined by the technology available to the video makers at the time. Lack of access to expensive cameras and editing technologies, national distribution channels and access to a wider audience, meant guerrilla television had to make do with limited technologies. Chapman argues that 'the development of a totally new style of media production surrounding half-inch video-tape was due both to the experimental inclinations of the early adopters and to the unique cultural and technical features of the new portable equipment'.[139]

Guerrilla television style was informed by the understanding that corporate television was structured as an opposition between 'people with transmitters', and the people with receivers.[140] The form and content of Guerrilla television, which was largely documentary, was

---

137 Clint Sharp, Email to videoblogging list, 14 July 2005, https://groups.yahoo.com/neo/groups/ videoblogging/conversations/messag es/16789.

138 Thomas Austin. '"...to leave the confinements of his humanness": Authorial voice, death and constructions of nature in Werner Herzog's' Grizzly Man'. In Thomas Austin and Wilma de Jong, (eds.) *Rethinking documentary: new perspectives, new practices*. Open University Press, Maidenhead, 2008: pp. 51-66.

139 Sara Chapman, 'Guerrilla Television in the Digital Age', *Journal of Film and Video*, 64.1-2 (2012) p. 42.

140 Chapman, 'Guerrilla Television in the Digital Age', p. 42.

dictated by the technological limitation the video makers were working within, as much as any political or philosophical conviction these 'video freaks' might have shared. Ironically, Boyle argues that the beginning of the end for TVTV, for a while the most media-friendly and controversial group of Guerrilla television, came with the commissioned to make a pilot for NBC, called *The TVTV Show*. However, with the perks and privileges of working for NBC, also came certain restraints and restrictions. Having to operate within a corporate framework and to the network's deadlines caused an enormous amount of friction within the group, and Boyle tracks how the community slowly grew apart. The rhetoric of the TVTV collective, and the Guerrilla television movement more generally might seem out-dated today, but their aim of utilising new video technologies to challenge the entire informational infrastructure of the media landscape, remains not only timely, but pertinent. In many ways, the digital video activisms we see today – and which was pioneered by the early adopters of online video – can be seen as the 'fulfilment of a radical 1960s dream of making "people's television".'[141] Although I wouldn't want to over-claim here or press this similarity too strongly, it remains suggestive.

Indeed, feminists have utilised video as a contribution to consciousness-raising of women and other oppressed groups. Whereas film is an expensive medium, video made it cheap and displaying it was easier. This, in conjunction with activist movement of the time, led to the creation of specific events, like the New York Women's Video Festival which ran between 1972 and 1980. This festival linked portable video, the women's movement, and the emergence of new cultural practices and new spaces for political contestation. For many women, creating video became a unique means of self-expressions (this is also the argument put forward by Alexandra Juhasz in her work on YouTube).[142] This was often achieved through 'sharing individual life experiences and analysing them collectively', allowing them to 'discover[…] their own subjectivity [through the idea that] personal testimony leads to theory and action'. Video likewise allowed women to explore their subjectivity, and the feminist political documentary (concerned with biography, characterized by structural simplicity, and eager to establish trust between the filmmaker and her subject) proved an especially flexible form.[143] There are resonances here with the way in which women videobloggers used the videoblog to explore, contest and question the traditional male 'public sphere' values by highlighting the personal, the particular and the domestic in their videoblogs, something I'll return to in later chapters.

Renov makes a strong argument that 'something happened' between 1970 and 1990 that facilitated a shift in the politics of documentary film making – from political and social commentary to more personal perspectives on culture and identity. He points in particular to the work of video artists Wendy Clarke, who began experimenting with the video diary format in 1977 as one example of the shift in documentary style and content in this period.[144] Renov argues that after the political storm of the 1970s, which the Guerrilla TV and the feminist movements

---

141 Boyle, 'Subject to Change'.
142 Alexandra Juhasz. *Learning from YouTube* [Video Book], MIT Press (BK) (2011).
143 Melinda M. Barlow, 'Feminism 101: The New York Women's Video Festival, 1972–1980', *Camera Obscura*, 18.3 (2003), pp. 3-40.
144 Renov, *The Subject of Documentary*, p 177-179.

had both been part of, the period after became rather more interested in the 'mundane'. Renov also points out how, in this later period, the documentary tradition moved away from an 'informed' and 'objective' style to a more individualistic perspective. Norris Nicholson makes a similar argument, when she states that 'early amateur film is one way of tapping into people's memories about themselves and how they relate to others in contrasting contexts'.[145]

At this point we might also make a connection to the 1995 BBC2 series, *Video Nation*. This featured 'ordinary people' with access to hand-held cameras who were encouraged to speak directly into the camera about their everyday lives and experiences, thoughts and feelings. Although the series was firmly in a public broadcasting tradition, it was different from earlier first person media in the way that it focussed almost exclusively on individual domestic issues and personal narrative accounts, instead of focussing on more structural issues. Arguably, *Video Nation*, which ran from 1995 – 2000, signalled, and possibly helped to contribute to, a critical change in the notion of the public sphere, paving the way for 'what Jon Dovey has described as 'first person media' forms, within contemporary lifestyle and docu-soap programming' and thus, creating audiences for the arrival of personal media diaries in the UK.[146] Looking back on these early experimentations with 'first person media' it is striking that many of the earlier notions of personal media as a reflexive practice were evident in videoblogging and social media.

The adoption of video and film technologies has been significant in the emergence of the practices explored so far. Blom persuasively argues that 'digital platforms… reduce the difference between film and video to a question of rhetorical (as opposed to technical) formatting.'[147] To explore some of these ideas and the effects of digital technology on the production of personal media I now want to contextualize some of the elements of digital technology that have contributed to this. As such, I now turn to the socio-technical considerations that make up the technical a priori of videoblogging. To do this, I briefly explore some of the genealogies of key technologies in the context of video and the internet.

---

145 Norris Nicholson, 'In amateur hands: framing time and space in home-movies', p. 199.
146 Nicole Matthews, 'Confessions to a new public: Video Nation Shorts', *Media Culture & Society,* 29. 3 (2007): pp. 435-448.
147 Blom, 'The Autobiography of Video', p.280.

3. BUILDING THE VIDEOBLOGGING INFRASTRUCTURE: A BRIEF HISTORY

The early development of the videoblogging community in many ways maps directly onto the growth of online video technologies on the internet. In this chapter I want to critically engage with videoblogging as a technical platform. I do this in part by looking at archived technologies, discourses and recordings of events, combined with an exploration of the research data gathered during the empirical study conducted over the course of my ethnography. As such, this chapter has two main functions. The first is concerned with mapping the development of a constellation of technologies. The second is concerned with how the videobloggers articulate their technical practices, which include the kinds of technologies they use, how they express their highly technical digital skills, camera skills, and how they organise around and through their social networks. Running through the analysis are the technical contours of the short-form digital film, usually under ten minutes in length, due mainly to technical limitations, narrative practices within videoblogging, as well as social norms and practice. This informs part of the self-description, or subject position, occupied by the videoblogger. This process of identity-making can be seen in relation to what we might consider a nascent form of database informed narrative, using digital tools to cut and paste film in innovative ways. This editing process opens up new and radical forms of video-reflexivity in the presentation of self. This is combined with reticular video-sharing fascilitated by bespoke tools and blogging platforms to distribute this through a shared community of practice.

There is considerable literature on the emergence of digital culture, life on the screen, communities and lived experiences online,[148] yet it is only in recent years that focus has started shifting towards a closer analysis of the material structures of the web.[149] The advent of software studies and infrastructure studies, network politics, tactical media and political economic studies of code and software, has meant that more attention is given to the structures that facilitate and shape digital media. The study of computational systems is made difficult by the fact that researchers often have limited or no access to what lies beneath the interface itself,[150]

---

148 See for instance Sherry Turkle, Life On the Screen. Identity in the Age of the Internet; Kennedy, 'Beyond Anonymity'; Rheingold, *Virtual Communities*; Jenkins, Convergence Culture. Where Old and New Media Collide; Castells, The Information Age. Vol. I: The Rise Of The Network Society, Castells, The Information Age. Vol. II: The Power Of Identity; Noble, Safiya Umoja. *Algorithms of Oppression: How search engines reinforce racism*. NYU Press, 2018; Abbate, Janet. *Recoding gender: Women's changing participation in computing*. MIT Press, 2012; Nagle, Angela. *Kill all normies: Online culture wars from 4chan and Tumblr to Trump and the alt-right*. John Hunt Publishing, 2017; Turkle, Sherry. *Alone together: Why we expect more from technology and less from each other*. Hachette UK, 2017; Pariser, Eli. *The filter bubble: What the Internet is hiding from you*. Penguin UK, 2011; Taylor, Astra. *The people's platform: Taking back power and culture in the digital age*. Metropolitan books, 2014; Carr, Nicholas. *The shallows: What the Internet is doing to our brains*. WW Norton & Company, 2011.

149 For instance, see Kirschenbaum, 'Extreme Inscription: The Grammatology of the Hard Drive'; Berry, *The Philosophy of Software: Code and Mediation in the Digital Age*; Alexander R. Galloway, *Protocol: How Control Exists After Decentralization*; Matthew Fuller, *Software Studies: A Lexicon*, Cambridge: MIT Press: 2008; Ian Bogost *Alien Phenomenology, or What It's Like to Be a Thing*, Minneapolis: University of Minnesota Press, 2012.

150 Ganaele Langlois, Fenwick McKelvey, Greg Elmer, and Kenneth Werbin. 'Mapping Commercial Web 2.0 Worlds: Towards a New Critical Ontogenesis'. *Fibreculture* 14 (2009): p. 1-14.

and indeed in my own work I have had to acquaint myself with unfamiliar technical details which are often obscure, difficult to understand and unfriendly for non-technical researchers. With this in mind, I introduce some of the major technologies underlying videoblogging and briefly describe their emergence and development. The aim is to contextualise these technical systems, but also to provide a map of the continuities and discontinuities that videoblogging, and particularly its technical side, have in relation to internet technologies.

In this chapter, I move rapidly through the history of a number of technical and social systems and due to limitations of space, I cannot hope to do them all justice here. Nonetheless, the aim is to provide some sense of the major events, technologies and movements that are important for the light they cast on understanding the rise of videoblogging, which is, of course, the focus of this book.

First, I want to spend a small amount of time thinking about the internet as a now well-known a global computer network. Often described as a network of networks, the internet was developed by Darpa in the 1960s. Its quasi-military origins show how 'military concerns and goals were built into the Internet technology… favour[ing] military values, such as survivability, flexibility, and high performance, over commercial goals, such as low cost, simplicity or consumer appeal'.[151] But much of the development of the DARPAnet was technical as well as militaristic, driven by engineers and mathematicians who were invested in the network through a love of programming, not a concern for military tactics. Decisions made early on to implement things like packet switching and networked computers were seen as technical problems, often divorced from their social context as a way to increase computing time and increase efficiency across the network.

But the internet also opened up, often inadvertently, new possibilities through its agnostic approach to centralisation, verification and hierarchy. That is not to say there are no hierarchies manifested on the internet, indeed that is patently untrue. Rather, earlier decisions on the technical structure allowed multiple points of communication, shifting to a model of data transfer and a paradigm of knowledge that was networked and distributed. This later created the ideal conditions for the spread of grass roots, viral media forms. It remains a curious historical artifact that the cold war should produce a counter-power in the form of a reticular system that the internet makes possible. Of course, this is the foundation on which videoblogging and other social media were built.

The origins of the ideas that informed the internet might be traced back as far as 1938, with H.G Wells' publication of *World Brain*, a concept that conceived of 'a complete planetary memory for all mankind'. Wells' ideas re-emerged in the writings of Vannevar Bush, whose *As We May Think* from 1945 described a collective memory machine for information storage

---

151   Janet Abbate, *Inventing the Internet*, Cambridge, MA: MIT press, 2000, see also John Naughton, *A Brief History of the Future*, London: Phoenix Press, 1999, Manuel Castells, *The Information Age. Vol. I: The Rise Of The Network Society*, Oxford/Cambridge: Blackwell, 1996, Manuel Castells, *The Information Age. Vol. II: The Power Of Identity,* Oxford/Cambridge: Blackwell, 2000. Castells, M. (2001) *The Internet Galaxy*, Oxford/Cambridge: Blackwell.

and retrieval called the *memex*. The traditional narrative about the origins of the internet tends to describe the 'demonstration of 4-node ARPANET network in 1969' as the 'epoch-making' moment. Campbell-Kelly and Garcia-Swartz argue that 'when the Internet took off in the early 1990s the world was covered by thousands of isolated networks and the integration of these networks into a global entity was likely to happen, whether ARPANET existed or not' due to the fact that linking up these systems was an obvious inventive step in the development of networking technology.[152] But we have to keep in mind the difference between the internet and the World Wide Web that was built upon it and which was inspired by these previous ideas.

The World Wide Web didn't emerge out of the ARPA research community itself, but from a separate group of computer scientists working at the European Organization for Nuclear Research, CERN, amongst them Tim Berners-Lee and Robert Cailliau. Berners-Lee developed the world wide web in response to the increasing difficulty of sharing information between scientists at dispersed universities and other institutions across the world. The World Wide Web also owes some debt to the work on hypertext developed by Ted Nelson, whose manifesto *Computer Lib* (1974) partly influenced Berners-Lee.[153] What was unique about the web as conceived by Berners-Lee, was that it did not require a directory of any kind, be it local or global. As Berners-Lee explains;

> Given the go-ahead to experiment… I wrote in 1990 a program called 'WorldWideWeb', a point and click hypertext editor which ran on the "NeXT" machine. This, together with the first Web server, I released to the High Energy Physics community at first, and to the hypertext and NeXT communities in the summer of 1991.

The 'specifications of UDIs (now URIs), HyperText Markup Language (HTML) and HyperText Transfer Protocol (HTTP) [were] published on the first server in order to promote wide adoption and discussion.'[154] Needless to say, their simplicity and ease of implementation meant that they were widely used, and usage accelerated over time.

It is also important to remember that sociality was happening across computer networks long before the development of the web. In fact, the first Bulletin Board System (BBS) went online in 1978 and grew increasingly popular as functionality improved. Initially, only one user could be online at any one time, but by 1994 it became possible for users of bulletin boards to connect to one another through low-speed telephone networks'.[155] In 1985, Larry Brilliant and Stewart Brand started the Whole Earth 'Lectronic Link (the WELL), which went on to become one of the most prolific, and certainly one of the most influential online commu-

---

152   Martin Campbell-Kelly and Daniel D. Garcia-Swartz, 'The history of the internet: the missing narratives'. *Journal of Information Technology*, 28.1 (2013), p. 18.

153   Abbate, *Inventing the Internet*, p. 214. See also Ted Nelson, Branching presentational systems-Hypermedia, *Dream Machines*, 1974, pp. 44-45 and Noah Wardrip-Fruin and Nick Montfort, *The NewMediaReader*, Cambridge, MA: MIT Press, 2003.

154   Tim Berners-Lee, The World Wide Web: A very short personal history, 1998, http://www.w3.org/People/Berners-Lee/ShortHistory.html, accessed 11 June 2014.

155   Campbell-Kelly and Garcia-Swartz, 'The history of the internet: the missing narratives', p. 26

nities at the time.[156] These early technical platforms that inculcate a sense of belonging, and hence a sense of community, soon gave rise to the emergence of community-formation as an explicit design goal. Of course we are familiar with this logic, which today is incorporated into platforms, but in these early days community often emerged organically.

By October 24th 1995, the formal definition of the term 'the internet' was unanimously agreed by the Federal Networking Council (FNC). The resolution states that the Federal Networking Council (FNC) agreed to define the term 'Internet' as 'the global information system that – (i) is logically linked together by a globally unique address space based on the Internet Protocol (IP) or its subsequent extensions/follow-ons; (ii) is able to support communications using the Transmission Control Protocol/Internet Protocol (TCP/IP) suite or its subsequent extensions/follow-ons, and/or other IP-compatible protocols; and (iii) provides, uses or makes accessible, either publicly or privately, high level services layered on the communications and related infrastructure described herein.'[157] In 1995, the number of commercial users also overtook the number of research and academic users.

Conflicting ideas about the internet have circulated since its emergence. As previously mentioned, John Perry Barlow's *Declaration of the Independence of Cyberspace* demanded autonomy from governments and nation states.[158] The declaration was part of the writings of a generation of thinkers influenced by the revolutionary rhetoric associated with the early web, drawn from, among others, William Gibson's *Neuromancer* (from 1984) and government discourse on the 'information superhighway'. A close reading of Barlow's text, however, reveals 'a wealth of contradictions and misdirection: newness is rooted in history; revolution is effected by commercial transaction; and liberal democracy becomes libertarianism'.[159] Nevertheless, the bodiless, immaterial world of distributed identities Barlow describes can be seen reflected in early writings on behaviour and communities online. Writers such as Sherry Turkle and Howard Rheingold both describe user practices and community bonds that are somehow intensified through digital technology. This utopianism is reflected through a discourse describing 'diffused networks [which] *equalize* social practices and values evolved in and around them' and describe '*all* virtual social practices [as] equalised in the sense of being "more equal than the real world"'.[160] It is interesting to note the degree to which Barlow's writing contributed to a conception of cyberspace and its users that emphasised immateriality and virtuality above materiality. We might note this moment as a significant marker for the emergence of the dichotomy within technical systems of the tension between the individual and community. This remains in place today in most technical systems, and of course reflects a wider contradiction manifest in liberal democratic systems within capitalism.

---

156   Rheingold, *The virtual community*, see also Fred Turner, *From counterculture to cyberculture: Stewart Brand, the Whole Earth Network, and the rise of digital utopianism*. University of Chicago Press, 2010.

157   Vint Cerf et al, Brief History of the Internet, *InternetSociety.org*, http://www.internetsociety.org/internet/what-internet/history-internet/brief- history-internet#History, accessed 24 June 2014.

158   John Perry Barlow, A Cyberspace Independence Declaration.

159   Aimee Hope Morrison, An impossible future: John Perry Barlow's 'Declaration of the Independence of Cyberspace', *New Media & Society*, 11.1-2, (2009) pp. 53-71.

160   Marshall T. Poe, *A History of Communications: Media and Society from the Evolution of Speech to the Internet*, Cambridge: Cambridge University Press, 2011, p 225.

These early systems had a strong feedback loop between community and network, with the network here understood as including the developers of the platform itself. As such, 'Web 2.0 platforms are not simply about facilitating user-produced content and carrying content across networks to large audiences or 'end-users'; rather, they are primarily concerned with establishing the technocultural conditions within which users can produce content and can be re-channelled through techno-commercial networks and channels.'[161] Indeed, a software platform has to work to inculcate a sense of community in users, understood here as a form of sociality, and into their technical processes. Or to put it another way, it is when the network and the community are brought together that a socially-oriented platform can emerge. Langlois et al put it aptly when they write, 'the ontogenesis of Web 2.0 is about the creation of inhabitable worlds within which users can exist and extend themselves according to specific technocultural logics'. Once a certain logic of sociality within technical systems had been identified, this notion of community was quickly incorporated into the development of online network platforms. In many ways, Web 2.0 was the first codification of this logic online, although of course this exploitation of the social inclinations of human beings had been used throughout the twentieth century in a number of marketing and PR processes for industrial production and consumption.

It is now common for technical platforms, when they are launched commercially, to alienate the original early community surrounding its technical development, and in many cases to offer little monetary rewards to the very people who were so instrumental in its early success. Examples abound of these ways of exploiting early adopter communities, Apple, for example, was heavily reliant on its early adopter community before it become successful.[162] Equally, we can consider the examples of Flickr, which originally had a means for the community to take a part in its governance. This practice was also followed by Facebook and Instagram, which, in the case of Facebook, later proposed to amend and remove this 'community' from the company ordinances in December 2012 when they began an IPO process, that is when they realised that community stood in the way of profits.

I now want to turn from this broad overview to think about the more particular case of technologies that were key to the development of videoblogging. For example, one of these is the video codec format technologies which were crucial for allowing the encoding ('co') and decoding ('dec') video. I want to spend some time talking about codecs mainly because they are key technologies – but also because they were highly unstable, constantly shifting, except at the time that videoblogging emerged. In some sense, due to a number of different external factors, codecs stabilised, which enabled users to get a grip on the technologies and utilise them to produce creative work.

The technical conditions for online video were represented by codecs and compression algorithms that were changing digital video. A codec is a device or computer program responsible for encoding or decoding a digital stream and a standard. It is a compression format – a way of

---

161 Langlois et al, 'Mapping Commercial Web 2.0 Worlds: Towards a New Critical Ontogenesis'.
162 This was detailed by Guy Kawasaki in relation to the mailing lists he used to direct the early adopter community in particular directions or to gain feedback on products.

storing data – and an implementation of a program that can read and write compressed files. After being compressed, files only retain some of the data from the original file (this is called a lossy format), so in some sense the codec could be considered a 'translator' that makes decisions about which data is included in the compressed file – so called lossy compression. To store large files on computers, or to transmit them across networks, requires that they are 'compressed'. This means that through clever mathematical equations, a digital file can be reduced in size, sometimes dramatically, and therefore assist in the sharing and transfer of files. Perhaps the most famous version of compression is that of MP3, which was able to reduce a file in size by more than half. This allowed music files to be fitted on a number of devices, but also shared widely on the internet.[163] Similarly, for video, compression algorithms made video on the internet (but also DVDs, BluRay and 4K video compression) possible. It goes without saying that video compression was a key technology that laid the foundations for videoblogging. But using video compression codecs is not just technical, it is also a social practice. There has to be some social agreement on which practices are reflected in the technical standards used – in order to create, use view and distribute the community work and ideas.

Ursula Franklin suggests that thinking about technology as practice 'links technology direct-ly to culture, because culture, after all, is a set of socially accepted practices and values'. Moreover, Franklin suggests that 'well laid upon practices also define the practitioners as a group of people who have something in common'. Further, she argues that 'the experience of common practice is one of the ways in which people define themselves as groups and set themselves apart from others'.[164] In terms of the videobloggers, this *setting themselves apart* is perhaps most clearly seen in their attitudes towards technology and video platforms, and one of the issues I want to spend some time on to show how video technologies and platforms developed in a crucial time between 2004 and 2007.

Today, there are a plethora of video codecs. Here, though, I wish to highlight QuickTime in particular. QuickTime was one of the fundamental technologies that formed part of the vid-eoblogging practice. Apart from a very small number of users who relied on Windows Media Player, the majority of the independent videobloggers I interviewed relied on QuickTime (both the application and the codec) in some way through their videoblogging practice.[165] As Cubitt argues, 'there is no internet without the standardisation of internet protocols; and there is no exchange of moving pictures without standardisation of the codecs on which the various proprietary players can function'.[166] I highlight QuickTime because it was such an important codec for the videobloggers to know and understand, and because, as it turns out, the development-cycle of QuickTime was significant to the videobloggers. QuickTime was also the first consumer-based video handler that actually worked, both as video support and as

---

163   See Jonathan Sterne. *MP3: The meaning of a format*. Duke University Press, 2012.

164   Ursula Franklin, *The Real World of Technology*, p. 15.

165   Andreas Haugstrup Pedersen, Cheryl Colan, Enric Teller and Raymond M. Kristiansen all explicitly mentioned it, but looking through their videoblogs, I found that a much larger number relied on this particular codec.

166   Sean Cubitt, 'Codecs and Capability', in Geert Lovink and Sabine Niederer (eds) *Video Vortex Reader. Responses to YouTube*, Amsterdam: Institute for Networked Cultures, 2008, p. 46.

a shared platform amongst a large group of users. Manovich argues that the 'introduction of QuickTime in 1991 can be compared to the introduction of the Kinetoscope in 1892: Both were used to present short loops, both featured images approximately two by three inches in size, both called for private viewing rather than collective exhibition.'[167] Manovich shows how the QuickTime and the Kinetoscope even appear to play a similar role in the cultural sense;

> If in the early 1890s the public patronized Kinetoscope parlours where peep-hole machines presented them with the latest marvel – tiny, moving photographs arranged in short loops – exactly a hundred years later, computer users were equally fascinated with tiny QuickTime movies that turned a computer into a film projector, however imperfect.

QuickTime was an extensible software framework that abstracted many of the complexities of multimedia formats. It not only supported the playback of video but allowed encodings of video and transcoding to other formats. The native video format for QuickTime was called QuickTime File Format, which was a 'container file' that stored different types of data, such as audio, video, texts or effects. Because QuickTime contained an abstraction of the underlying formats, it could support abstract references and edit lists – this made QuickTime ideal for editing video. Its abstraction affordance meant that other formats could be 'plugged in' to the framework and it could therefore handle other popular formats like Asf, DivX etc. Indeed, in many ways, QuickTime was the 'killer app' for videoblogging.

QuickTime was originally designed by Bruce Leak and was first shown to the public at the World Wide Developer Conference in May 1991. During Apple's onstage presentation, QuickTime was displayed playing Apple's iconic 1984 advert playing directly off the computer on the stage. As has become usual with Apple's big launch presentations, the event was a huge success and QuickTime was considered an astounding technical breakthrough. The first generation of QuickTime (version 1.0) displayed an aspect ratio of 320 x 240 pixels, and had a frame rate of 15 frames per seconds, fairly primitive to us today, but a real technical achievement at the time.

The next year, 1992, Apple launched QuickTime 1.5, which added the Cinepac codec and vector-quantization. Cinepac was a lossy video codec that had previously been used in, amongst others, the Atari Jaguar. This allowed for more compact video compression. The 320 x 240 ratio remained, but QuickTime now supported 30 frames per second. Apple also added text tracks, and released their first Windows compatible version of QuickTime (1.0 for Windows). This version included Cinepac and INDIO (from Intel). In February 1994, Apple launched QuickTime 2.0, which supported the addition of music tracks in addition to the already supported video and text. With this, QuickTime was becoming a fully integrated multimedia format. In the same year, Microsoft launched their competitor Video for Windows (version 1.0), using Microsoft's own RLE and Video Codecs, but these were woeful in comparison, having few of the technical breakthroughs of QuickTime.

---

167 Manovich, *The Language of New Media*, p. 313.

QuickTime 2.5 was launched in 1995, and supported sprite tracks (which allowed the use of animation to be superimposed over the video) and an early version of Virtual Reality (VR). In the same year, Microsoft launched Windows 95 which came with the Direct X codec – an important competitor technology. The languages Java and Javascript were also introduced in 1995. In 1997, QuickTime MPEG was launched, which basically allowed and supported the playback of the MPEG codec. This is significant because the MPEG format was an important industry standard. 1998 saw Apple launching QuickTime 3.0, which added the ability for QuickTime to understand GIFs, JPEGs and TIFFs. Perhaps more importantly, QuickTime 3.0 allowed the user to output video directly to Firewire, cutting down export time dramatically. QuickTime 3.0 also included support for the Sorenson video codec, which meant QuickTime could now support fully professional codecs.

In June 1999, Apple launched both QuickTime 4.0 for Mac and QuickTime 4.0 for Windows. This iteration supported MP3 and video streaming. It also supported connecting to a Quick-Time streaming server. Here, one of the fundamental building blocks for the live streaming of audio-visual data across the internet was laid. In December 1999, Apple launched QuickTime 4.1, meaning Apple released two big updates this year. This was a major update, allowing the processing of video files larger than 4 GB. The update introduced variable bitrate for Mp3 files, allowing better quality files to be produced. In 1999, Apple also launched iMovie, a video editing software aimed at consumers, not professional filmmakers. This software radically simplified video editing by building on the abstraction that the QuickTime framework created. Needless to say, for videobloggers, iMovie enabled a more rapid and professional looking production of video and was widely used.

QuickTime 5.0 was launched in 2001, which allowed MPEG 1 video playback (for both Mac and Windows). Apple added Sorenson video 3 playback, Flash 4 playback and export, and had a new VR engine. By supporting real-time rendering of effects and transitions in DV files, QuickTime 5.0 was the first launch that seriously developed QuickTime's potential as a video *editing* software, and not just a media player. The elements of technology for supporting videoblogging were therefore strengthening into a comprehensive technical system. In 2002, Apple launched QuickTime 6.0, supporting MPEG 4 playback, import and export, as well as support for Flash 5, JPEG 2000 and MPEG 2 playback. Apple also included support for Instant On Streaming Playback, which would change the way video content could be consumed online. Also launched, but not by Apple, was the RSS 2.0 feed specification and many implementations of it were supported on websites and blogs, enabling the syndication and distribution of videoblogs. This was another key technology for videoblogging.

Additional support for AAC/AMR codecs, which increased the quality of compression for audio output, was introduced in June 2003, when Apple released QuickTime 6.3. Apple also included the first support for mobile formats, the 3gPP codec,[168] which supported mobile video camera formats from brands such as Nokia and Sony Ericsson. This allowed seamless

---

168   3gPP was the industry's first mainstream solution to support the third generation partnership project standard, which allowed a foundation for the delivery and playback of rich multimedia content over wireless networks.

movement of files between mobile and computer, allowing not only playback possibilities, but also more logical storage and archiving of mobile video files.[169] In October of the same year, Apple launched the Pixlet codec, allowing QuickTime to process High Definition (HD) video files. By December, QuickTime 6.5 was launched, reinforcing Apple's support for 3gPP (mobile), AMC (audio) and Apple lossless format. Thus we can see that Apple yet again moved the bar in terms of democratising its software, which was usable by professionals and consumers, and laying the foundations for increased streaming services across wireless networks. Indeed, 2003 was also the year Chris DeWolfe and Tom Anderson launched Myspace, which, for a short period before Facebook and Twitter, would become one of the largest social networks on the internet, as well as one the first sites to promote video content.

In 2003, Apple released Final Cut Pro 4, a professional video-editing software suite which included a package of additional applications, *Compressor* for transcoding between video formats, *LiveType*, *Soundtrack,* and *CinemaTools.* Apple also launched Final Cut Express, a cheaper and slightly downgraded version of Final Cut Pro. Final Cut Express became a useful tool for those within the Videoblogging community who wanted to edit their videos but who either didn't have the technical expertise or financial ability to get to grips with Final Cut Pro. Final Cut Express allowed more advanced editing than iMovie, producing a more professional looking result and again found an important user base in the videoblogging community.

The term 'podcasting' was coined by Ben Hammersley, a technology writer for the Guardian, in 2004, when he 'rhetorically asked what the emerging practice of amateur online radio should be named: 'Audioblogging? Podcasting? Guerilla Media?"[170] Podcasting was the creation of

> A digital media file, or a series of such files, that is distributed over the internet using syndication feeds for playback on portable media players and personal computers. Like 'radio', the term can refer either to the content itself or to the method by which it is syndicated... The host or author of a podcast is often called a podcaster.[171]

As such, podcasting can be seen as closely related to both blogging and videoblogging (there also exists the term audio-blogging, which indicates that audio files are regularly embedded in a users' blog, much like videos are embedded in the videoblogger's videoblog). Sterne et al argue that podcasting is a conflation of iPod and broadcasting and divide podcasting into practice and product. They further observe that podcasting continues to work through the division between producer and consumer – that it is not merely an extension of blogging culture.[172]

---

169 These video files were very small, with very low resolution, so were perfect for device-to-device sharing, but not much else. Nonetheless, the collapse in formats between computation and telephony was an important anticipation of the later moves by Apple in mobile technology.

170 Jonathan Sterne, Jeremy Morris, Michael Brendan Baker, and Ariana Moscote, 'The Politics of Podcasting', *Fibreculture*, issue 13 (2008).

171 Jonathan Sterne, *MP3: The meaning of a format.*

172 It is interesting to note the explosion of podcasting media in 2017, with podcasts such as *RadioLab, Radiotopia, Invisible 99, My Dad Wrote Porno* and many others getting a mass listenership. However, its political economy remains shaky.

After the launch of YouTube, a number of competing video platforms were launched in 2005. In April, Dailymotion was launched, a French video sharing website founded by Benjamin Bejbaum and Olivier Poitrey. Other examples of video platforms include Veoh (founded by Dmitry Shapiro in September 2006), Vimeo (founded November 2004, VideoEgg (founded by David Lerman, Matt Sanchez and Kevin Sladek in early 2005).[173] In July, News Corporation bought Myspace in a shocking $580 million deal. Since February 2005, Myspace users' had the ability to embed YouTube videos in their Myspace profiles and realizing the competitive threat to the new MySpace Videos service, Myspace banned embedded YouTube videos from its user profiles. MySpace users widely protested the ban, prompting Myspace to lift the ban shortly thereafter. However, News Corporation failed to capitalise on Myspace's potential, and it was soon overtaken by its rivals.

Apple launched QuickTime 7.0 on April 28th 2005. This upgrade introduced the codec H264,[174] which was to become the standard format for audio-visual digital content across all of Apple's mobile media devices (including the iPhone, iPod touch, iPad, and Apple Watch). It would later become the industry standard format for displaying audio-visual content on the internet, but at the time it was widely derided as poorly supported in contrast to the flash '.flv' format. Ironically, in QuickTime 7.3 Apple dropped support for the flash format altogether. Apple also upgraded to iMovie HD, which included support for HDV (720p and 1080i) and introduced a new feature called 'Magic iMovie' – streamlining the video editing process by automatically inserting a pre-selected video-transition between clips. The H.264 format was important as it allowed high quality video at lower bitrates than other standards. It was half the bitrate of MPEG-2, H.263 or MPEG-4 part 2. It's best known for being the video encoding standard for Blu-Ray discs and was well-designed to support streaming video. It is also notable for its ability to support 4K UHD video and in this sense was a very forward-looking technology.

In 2009 the discourses around online practices shifted from participation to consumerism. The focus on participation and involvement that had dominated media discourse since 2005 gave way to studies showing how much online content people were consuming, how many hours of video were being watched on YouTube and so on. This shift is mirrored by the development of QuickTime. After four years of few major updates, QuickTime X launched. This was significant, moving QuickTime from being a specialised tool to a social media oriented application. In this upgrade, Apple introduced visual chapters and the ability to perform more complex editing from within QuickTime itself. It also supported screen capture, the ability to record the screen of the computer whilst the user is performing other tasks, and support for capture of video and audio streams. It increased GPU acceleration and improved live streaming. This version of QuickTime, which had been completely re-written in order to support 64-bit audio and video codecs, dropped some of the earlier codecs. Perhaps most interestingly, however, QuickTime now allowed direct sharing to YouTube, bypassing the previous complex

---

173   There are too many to list here, but a few important ones are Archive.org, blip.tv. Dailymotion, Facebook, Funny Or Die, GodTube, Hulu, LiveLeak, Mefeedia, Openfilm, and Photobucket.

174   H264 is a video-compression format. It is particularly good because it is able to produce high quality video in relatively low bitrates.

system of compression and codecs, essentially allowing anyone with little previous knowledge of video formats to export video *in the correct and optimised format* directly to YouTube. In other words, one expert layer of knowledge about the export of audio-visual content via QuickTime was abstracted away, transforming the process of creating, uploading and sharing video to the internet. Video-sharing's technical a priori was now in place.

Gradually, corporations and industry started to see the potential profit from online video distribution. For example, in February 2007, Netflix, the online movie-rental service, which had been posting DVDs to subscribers since 1994, introduced video-on-demand to its subscribers. In December 2007, the BBC iPlayer was launched; a Flash based video streaming service giving users online access to BBC programmes. The service had been in 'beta' since the summer, and was criticised for only working with the Windows XP operating system. As a publicly funded public service broadcaster, it was very odd for the BBC to miss an opportunity to develop the spirit of community and diversity represented by the GNU/Linux and open web. It goes without saying that Microsoft at the time represented a monopoly on user desktops. After a petition signed by over 16,000 people, the government said the BBC would ensure the iPlayer worked with other operating systems. In October, the BBC entered a strategic relationship with Adobe, in order to provide streaming across multiple platforms (Macintosh, Linux and Windows). This relationship was 'part of the BBC's strategy to reinvent bbc.co.uk to ensure that all its rich-media content is accessible to the widest audience possible'.[175] When the iPhone 3GS (the first in Apple's iPhone range capable of shooting video) was launched in 2009, the possibility for short-form digital film went truly mainstream. The Apple App Store opened in 2008, and brought with it a potentially massive market for film editing apps.

Unfortunately, one cannot talk about online video without talking about the elephant in the room, YouTube. Not only does YouTube dominate online video consumption, but the desirability of its audience compels others to chose the platform to upload their videos. Likewise, YouTube also tends to dominate academic discussion of online video, now of course naturalized to digital video. The way in which digital technologies have a tendency to monopoly as platforms is an interesting research question – but its oversized representation in academic discussion is something this book aims to push back on. Nonetheless, to do justice to the development of videoblogging, YouTube has to feature, if only tangentially. With this in mind, I want to quickly sketch the technical milieu that soon came to overwhelm and undermine grass roots videoblogging.

YouTube grew at an incredible rate between 2006 and 2008, and in only a few years the site completely dominated the online video sphere. In 2008 alone, YouTube received around '64 million unique visitors a month and [was] the third most visited site in the United States after Google and Yahoo'.[176] There is no doubt that this growth led to many changes to the

175 BBC Press office, 'BBC enters strategic relationship with Adobe to enhance BBC iPlayer and bbc.co.uk', *BBC Press Office*, 2007, http://www.bbc.co.uk/pressoffice/pressreleases/stories/2007/10_october/16/ adobe.shtml, accessed 13 June 2014.
176 Matthew Mitchem, 'Video Social: Complex Parasitical Media', in Geert Lovink and Sabine Niederer (eds) *Video Vortex Reader. Responses to YouTube*, Amsterdam: Institute for Networked Cultures, 2008, p. 278.

site itself. In 2005, for example, it was still possible to upload a video and watch it hover on the 'recently uploaded' tab for at least an hour or so. This feature was later removed, as the stream of uploaded videos started moving so quickly that it was impossible to keep up. This has now been replaced with a 'recently uploaded – recommended for you' feature, based on your viewing history, similar to Twitter's 'in case you missed it' feature. By 2014, YouTube boasted an impressive 1 billion unique visitors a month, and by 2017 a staggering 3.25 billion hours of video were watched on the site every month. YouTube might not be the haven of user-generated content it once was, as Geert Lovink reminds us, 'YouTube's slogan, 'Broadcast Yourself', is put into action by less than 1 per cent of its users'.[177] Rather, he argues, 'in this Long Tail age, we know that it's mainly about "Broadcasting to Yourself"'. In many ways, then, YouTube has developed and grown into a platform which is 'negotiating and navigating between community and commerce'.[178]

YouTube is often talked about in popular culture as if it is a library, an archive or a laboratory, and sometimes as if it is a medium like television. Although cultural contexts give the site different meanings, from a strictly computer-science viewpoint, YouTube is nothing but a database.[179] This reflects Lovink's comment from 2008 that 'we no longer watch films or TV, we watch databases'.[180] Attempts have been made to tackle the platform analytically, providing useful overviews of the service, it's users and cultural significance. These studies often do so at the cost of much detailed investigation into the specifics of the platform. Jean Burgess and Joshua Green's important text on YouTube gives an impressive snapshot of the platform. They create a typology of the videos found on YouTube, from corporate advertising campaigns, via music videos, fan videos and vlogging. This survey is incredibly valuable as it gives us an indication of where the platform was at the time and how much it has changed since.

In 2008, over half the videos on YouTube were user-generated, 40% of which were vlogs.[181] Vlogging was a relatively established practice amongst the early adopters on YouTube. However, traditional content, defined as 'videos originally produced within the established media industry' ranked higher than the user-generated content in terms of number of views and favourites. On the other hand, user-generated content far outweighed the traditional when it came to most discussed and most responded to, thus reinforcing the value of vlogging for a sense of community.

Patricia Lange, on the other hand, points out a number of what she calls (mis)conceptions about YouTube. The first is that YouTube is a video sharing site. She argues that in addition to sharing videos there, 'for a subset of participants, YouTube is an imagined community of people who share an interest in video making or communicating through interactive video'.[182]

177   Geert Lovink 'The Art of Watching Databases', in Geert Lovink and Sabine Niederer (eds) *Video Vortex Reader. Responses to YouTube*, Amsterdam: Institute for Networked Cultures, 2008, p. 11.
178   Pelle Snickars and Patrick Vonderau, *The YouTube Reader*, Stockholm: Mediehistorisk arkiv, 2009, p.11.
179   Snickars and Vonderau, *The YouTube Reader,* p. 13.
180   Lovink, 'The Art of Watching Databases'.
181   Burgess and Green, *YouTube,* p. 43.
182   Patricia Lange, '(Mis)Conceptions about YouTube', in Geert Lovink and Sabine Niederer (eds) *Video Vortex Reader. Responses to YouTube*, Amsterdam: Institute for Networked Cultures, 2008, p.88.

As such, YouTube is arguably *more* than a video-sharing site. The second (mis)conception is the desire for researchers to study 'ordinary people' on YouTube, arguing that 'if you are posting videos on YouTube, you are arguably no longer ordinary, if by ordinary we mean a person who has no special interest in or connections to intensive media-making'. Lange argues that the technical requirements, time and effort it takes to post videos, coupled with the fact that only a small percentage of registered YouTube user actually post videos at all, means the idea of studying 'ordinary users' is itself flawed. Thirdly, Lange argues that contrary to the fact that most users simply go to the site to watch particular videos, YouTube is a community, populated by users who invest in each other and each other's content. As she argues, 'the suggestion here is not that all people on YouTube feel part of a community or even part of a specific community or group of friends. The contention is rather that not all people who watch videos on YouTube are casual two-minute viewers of specific videos'.[183]

By January 2009, it was estimated that 100.9 million viewers watched 6.3 billion videos on YouTube.com (62.6 videos per viewer) for a 43 per cent market share. In comparison, Fox Interactive Media ranked a distant second in terms of videos viewed, with 552 million videos (3.7 per cent). On a global scale, 77 per cent of the total US Internet audience watched online video for an average of six hours in January 2009.[184]

Towards the end of 2009, what we see is a shift in the way social media use was being reported; whereas so far the focus had been mainly on participation, and the way in which new participatory media opened up far wider audience interaction, at the end of 2009, the focus started drifting towards 'engagement', a euphemism for consumption. To illustrate, in January 2009, YouTube announced a new partnership with Apple, offering users 'a dynamic, lean-back, 10-foot television viewing experience through a streamlined interface'.[185] This announcement meant the integration of YouTube with Apple iTunes, allowing users to watch YouTube videos directly on their televisions, further blurring the distinction between online and offline content, as well as the distinction between online and offline behaviour. YouTube's expansion into 'offline' media continued with the announcement, in April 2009, of a partnership with Sony 'to expand its library of movies and TV shows'. The extent to which YouTube is an accepted part of the media landscape is also reflected in the decision of the Library of Congress to create its own YouTube channel. During spring 2009, the Library announced that it would begin to upload millions of clips to YouTube.

Since 2010, online video moved in two directions. In terms of viewing online video, increased bandwidth has meant a massive increase in real-time streaming of either live or archived data. This has made viewing content online easier, more readily available and, with services such as Netflix, Hulu, BBC iPlayer Apple iTunes, and HBO Online, bringing a much wider range of content to the user. Some of these services, like the BBC iPlayer, are 'free' (or, in the UK at least, funded by the TV licence), whereas Netflix and HBO online charges a monthly

183 Lange, '(Mis)Conceptions about YouTube', p. 96.
184 William Uricchio, 'The Future of a Medium Once Known as Television', in Pelle Snickars and Patrick Vanderau (eds) *The YouTube Reader*, Mediehistorisk arkiv, 2009, p. 27.
185 Snickars and Vonderau, *The YouTube Reader*, p. 11.

subscription fee. Other services, such as the UK-based BlinkBox (rebranded as TalkTalk TV Store in July 2016), charge users per episode, series or film. On the other hand, sites such as YouTube allow its users to upload videos up to 15 minutes long and files larger than 20GB. Video-sharing also moved out of the browser and into mobile applications, which are highly personal (also see Lovink on what he calls *'totale Mobilmachung'* of visual culture).[186] Similarly, Nanna Verhoeff argues that 'screens are objects, technologies, apparatuses and machines of vision, all at once.'[187]

To complete this compressed history of digital video, more recently, in September 2011, Snapchat was launched. Initially named *Picaboo*, Snapchat originally allowed users to share images that would self-destruct after a few seconds. The app has since introduced video-sharing and 'stories' – where users can post updates throughout the day. To increase the sense of immediacy, all images and videos posted to the story are deleted after 24 hours, though later software updates allowed the user to save their stories within the application, or download onto their camera roll. In 2012, two new video processing applications (apps) were also launched,[188] and which also commodified something akin to the videoblogging aesthetic. Vine, a short-lived but much loved video sharing app, allowed the user to record 6 seconds of video by tapping the screen (which operated as the viewfinder) and another video processing app, Light, released only months before. Light created short, stop-motion videos by recording one frame a second for approximately ten seconds. Both Vine and light were great examples of tools of interest to those fascinated with 'light weight, ready to hand video documentation practices that want to seriously engage with and intersect the everyday' in a way similar to that trail blazed by videoblogs.[189]

Meanwhile, QuickTime continued to be developed by Apple, and in March 2012, QuickTime 10.2 was launched, supporting more social sharing, allowing users to share their videos instantly to either email, YouTube or Facebook but also directly to devices, such as iPhone, iPod and Apple TV. The history of QuickTime documents a codec that developed from a very technically complex software package (media player and codec), requiring expert knowledge of the requirements of formats and compression, into an abstracted social media aware framework, allowing the quick and easy processing of audio-visual data. In its last iteration, QuickTime also made sharing data across the internet very simple. What is interesting is that in the period between 2005 and 2009, in which QuickTime was, by any means, a stable codec, with relatively minor upgrades, the videoblogging community was at its most active. I merely note that the relative stability of QuickTime might have contributed to the emergence and relative success of videoblogging. A lot of the discussions early on within the community circled around the problem of negotiating a rapidly changing technological landscape and

186 Geert Lovink, 'Engage in Destiny Design: Online Video beyond Hypergrowth', in Geert Lovink and
     Racheal Somers Miles, (Eds) *Video Vortex Reader II: Moving Images Beyond YouTube*, Amsterdam:
     Institute for Networked Cultures, 2011.
187 Nanna Verhoeff, *Mobile screens: The visual regime of navigation,* Amsterdam University Press, 2012, p. 16.
188 Vine amassed over 40 million users in its first year although there is some contention about this figure,
     as well as a question to be raised about how many of those are active users.
189 Adrian Miles, 'Vine and Light (a poetics of the sublime ordinary)', 29 Janary 2013 from http://vogmae.
     net.au/vlog/2013/01/vine-and-lightt-a-poetics- of-the-sublime-ordinary/.

QuickTime made this relatively easier. For the majority of this chapter of the videoblogging 'era' one of the most important technologies used by the community was actually relatively stable. The conditions of possibility for the videoblogging practice rests partially upon the fact that Apple slowed their QuickTime releases as they were in the process of modernising their operating system and hardware.[190]

In 2013, Instagram, an established photosharing site recently purchased by Facebook, launched video as part of their service. This allowed up to 15 seconds of video to be recorded. The method of capturing video in Vine and Instagram (tapping finger on viewfinder in Vine, and pressing and releasing finger on record button in Instagram video) produced a similar aesthetic. This created a comparable effect to the fast-edits of early videoblogging. Whereas it could take the videoblogger a long time to create this effect in software packages such as iMovie, Final Cut Pro or QuickTime, here the process was automated and user friendly. In many ways, then, the more recent applications and software packages that handle online video, have taken the videoblogging practices, automated, simplified and streamlined them, so that the videoblogging aesthetic is now available at the click of a button.

Videoblogging remained a marginal practice for a long time, although recent years have seen the success of a younger generation of videobloggers who are creating global brands for themselves, see for instance Michelle Phan, a beauty vlogger who has an impressive 6.7 million subscribers.[191] Phan posts tutorials about makeup and posts life advice to her follow- ers. Another example is British vlogger Zoe Elizabeth Sugg, better knows as Zoella, who has monetised her beauty and lifestyle YouTube channel into a multi-million pound business.[192] Since becoming 'internet famous', she has written a book, launched her own line of beauty products, started a WH Smiths book club and designed a range of stationary for them. Her YouTube channel attracts over a million views per episode, and she can charge up to £20k for endorsements on her channel or Instagram page. Clearly, video online has changed dramatically in just a decade.[193]

One of the interesting things about the period 2004-2009 is the extent to which the self-iden- tity of the videoblogger and the platform technologies were continually contested by the community. Even as the technologies began to encode certain practices, the generally high technical competence of the videobloggers meant that they could always choose to reject or unpick a particular delegation of their practice. This placed the videobloggers in an inter-

---

190 Here I refer to their paradigm-shifting move from Power PC to Intel, a process first made public at the World Wide Developer Conference in 2005. The process was completed in August 2009, with the release of the 'Snow Leopard' upgrade to the Mac operating system.
191 https://www.youtube.com/user/MichellePhan.
192 https://www.youtube.com/user/zoella280390/.
193 YouTube is also host to a number of political and activist video makers, allowing small grassroots organisations like Novara media to flourish. Novara media tell stories about racism and climate change with the goal of 'elevating critical perspectives' they claim you are unlikely to encounter in the mainstream media. Although there is no space to explore this in more detail here, it is worth mentioning that YouTube, in it's apparently neutrality regarding political affiliation, also plays host to a range of conservative and Alt-right channels, like the Canadian political activist Lauren Southern, who has become both popular and influential.

esting position of power in relation to the platform developers (who also often included the videobloggers themselves). In effect this often meant that the developers had to woo the videobloggers and thus enrol them into using their systems by making the platform technologies themselves 'looser' and hence more customizable. This also meant that the ability for this platform to create any sense of lock-in, or loyalty, was limited – which also potentially lessened any commercialisation strategies by the platform developers. This looser, open development method has resonance with free and open source software, and it is certainly the case that videobloggers had a relatively sophisticated understanding of, for example, intellectual property rights. YouTube, on the other hand, with its flash-based technologies and practices was swallowed by Google where it developed into a much more mainstream short-video platform.[194] YouTube is also more clearly structured around a traditional notion of what video 'should be' in as much as it is structured heavily around 'hits', internet memes, popularity and 'likes'. YouTube tried to incentivise their users in other ways. The YouTube revenue-sharing program, which was launched in 2007, paid money for people to distribute their content on the platform. 'Once a creator signed, Google would load up the channel with advertising, take a 45 percent cut of the resulting revenue, and hand over the rest. For many YouTube creators the money was an incentive to keep going but wasn't enough to live on. They still had to hustle'.[195] But this point here is no doubt that the sphere of video as a grass roots experimental community was mostly over.

Today we tend to take for granted these earlier technical systems, particularly important issues like the slow refinement of the video codecs that made online video possible at all. Nonetheless, as I have tried to show in this chapter, a number of technical preconditions, none of them easy, had to be resolved before they could be combined to create the beginnings of a video platform. A platform is a standardised technical architecture that simplifies, standardises and systematises a constellation of technologies. Once this is done, the drive to monopolise the platform takes place, and hence aggregate a massive user base which can then be monetised, for example through advertising. The classic instance of this process is, of course, YouTube which seeks very aggressively to preserve its quasi-monopoly over social media and hence to reap the profits from almost complete control of video online.

---

194 Of course, 'open' platforms also have the possibility, and frequently attempt, to monetize their services, see for instance the success of Ubuntu and the Android operating systems.

195 Felix Gillette, 'Hollywood's Big-Money YouTube Hit Factory', Bloomberg Businessweek, accessed 08 September 2014 from http://www.businessweek.com/articles/2014-08-28/youtube-hollywoods-hit-factory-for-teen-entertainment.

4. FROM VIDEO-IN-BLOGS TO VIDEOBLOGGING

In this chapter I want to spend some time connecting the previously discussed technologies to their manifestation in particular videoblogging practices. The aim is to highlight the socio-technical aspect of videobloggers and to ensure that the cultural practices and the technical practices are fused in the account I am making. This is important because the videobloggers encountered the limitations, breakdowns and glitches of their technical milieu in their everyday practice – the technical was intimately related to their work. But further to this, a number of the videobloggers were also developers and programmers, and were keen to develop and iterate the tools they used and share them more widely in the videoblogging community. In this respect, they are very different from the videobloggers who are in evidence today on YouTube. The Youtubers benefit from the ease and abstractions of the platform, without much regard for the underlying video technologies – indeed, they do not need to. However, back in 2004, the milieu was remarkably different, with a plethora of formats, standards, software and the limited bandwidth as previously discussed. It is through a combination of cultural practices and technical restrictions that videoblogging emerges as a practice, and goes on to flourish for a number of years before being swept away in the double whammy of social sharing sites and an avalanche of vernacular video that proliferated in the post-YouTube era.

Much of the videoblogging community behaviour and activity is situated in relation to discussions around working with an underlying set of technologies in a competitive and collaborative atmosphere aimed towards the development of a platform. This included the articulation of competing and often normative ideas of how a video platform 'should be', and eventually the emergence of a *platform imaginary* (see figure 3), that guided the implementation and content creation practices in videoblogging. This imaginary was constructed through discourse and computer programming code and supplemented through demo websites, prototypes and mock-ups. Usually, but not always, the platform imaginary was guided by a few key individual developers and users, and some companies, but in many cases the companies did not understand the platform imaginary. This is fairly common, seen for example on Twitter, in the way the early users' practices developed the @mention and hashtag functionality, and to which the company at first didn't pay attention to because it was considered to be 'too geeky'. Equally, a set of norms developed quite quickly around videoblogging and a number of developers and companies attempted to build software around these emerging practices. Similarly, the early Twitter platform had very little functionality for sociality and was conceived as a communications channel. The very active early adopter community therefore developed a new set of practices, such as re-tweeting (RT), mentioning (@-mentions) and hashtags (#) to make up for lack of technical functions. These were later absorbed into code in the current system. This kind of appropriation of user innovation is very common on technical platforms.

Companies like Microsoft employ proprietary, or closed, code for most of their software packages, and, likewise, companies like Facebook and Twitter are notoriously protective of their technical systems. Within these, the abstraction of technical processes (as seen with the emergence of Web 2.0 technologies) creates new user experiences built around convenience when using the web. For instance, compare the action of posting a video on a website before the emergence of Web 2.0 – copying a link, pasting the link (with the correct html) into your website or blog, then either waiting for someone to visit your site or emailing a link to this particular page (via your email) to a number of contacts, all entered by hand – with the much simpler 'one-click' embedding of a YouTube video directly onto the Facebook Timeline, instantly shared with your Facebook friends. Compare this again to sharing a brief video clip with all your friends via Snapchat, or Instagram stories – where short videos are instantly pushed to all their devices. This has profound effects on the experiences of the users, and should have profound effects on the way in which these technical systems are studied; What we need to do is 'to challenge our perception of the Web as rooted within the visual aesthetic of the user interface'.[196] A platform-based methodology is a way to uncover these underlying processes that tie the various 'modular' elements of Web 2.0 world together, allowing for critical analysis of protocols and the way they are 'articulated so as to channel information in specific ways and this enacts specific economic, legal and cultural dynamics'.[197]

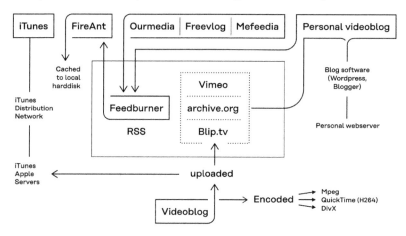

Figure 3: A schematic overview of the videoblog platform, 2005.

Langlois et al calls this going 'beyond and below the user interface'. Here I draw on software studies and related approaches to examine the technical and social elements of platform-based communities. The aim is to try and locate the interconnections and co-constructions of the 'network' and 'community'. I do this by analysing the communities in question at a point *before* the 'corporate colonisation' takes place. In other words, I look at the constellation of technical systems and user-practices of the early adopter communities in a period of instability, before the platforms have been set in place, and at a point where individual users still have the power to influence changes on the building of the network. For these purposes, I use *network* to refer to the material level of the technical-social level and *community* to refer to the socio-cultural level of the socio-technical associations that form in these technical-social assemblages. It is important to map the way in which the technical

196 Langlois et al, 'Mapping Commercial Web 2.0 Worlds: Towards a New Critical Ontogenesis'.
197 Langlois et al, 'Mapping Commercial Web 2.0 Worlds: Towards a New Critical Ontogenesis'.

level, as network, is co-constructed, and yet constantly iterated by the early-adopter community who populate it. Additionally, I am interested in the way in which mediators (like apps), function to mediate the interface between the network and the community, and in some cases intensify, shape and facilitate particular forms of sociality on the network.

So now I want to use this approach to look at videoblogging itself, drawing on the empirical data gathered through my virtual ethnographic fieldwork. Looking at different aspects of the videoblogging practice, I start with its technical foundation. I look closely at how the technologies available to, created and maintained by the videoblogging community were conceptualised and discussed. This helps explore the emergence of a videoblogging platform imaginary. But although this technical knowledge is necessary to gain a deep understanding of the videoblogging practice, it is not sufficient unless we also look at how these technological structures are negotiated and the conditions under which these practices emerge. Participatory culture was not created by Web 2.0 platforms such as YouTube, rather, platforms such as YouTube were so quickly accepted by the mainstream because for decades groups of participatory cultures had prepared the way for the early adoption of these kinds of platforms.[198]

From a purely screenic perspective, a videoblog is a blog that uses video as its main form of expression. The videobloggers used a variety of blogging software, most notably Blogger, although many converted to Wordpress as that platform grew in popularity.[199] Blogs settled into a particular design in the early 2000s, where the sidebar contained links to other blogs usually related to the one being read. This was called a 'blogroll' and was a popular way of building comments about and a readership for blogs. The sidebar also signalled to the reader the kind of context the blogger liked to position herself in (e.g. 'mummy-bloggers' would link to other 'mummy-bloggers', fashion bloggers to other fashion sites and so on). The sidebar of a videoblog often had additional information about the videoblogger, such as other sites they maintained, a blogroll of other videoblogs they liked or would recommend, and links to community websites, services and platforms. Similar to a blog, the videoblog had an available archive, a profile page and a profile image.

---

198 Henry Jenkins, 'What happened before YouTube?', in Burgess, J. and Green, J. (Eds)
      YouTube. Digital Media and Society Series, Cambridge: Polity, 2009, p. 109-110.
199 Possibly this was because Wordpress was open source, whereas Blogger was proprietary software.
      Blogger was the first truly mainstream blogging software, allowing anyone to create and maintain a
      blog without needing any prior technical knowledge of web design, programming or coding Infinitely
      customizable, Blogger grew exponentially after being purchased by Google in 2003.

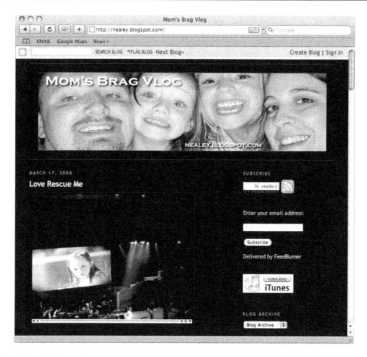

Figure 4: *Mum's Brag vlog* by Erin Nealy.

A blog could be said to be made up of four main components. There was the main body of text, which would contain the most recent post at the top (figure 4), with subsequent posts displayed below. There was a sidebar (figure 5), which contained the blogroll, advertising, a search bar, link to a profile page, subscriber button, and various other information. There was also an archive, which gave access to the previous posts on the blog, and finally, there tended to be a comment section, which allowed other readers to post text and engage in debate on the blog. By 2003 these had become fairly standardised and with the emergence of blogging platforms such as Blogger and Typepad, became very common layout templates on blog systems. It was therefore natural for the videobloggers to build on these existing structures when they first started posting videoblogs.

Individual posts on a blog were time stamped with information such as the date and time the video was posted, which video formats the videoblogger made available, a short description of the video (including credits to musicians of music hosting companies), how many comments had been left, and a permalink to the post (figure 4). For example, a post might link to four different video formats or codecs, such as QuickTime, Windows media player (WMP), DivX or flash. The most common format was QuickTime, due to the reliance on Apple hardware and software to create the videos, but other formats were often included to widen the possible audience.

Figure 5: Typical videoblog post. Sidebar with blogroll.

Videoblogs generally featured short videos, each one usually between 1-5 minutes in duration, which could be viewed, commented on and downloaded by users over the internet. The ability to download videos from videoblogs was an important technical requirement. This was because the de-coupling of the video from the videoblog was a necessity for syndication, which formed the basis for dissemination of videoblogs at the time. It also stood in direct contrast to other, proprietary video platforms such as Vimeo, Veoh and YouTube, which prevented the user from downloading content.[200] The content of videoblogs varied greatly, from personal diaries to news programs, sci-fi shows and more artistic videos. The videoblog tended to have the author's posts in reverse chronological order, with the newest at the top (figure 5). This aided the user with finding the latest blog post or video and helped to drive user 'traffic' to the content and gave a sense of newness to the blog.

---

200 There are technical solutions to this today of course, sites such as Tubesock and KeepVid are some examples of clients that allow you to circumvent this. Tubesock (http://stinkbot.com) and Keepvid (https://keepvid.com) were both designed to download and convert content from YouTube or other flash-based video sites into other formats. They were especially popular with people who liked to view their video content on devices such as the video iPod. These sites are still active today. In the case of Veoh, it was founded by Dmitry Shapiro in September 2005, Veoh combined user-generated content with professionally produced network content from among others CBS, ABC and ESPN. Veoh transcoded user-generated content into Flash and was not considered a good option within the videoblogging community. Veoh filed for bankruptcy in February 2010, before being acquired by Israeli start-up company Qlipso in April 2010.

I want to spend a little time exploring further some of the technical affordances, specifications and protocols that served to stabilise the videoblog form. At a time of fervent development of technologies around video and moving images, particularly in relation to codecs (used for video compression), it is hard to remember just how confusing and fragmented video in the web was during this time. Not only were there competing standards, codecs, encoders and formats, but there were also a multitude of different players, plug-ins and applications that introduced their own idiosyncrasies as shown in the last chapter. For example, the flash (.flv) format was written for desktops and was very frustrating to use (most videobloggers at this time avoided it) and was highly processor intensive – a reason that Steve Jobs banished it from the iPod and iPhone. Taken together, these technologies slowly combined to create what Kittler called a technical a priori, that is the establishment of a common set of technical standards which serve as foundations on which action and cultural practice might take place.[201] Bernard Geoghegan argues that a 'technological a priori defines the scope and logic of distinct cultural formations and epistemes'.[202] In this case, standards grew out of a number of cultural techniques that were shared amongst the members of the videoblogging community. As Adrian Miles, videoblogger, early community member and academic reaserching hypertext, narrative and technical systems, explained, 'in terms of codecs and picking up an earlier question about standards. I use [QuickTime] for everything because I do interactive work and it is the best architecture... The codec isn't great but it... means any mpeg4 compliant client can view it, anywhere.'[203] In many cases these technical standards were defaults in video software or the common codec or format used in industry, e.g. QuickTime was the default codec in iMovie. But in a similar fashion to discussions over open source software, videobloggers would question the use of closed codecs or software platforms.[204] For example, as one of the videobloggers, Jay Dedman argued;

> I know a big question is simply: why should I care about open codecs? Aren't codecs free now? Flash and QuickTime are monetarily free for the most part. It's difficult to find arguments for this now. The concern is when either/both these codecs become totally dominant...and web video is the new TV for lack of a better word. We need an open codec to either challenge the status quo...or be a solid alternative.[205]

At the time, there were many incompatible video standards, and rapid updates, alongside the paucity of bandwidth on the internet, which combined to render much video unwatchable or difficult to view. It is no surprise then that the videoblogging community began to slowly

---

201 A condition of possibility for knowledge in the Foucauldian sense. See Jussi Parikka, 'Friedrich Kittler - a media anthropology without the Man?' (2011) http://www.media-anthropology.net/ file/parikka_kittler.pdf.

202 Bernard D. Geoghegan, 'After Kittler: On the Cultural Techniques of Recent German Media Theory', *Theory, Culture & Society*, 30. 6 (2013) pp. 66-82.

203 Adrian Miles, Email to Videoblogging list, 18 June 2004, https://groups.yahoo.com/neo/groups/ videoblogging/conversations/messages/44.

204 There are a number of free software or open source video codecs today, but perhaps the Ogg Theora is the one most well known (it is mentioned 213 times on the videoblogging email list). It was made available as an alpha in 2002 but was still in beta until 22 September 2007. At the time Ogg Theora was not well supported and consequently little used.

205 Jay Dedman, Email to Videoblogging list, 27 January 2009, https://groups.yahoo.com/neo/groups/videoblogging/conversations/topics/73905.

coalesce around a series of informal standards in relation to their work. These standards created certain digital artifacts embedded in the videos which also created a distinctive digital video aesthetic. This aesthetic featured high-compression and therefore pixelisation, low frame rates and often muffled or distorted sound. Miles argued that most of the presets within video-editing software packages 'treat things like 'dialup' as a compression setting so that video will stream in real time at that data rate, so it has to compress very hard to achieve this. But you're not trying to real time stream, you're progressive streaming… If they want it, they will wait.'[206] By progressive streaming, Miles is referring to the two major ways in which video is encoded, either as progressive, that is the image is downloaded completely as an image, rather like a photograph, before displaying the frame, or interlaced, where alternating horizontal lines of video are displayed. In the second case, the illusion of a higher resolution is made because the flipping between frames (one is the horizontal lines 1, 3, 5, 7 and so on, and then the other 2, 4, 6, 8, etc.), however the image does appear to jump and move around if our eyes catch the interlacing taking place. In the case of progressive video (and the reason why video is marked with a 'p' as in 480p, 720p, 1080p) the image is sharper and realistic, whereas in interlaced (where video is marked 480i, 720i, 1080i) the image is sent at half resolution on alternate frames. Clearly then, interlaced video will download much faster than progressive, but with markedly lower quality, and this would be *in addition* to the digital artifacts made into the video by the video compression codecs. It is therefore interesting that videobloggers believed they were maximizing video quality in preference to the problems they associated with real-time streaming. When downloaded, they argued it would be of higher quality and more enjoyable to watch as a visual medium, which is ironic when we now look back on these videos and observe their comparatively low video quality and the various video digital artifacts that were common in these early video codecs.

Discussions around standards were very common in the videoblogging community. For example, the size of the window for the video, that is, the number of pixels in the x and y plane that made up the image, was widely discussed. This determined the size of the video but also the complexity of the video content and hence the amount of time it would take for the editor software (e.g. CPU processor time) to export a video that could be distributed via blogs and online more generally. The compromise between video size and quality was a perennial issue in relation to videoblogging and defined, in many cases, the aesthetic of the videoblog. The 'typical' videoblog was distributed with a resolution of 320x240 pixels, which is essentially half the size of the visible portion of a standard television signal in North America, otherwise referred to as NTSC. These videos tended to display at 15 frames per second. In fact 640x480 is the standard definition, 4:3 aspect ratio NTSC video, so by halving the pixels the videoblogger halves the data needing to be compressed and sent. The 480 lines is standard definition (SD) video and anything above 480 horizontal lines (usually 720 or 1080 for consumer videos, camcorders or cameras) is high definition (HD) video. Settling on 320x240 pixels for the size of the video file, was a standard format that emerged out of these compromising technical affordances (size of file, speed of processing, ease of distribution) and cultural preferences (video aesthetic, length of video, complexity of material). Agreeing

---

206 Adrian Miles, Email to Videoblogging list, 22 July 2004, https://groups.yahoo.com/neo/groups/
videoblogging/conversations/messages/38 7.

on a standard preference also became a marker of membership of the videoblogging sub-groups and became a relatively standard format for distributing videoblogs.

It is amazing how fast video has developed such that we might talk about the softwarization of digital video. There has been a disappearance of the 'prosumer' video camera and its replacement with the digital video (though of course, the digital camera and the digital mobile phone remain pieces of hardware). This predates the launch of the iPhone in 2007 and other video-capable smartphones that have since become the de facto device(s) for capturing everyday video. Indeed, videobloggers had a keen interest in small, portable digital video cameras that could create video quickly and transfer it to a computer with ease.

At the time of my interviews, only one of my informants shot videos on a 'professional' camera (Roxanne Darling) and only two recorded video on a mobile phone, using the Nokia N95 (Steve Garfield and Rupert Howe), with three others (Andreas Hagustrup Pedersen, Sam Rein-sew and David Howell) explaining that they combined mobile phone with a hand-held camera. Casey McKinnon, who aimed to build a career from her videoblog sci-fi show, *Galacticast*, shot video on a HD digital camera. A small group shot on 'digital cameras' (Loiez Deniel, Juan Falla, Jen Proctor, Gromik Nicholas and Raymond M. Kristiansen) and the rest referred to their recording equipment as 'hand-held' (Richard BF, Richard Hall, Mary Matthews, Markus Sandy, Erin Nealy, Daniel Liss, Cheryl Colan, Bekah Havens, Erik Nelson, Paris Marashi, Zadi Diaz), either a 'small, fits in handbag' (Brittany Shoot) or the most popular camera among the videobloggers at the time, the Sanyo Xacti digital video camera (Ryanne Hodson, Gena Hackett, Jen Gouvea, Enric Teller).

The Sanyo Xacti digital video camera actually became iconic within the videoblogging com-munity. This was because in so many ways it was *not* different to traditional video cameras. The Xacti was designed to 'function like a tiny camcorder, with a flip-out LCD view screen and a camcorder-style ergonomic design [which made] shooting video from different angles and getting yourself into the shot much easier.'[207] The camera was L-shaped, with the body resting nicely in your hand (pistol grip) and the screen and viewfinder folding open to one side, making it easy to watch footage while shooting, while also making sure you were in frame at all times. This made the classic videoblogging shot extremely easy to achieve, and was perhaps one of the reasons for its success within the videoblogging community. The classic videoblogging shot was filming yourself using your right arm stretched out in front of you, and pointing the camera at yourself, the kind of image that has become immortalised in the notion of the 'selfie' today. The Xacti allowed you to flip the viewfinder towards your face, which made it easier to film yourself. Importantly, the Xacti was one of the first video cameras to move away from physical media. The camera relied on digital storage, and did not use videotape or discs, storing video on a flash memory card, making it easy to transfer to a computer.

Some videobloggers used the built in webcam in their laptops to record videos, although none of my informants did this. The webcam is often conceptualized in terms of voyeurism and exhibitionism, and as Tina LaPorta's work shows, 'while the home represents a private space

---

207 Hodson and Verdi, *Secrets of Videoblogging*, p. 53.

and the Web a public site, webcams become a window or an invitation to look, to gaze upon everydayness of the inhabitants.'[208] Jimroglou's feminist critique of JenniCam argues that it was 'not only the woman in front of the camera, but it is the woman behind it too. [She] is both viewer and viewee: she occupies the hybrid position of both object and subject; she is composer and is composed' thus offering a 'fruitful as a tool of feminist transformation'.[209] In contrast, videobloggers tended to prefer to use hand-held video cameras and they also shied away from the 'webcam' association of web cameras on laptops.

There were links made by videobloggers in my interviews between the relative mobility working a laptop affords and the production of video on-the-go, something many videobloggers reported as being important to them (Susan Pitman, Juan Falla, Jay Dedman, Erin Nealy, Rupert Howe, Jen Gouvea). There was also a tension between the cultural idea of Mac users as more 'creative' than PC users, and although the majority of the videobloggers used a Mac, there are clear examples of those producing not only 'regular' videoblogs, but videoblogs considered 'artistic' (for example, Adam Quirk), using Windows. Out of the 34 videobloggers I interviewed, three quarters used a Mac, and three videobloggers combined a Mac and a Windows machine (Cheryl Colan, Markus Sandy, Richard BF). Five videobloggers relied solely on the Windows operating system (Raymond M Kristiansen, Gromik Nicholas, Adam Quirk, Gena Hackett, Susan Pitman). Amongst the Mac users, 22 videobloggers used laptops, and the rest relied upon desktops, whereas two Windows users used laptops, and the others used a combination of laptops and desktops. It is interesting to note that FireAnt was only ever released for the Mac, despite promises of making it available for Windows, and that the links between the Mac and videoblogging were reinforced by the use of QuickTime.

Ironically, this technical specificity wasn't really remarked upon by the videobloggers, beyond a comment by Casey McKinnon about the need to switch from one to another for professional reasons; 'for the first year and a half, we used a PC,' she told me. 'However, due to the demands of our new HD camera we are currently making a switch over to Mac in order to use Final Cut Pro out of the box. Adobe Premiere Pro doesn't have the HD quality we need'. Software such as Apple iMovie (used by Rupert Howe, Cheryl Colan, Ryanne Hodson, Markus Sandy, Jay Dedman, Adam Quirk, Erin Nealey, Steve Garfield) was one of the most popular software for editing video within the videoblogging community, despite being the more 'simple' compared to Final Cut Pro (used by Daniel Liss, David Howell, Richard BF, Casey McKinnon, Jen Gouvea), Windows Movie Maker or Premiere (Enric Teller), which required more advanced technical skills. iMovie allowed the user to record video files directly from either the webcam or an attached camera (like the Xacti) or import video files. It used a simple editing layout (figure 6), with the captured footage on the right side of the screen, each video file resting in a window of its own. The bottom panel showed a timeline of the footage the user was editing together, and the video would playback in a large window to the left. The editing field also contained two audio-tracks, for added music or voice-overs. In essence, it was very much the ideal video-editing software for the everyday life aesthetic that was widely reproduced in the videoblogging community.

---

208 Margot Lovejoy, *Digital Currents; Art in the Electronic Age,* London: Routledge, 2004, p. 264.
209 Krissi M. Jimroglou, 'A Camera with a view JenniCAM: visual representation, and cyborg subjectivity', *Information, Communication & Society*, 2. 4 (1999), pp. 439 - 453.

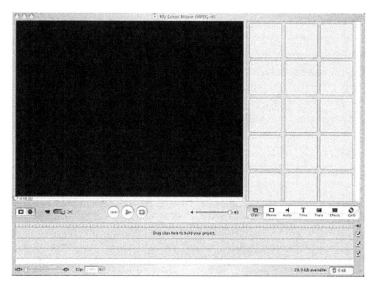

Figure 6: Screenshot of iMovie HD (version 5, January 2005)

In iMovie, below the captured or imported files the videoblogger had easy access to photos or music stored on the laptop, as well as access to effects, title cards and the export to DVD button. This simplified framework for presenting data made producing the videoblog simple and many videobloggers found it a more creative approach to working.

There was a suspicion in the videoblog community, however, that despite being both accessible and intuitive, iMovie was inferior software compared to professional software Final Cut Pro; as Daniel Liss told me, 'once—I could even tell you which video—I was away at my parent's [without] a computer and I used iMovie on my mom's laptop. And it was a scarring experience. Yuck'. There was also a sense that iMovie was less serious, and thus more playful perhaps than it's more professional counterparts; 'I edit with iMovie' Cheryl Colan told me, 'whose effects are terribly cheesy. I frequently abuse transitions and wipes because I think they are campy and funny. What's not to love about a transition that's an ever-widening heart shape? Or a barn door? I'm a big fan of iMovie's shooting star effect because it's absolutely ridiculous. I can't figure out it's real purpose.' This dichotomy between amateur and professional, serious and frivolous constantly played out in the videoblogging community discourse and practice.

Videobloggers often described their computers. They were extremely passionate about their systems, and it seemed to have replaced the television as the central technology in the living room. This was new and surprising in 2005, and anticipated many of the subsequent changes in media consumption that we see today. More importantly, the videobloggers' focus on their computers was an early example of computational visual media –videobloggers quickly moved to digital video cameras, with no physical, analogue tapes. Videoblogging was a truly digital practice, with the content captured, edited, produced, disseminated and consumed entirely on a digital platform. The computer occupied a similar position in the videobloggers' homes, as the television traditionally held. 'It's the "centre of attention" of the living room,' Juan Falla told me, 'we not only use the computer to edit or connect to the internet, but we use it to listen to music and watch DVDs. So we use it for everything. Every time I arrive home, I turn it on and put music on.' Further, they explained, 'the TV is in our room. We watch A LOT of TV. I'd say minimum 3 hours a day. But, if we have friends, we do everything in the living room WITH the computer, not only listening to music but watching videoblogs or videos from YouTube, etc.' In other words, the computer and the content found on the internet is increasingly, for Falla, competing with 'traditional television' for the attention of the viewer. Videobloggers were in some sense early adopters of digital cultural practices that have become dominant today. Their practices signalled the merging of television and the computer that has later manifested itself in the form of 'streaming' boxes like the Apple TV and Fire TV.

The videobloggers often described their computers as more important than their cameras. They highlighted the computer within their living space, calling it a 'centrepiece of the room' (Steve Garfield) or 'pretty prominent. You see my computer set-up as soon as you enter my home' (Zadi Diaz). Describing their work space, Ryanne Hodson also explained that 'we spend most of our time in that room. It's also connected to the kitchen, there is no wall separating it, so we eat and work on our computers, it's quite nice'. The computer had replaced the television as the centrepiece of the videoblogger's living space. This is reminiscent of Ballard's prediction from 1984, that one day

> Everybody will be doing it, everybody will be living inside a TV studio. That's what the domestic home aspires to these days; the home is going to be a TV studio. We're all going to be starring in our own sit-coms, and they'll be strange sit-coms, too, like the inside of our heads. That's going to come, I'm absolutely sure of that, and it'll really shake up everything...[210]

The videobloggers very much lived the coming world of online video in their everyday practices – even if the tools were still relatively primitive by todays standards.

I now want to turn my attention to the textual practices of the videobloggers and how they used various forms of writing systems, such as email, to build, develop and strengthen the videoblogging community. In the period between 2004 and 2007, the videoblogging community went from a small group of enthusiasts to a vibrant community of users. The group met online on each other's blogs and videos but also through the Yahoo group email list. The Yahoo group was the heart and soul of the videoblogging community. New members were always greeted by at least a few members, and encouraged to share links to their blogs, RSS feeds and personal information. To begin with, the email list recruited mainly through word of mouth and friends of friends. It was established on June 1st 2004 and is still going today, although now with much less activity. As of the end of November 2017, there are 2750 members still signed up to the list, and almost 80k messages in total have been posted to the list.[211] The most active period on the list was between December of 2004 and August

---

210 James Graham Ballard, 'Interview with JGB by Andrea Juno and Vale', *RE/Search*, no. 8/9, 1984.
211 As of November 2017, there were 79627 messages posted to the group, the last one posted 13th of July 2016.

2007, which saw the list receiving >1000 posts per month, impressive by email group standards. The high point was in June 2005 when the email group received the highest number of posts (2974 posts). If volume of posts can be seen as an indicator of 'community participation', this period was probably the most active (figure 7). In more recent years the list has seen months go by with only 3 or 4 posts, quantitatively demonstrating the way in which the videoblogging community had changed and slowly declined.[212]

	Jan	Feb	Mar	Apr	May	Jun	Jul	Aug	Sep	Oct	Nov	Dec
2016		11	2				6					
2015							4			2		
2014					25	21	5	1				1
2013	13	3				6	2		4	16	1	
2012	8	16	5	13	4	14	4			44	3	3
2011	59	47	72	38	104	11	10	75	33	65	135	22
2010	283	262	89	320	160	207	134	72	63	79	295	66
2009	379	246	347	302	168	207	178	249	227	343	293	167
2008	995	926	518	574	265	437	442	400	306	434	478	374
2007	1778	1412	1521	1141	830	1119	1155	1114	757	840	763	752
2006	2257	2114	1876	2481	2212	2051	2416	1671	1790	1609	1399	1422
2005	1967	1774	1660	1751	2346	2974	2899	2951	1926	2357	2370	2861
2004						224	264	541	307	282	422	1078

Figure 7: Number of emails posted to the videoblogging email list (June 2004 – July 2016). Screenshot taken from Yahoo.

The email list occupied a crucial position in relation to videoblogging and the videoblogging community. It functioned as the initial meeting point for the videobloggers, a digital *agora* in which the community gathered (albeit asynchronously), and it acted as the main communication channel between the early members. On the list, the videobloggers would discuss their equipment, cameras, codecs and working practices as well as their engagement with a selection of third-party applications, such as FireAnt and Feedburner. It was a crucial part of a videoblogging platform – at least in as much as the rest of the videoblogging technology was relatively underdeveloped and dispersed. Indeed, the email list was very stable. The list was

---

212 Table retrieved 16 October 2017 from http://tech.groups.yahoo.com/group/videoblogging/.

very much the public hub of the videoblogging community, rather like a café, lobby or meeting place; where ideas were exchanged, expertise sought and shared, problems discussed and arguments debated. As Steve Watkins explained 'the videoblogging group is about far more than the technologies necessary to videoblog.' It was also a place for people to form friendships and discuss 'incompatible ideas about what videoblogging will be to them, ideas that clash with some fundamental beliefs about what videoblogging is to the established/vocal crowd.'[213]

The list also served as a community memory, as a repository of knowledge, and as an archive of problems and solutions which was useful for new members. The group members helped each other out, and there was a sense of excitement about what people would come up with next;

> There were the technical people that were solving problems and then there were guys like me that were more about just trying to have fun and get people to think of ways of making video that they had never thought of before. When Michael [Verdi] and Ryanne [Hodson] would come up with these settings, they would then tell everyone how to do it and it would solve everyone's problem. Then everyone's quality automatically would just go up overnight. That was the cool thing about the group.[214]

The list was a public email group, with an open, accessible archive of every post written since 2004. As is standard with most Yahoo groups, the software allows functionality in additional to email. This included a public calendar, though this was not enabled by the moderators, a polling system, used a number of times between 2005 and 2007, a links section, also quite heavily used, and members had access to a database-area. In the database-area, the video-blogging group had four sub-groups; i. *Videoblogging directory*, a list of every videoblog in the vlogopshere catalogued at the time (95 entries); ii. *Giving back* a smaller sub-set (six entries) where some videobloggers have offered services to other videobloggers,[215]; iii. *Birthdays*, a list of member's birthdays (12 entries); and iv. *Location,* contact list (10 entries), containing information such as email address for user, what platform she uses, software usage, country, state, videoblog or company name and phone numbers.

The information posted in the database area is a useful indicator of the role the email list played in the early days of videoblogging. Although only a few entries were made between 2004 and 2005, at first the database was used to collect and organise information about the fledgling community. But this was soon superseded by the more narrative content of email exchanges via the mailing list and the database activity never became the norm among the later members of the community. It is interesting to note that, as Enric Teller pointed out, 'most people define videoblogging as having control over the production and distribution of their rich media work', and this led to a paradoxical distrust of public web resources that the

---

213 Steve Watkins, Email to Videoblogging list, 15 July 2005, https://groups.yahoo.com/neo/groups/
     videoblogging/conversations/messages/16 975.
214 *The Web Ahead*, 'Videoblogging with Jay Dedman, Ryanne Hodson and Michael Verdi' [transcript],
     accessed 16 September 2014 from http://5by5.tv/webahead/76.
215 For example, as one member posted; 'I will happily whistle, record and email an mp3 tune for anyone
     on this list (kindly indicate 'mood' or public domain tune, and length)', see https://groups.yahoo.com/
     neo/groups/videoblogging/database/4/edit.

videobloggers do not directly control individually. This emphasis on control translated into control of personal and potentially sensitive information, like birthdays and geographical location, and although many videobloggers displayed this information quite prominently on their own videoblogs, they hesitated to enter it into a public/ corporate system like a Yahoo group.

The first messages on the mailing list give a snapshot of a community in very early development. For example, the second post to the list immediately mapped out the technical challenges faced by the videobloggers and the poster articulated some of the technical issues facing anyone wanting to post video on the internet in 2004. I quote in full as I think it gives a good flavour of the very early discussions;

> i. Technically, the process takes too long (capture, import, optimize, write some HTML, post); ii. Existing servers don't allow much bandwidth and storage space. You'll either get screwed because too many people watch your posts, or you have to erase your archive video because you're out of space; iii. What is the language of videoblogging? Is it little movies? Or moments from your life?[216]

Topics such as these were a constant theme in the conversations about the practice of videologging. As previously discussed, the technologies available to non-professional media creators at the time were limited, under-developed and expensive, and the opportunities that were seen to be opening up in relation to the rise of Web 2.0 technologies gave the videobloggers a sense of being part of an exciting change in media.

As with any new medium, discussions on the list were fervent around the definitions and practices of videoblogging. Was it web video? Was it television on the internet? Was it a new form of documentary, a new form of art, or was it a political tool for taking on the media industry? Depending on where one fell on those issues, how did that influence how one videoblogged? Should one draw on televisual aesthetics? On cinema? Or – as some argued – was videoblogging more like Astruc's notion of writing using video, and what did that mean for the look, the feel and the sound of the videoblog? These discussions had a sense of urgency with some videobloggers arguing that 'the first successful movies – i.e. the first moving pictures accepted as motion pictures – were not applications of a medium that was defined by their giving significance to specific possibilities. Only the art itself can discover its possibilities, and the discovery of a new possibility is the discovery of a new medium.'[217] This initial burst of excitement around a new medium was important for inspiring the community and giving a sense of transformation and possibility that is crucial to any social movement.

As well as using email, videobloggers voiced their opinions in the videoblogs themselves, thus spawning a new genre of videoblogs – what one could call meta-videoblogs, or videoblogs about videoblogging. This was exemplified in 2005, when Michael Verdi, an active member

---

216 Jay Dedman, Email to Videoblogging list, 1 June 2004, https://groups.yahoo.com/neo/groups/
       videoblogging/conversations/messages/2.
217 Stanley Cavell, *The world viewed: Reflections on the ontology of film.* London: Harvard University Press,
       1979, p. 32.

of the group and co-founder of Freevlog, posted his seminal and hugely influencial video; *Vlog Anarchy*. Filmed in his home, Verdi presents what can only be described as a manifesto against manifestos, a call for the community to stop trying to define what videoblogging is. In the raw, unedited piece, Verdi laments the tendency among the early adopters to 'lock the medium down' and through definitions and discussions limit its potential. Instead, he calls for the community to 'play with it', to let it 'breathe and live and grow'. The video became notorious within the community, and was referenced two years later in Rupert Howe's entry for the Vlog Deathmatch challenge, one of many community events organized by the Video-blogging community. This took the form of karaoke which was then voted on to determine the best video.[218]

Although the majority of early videoblogs fell into what I categorise as 'personal' video, Rocket-boom was one videoblog that was distinctive and new. Andrew Michael Baron founded Rock-etboom in October 2004, and until it closed down in November 2013, produced short videos that parodied traditional newscasts through a technology-oriented comedy show. Rocketboom was originally hosted by Amanda Congdon (from October 2004 – July 2006), though over the years it had a number of presenters, including Joanne Colan, Mememolly and Keghan Hurst. Over the course of 2004, Rocketboom became very popular, to the extent of being featured during Steve Jobs' iPod presentation for Apple in October 2005. By December, Rocketboom claimed that it cost about $20 to produce an episode, yet they were able to reach an audience the same size as shows such as 'Crossfire' on CNN, a remarkable achievement. In September 2005, Business Week covered the faux news show in a magazine feature that the Internet was becoming more videocentric. Rocketboom was therefore one of the first videoblogs to 'break out' and find popularity beyond the videoblogging community, even being featured on American TV drama CSI in February 2006. Many of the members of the videoblogging community, including Zadi Diaz, Richard Hall and Steve Garfield, provided 'raw footage' for Rocketboom which also worked to draw attention – and viewers – to their own sites.

A key technology in the technical constellation around videoblogging that helped simplified video distribution, was Feedburner. It was founded in 2003 by Dick Costolo (later, CEO of Twitter 2010-2015), Eric Lunt, Steve Olechowski and Matt Shobe, and launched in 2004. The importance of Feedburner lies in taking a website address and generating an RSS feed for the user. [219] At the time, RSS (really simple syndication) was the main technology for 'pulling' data from the web, particularly blogs, into a computer. Feedburner was the first company to make this process a user-friendly experience, and provided the members of the videoblog-ging community with the ability to generate an RSS feed from their videoblog, which could be picked up by content platforms such as FireAnt or iTunes. Feedburner became hugely important in the distribution of videoblogs, and a number of my informants relied heavily

---

218 Vlog Deathmatch (http://vlogdeathmatch.blogspot.co.uk) Howe's entry *Anarchy in the UK* was built shot, edited and uploaded on his Nokia N96, as he travelled around London showing sites such as Parliament, Big Ben, Downing Street and the London underground, while miming into his phone. With its stripped back production values and low quality sound and image, it paid homage to Verdi's argument that videoblogging "can be as punk rock as we want it to be".

219 RSS (Really Simple Syndication) has a long history, with early iterations seen in the 1990s. RSS 2.0 which is referred to here, was developed by Dave Winer and released in September 2002.

on their 'feeds' for distributing their videos, but also for watching other videoblogs. The importance of RSS feeds and Feedburner in particular to the videoblogger could perhaps be summarised by this email exchange from September 2005, after a new videoblogger announced her arrival in the vlogosphere.[220] Within 15 minutes of posting, there was a reply; 'I went to your site, but I couldn't find your RSS feed in order to subscribe to your videoblog'.[221] Feedburner therefore became a necessary link in the distribution chain of videoblogs, and in some senses it was *the* mechanism for linking content between the videobloggers and their audience. In consequence, Feedburner was acquired by Google in 2007, for a reported $100 million. However, with the rise in real time streams like Twitter, RSS became less important to most websites, who moved to push notifications instead. By buying a competitor to YouTube, Google ensured that there was no alternative to the streaming video platform. On May 26th 2011, Google deprecated the Feedburner API, and in October 2012 it shut it down, reflecting a not unfamiliar story of big corporations using their buying power to shape the technical systems for their own benefit.

One of the main consumer oriented technologies that was designed by developers and that was closely linked with the videoblogging community was an RSS video player called FireAnt. The first beta was released in 2005.[222] FireAnt was a desktop application that subscribed to RSS feeds and allowed the user to play videos on the desktop. As one videoblogger explained, 'the point of using an in-computer aggregator program like FireAnt would be the added benefit to the user that 'new video (and other) posts are automatically downloaded'.[223] This automatic downloading of new episodes made following videoblogs much simpler. It also created a helpful abstraction from the inherent complexity and messiness of web-links and surfing between blogs. Users would be able to identify new videos and keeping up with episodes would be much less of a chore.

These kinds of user interfaces are interesting in a number of respects. Of course, by simplifying the technical process for the user they can massively expand the audience beyond the technically competent user. However, the act of abstracting away the underlying blogs in some sense breaks an important link between the personality of the videoblogger and their videos, removing the surrounded context the blog provided on the webpage. But it also breaks a link with the comment culture that was manifest in the blog-form, and took the form of personal comments and criticism under each video post. FireAnt therefore represented a shift, barely perceptible to the videobloggers of the time, from a web-based medium to a video-centric media form. Of course, the temptation with a video-centric metaphor was

---

220 Just like the 'blogosphere' became a collective term used when talking about the network of people who write and read blogs, the vlogosphere became a term for the collective practice of videoblogging, be it producing or simple consuming the videoblogs.

221 Joshua Kinberg, Email to Videoblogging List 12 July 2005, https://groups.yahoo.com/neo/groups/videoblogging/conversations/messages/16 402.

222 FireAnt, gets its name from a recursive joke often found in computer science and programming circles. FireAnt actually stands for Fire Ant's Not TV (this is similar to the recursive slogan for GNU: 'GNU's Not Unix').

223 Jan McLaughlin, Email to Videoblogging list, 21 August 2005, https://groups.yahoo.com/neo/groups/videoblogging/conversations/messages/20 517.

to look to television and film to inform the design patterns and unsurprisingly, the notion of a 'channel' became an important new way of presenting videoblogs. This too changes the way the user interacts and thinks about videoblogs – from discrete stories or moments to an unceasing stream of content, and where the user can flick the channel at the onset of boredom.

Figure 8: FireAnt RSS videoplayer with pre-selected channels

FireAnt came with twenty pre-selected video 'channels' (figure 8), including the popular Rocketboom, but the user could subscribe and unsubscribe to as many other channels as she wanted. The pre-selected channels made some of the videoblogs very popular, and featured videobloggers who were very active in the community. I asked Jay Dedman, one of the developers of FireAnt, about the pre-selected channels, and he told me that;

> The feeds we chose for FireAnt were at first all the ones that existed! Difficult to imagine. We would add feeds as people made them…Then as there were more and more RSS feeds, we kind of just chose a set of feeds that had a mix of content so a new person could get a sense of the excitement we all felt. It certainly wasn't scientific or well-planned. In those days, we were kind of flying by the seat of our pants.

In its early development, as the platform was still under construction, it was marked by uncertainty and tentative development. There was a trial and error exploration in both the technical and social aspects of videoblogging but also a touch of naivety about turning videoblogs into television, however inadvertently.

Some of the featured videobloggers (like Jay Dedman and Ryanne Hodson) had also been part of developing FireAnt, and were early beta testers. In fact, many of the announcements about updates to the FireAnt software, were made by non-programmers or members of the community. In return, these videobloggers made frequent videos promoting FireAnt, so in a sense there was a kind of gift economy within the community at this point. By gift economy I refer to the way in which services like these were performed without expectation of pay or reward. The early adopters would also be defensive and protective about the FireAnt software, feeling it was part of the community.[224]

The functionality of FireAnt was described by one of the founders, Joshua Kinberg, in an email in July 2005. He explained that FireAnt allowed the user to 'subscribe to any RSS 2.0 feed, with Bit Torrent built in.'[225] It could playback most media formats, and sync media to iPods or Sony Playstations. FireAnt allowed you to organise your content with tags, had built in Yahoo video search and its 'integrated directory of videoblogs [was] constantly improving and expanding'. It further allowed the user to 'preview anything before downloading, or schedule automatic download and notifications of new content'. While reflecting on this period in videoblogging practice ten years later, one videoblogger said that the 'community was largely fuelled and glued together by our excitement about the newness of it all. It wasn't about the content. We were video hackers'.[226] The development of software like FireAnt added to the sense that videoblogging was a growing and important new medium.

In October 2005, Apple announced that they would start distributing video 'podcasts' in their iTunes store. This new distribution network would be available to anyone, amateurs and professionals. This opened up distribution via the internet and further simplified the process. Content creators no longer had to learn about RSS syndication or the technical specifications of particular codecs in order to distribute their work. Of course, Apple was keen to embrace online video throughout its networks, codecs and technology platform, and thus cement their control of the 'media hub' they controlled with iTunes. It is also important to note that little commercial video or film was available at the time due to licensing issues by the film and television industry who were terrified of a Napster-like collapse of their industry. This helped fuel consumption of videoblogs and related video resources. Apple created an iTunes-ready format and provided all the technical means necessary for distribution through their 'music' store. It was also a way for Apple to experiment with video and film delivery and distribution systems without waiting for the film and television industry to give them permission to do so. For example, early video did not make use of Digital Rights Management (DRM), which simplified their technical systems. This was noted within the videoblogging community, particularly by Dedman, who noted that 'now that iTunes etc is making videoblogging/podcasting popular... new people are coming in who don't really care of what came before them. And that's their right. So those of us who have been around, we know who we are. Isn't it cool it's getting so out of control? It's really happening.'[227] With hindsight we can see that rather than getting out of control these moves by Google and Apple were in reality meant to reduce the 'out of control' anarchy of video and podcasting by effectively monopolising the distribution networks.

---

224 Adam Quirk, Email to Videoblogging list, 15 June 2015, https://groups.yahoo.com/neo/groups/
      videoblogging/conversations/messages/14 050.
225 Bit Torrent is a communication protocol used for sharing content across peer-to-peer networks. See
      http://www.bittorrent.com.
226 Rupert Howe, Email to Videoblogging List 30 May 2014, https://groups.yahoo.com/neo/groups/
      videoblogging/conversations/messages/79 558.
227 Jay Dedman, Email to Videoblogging list, 16 December 2005, accessed 18 July 2014 from email digest.

As Michael Verdi, Ryanne Hodson and Jay Dedman later reflected in a special issue of the web series *The Web Ahead*,

> When the Apple store opened in New York, down on Prince Street, we were doing these events down there where they were asking us or we asked them if we could come and talk about videoblogging. And they were like, "Yeah, sure, no problem." So we would try and explain what we were doing to people and we would have a whole crowd of people off the street, they all had their Macs, everyone seemed interested and excited but it was so complicated trying to explain to them how to do this… Film it on your camera, import it into iMovie or Final Cut, you have to edit it, you have to export it in this certain way, you have to take a screenshot and you have to embed that, you have to link this, you have to hand code this RSS feed. I mean, it was just so crazy. That's when Ryanne and Michael made a site called Freevlog. And that really I think was the point where videoblogging started really spreading fast.[228]

At the time, RSS 2.0 was seen as the future of media distribution on the web. Tags allowed the categorisation of content into different taxonomies of media, as well as the increased usability of the archive. Kinberg emphasised that FireAnt could play any media format – and this was clearly in competition with YouTube, which was criticized for taking whatever format the user uploaded and converting it to Flash, a format shunned by the videobloggers due to its perceived low-quality and being a closed format. This distinguished FireAnt from iTunes, which had specific Apple requirements for the format that could be uploaded. FireAnt was very much a product of and for the videoblogging community. Any changes to functionality or features were completed in dialogue with the community. The updates were regular and the developers wanted testers. They encouraged the users to push the software to its limits, as they would say 'bang on it. Try to break it. We want your feedback.' The co-dependent relationship between FireAnt and the videoblogging community can be seen further in an email from Kinberg in June 2005, 'many of you have helped us test FireAnt and we thank all of you for your help, advice, and suggestions.' [229] Kinberg positioned the videoblogger creator as a crucial actor in the development of FireAnt, calling them 'the power under the hood', who have 'energy and passion'. FireAnt, he claimed 'listen' to'and 'carefully consider' all the videobloggers' 'help, advice and suggestions'. FireAnt assisted the videobloggers in getting their videos out there, but the videoblogger reciprocated by promoting FireAnt on their videoblogs and by being unpaid beta testers.

Interestingly, despite its popularity, few people (Erik Nelson, Erin Nealey, Richard BF, Ryanne Hodson) specifically mentioned using FireAnt in their interviews; 'I have like almost 200 feeds in my FireAnt and I'm so behind', Hodson told me. When asked how he watched videoblogs, Richard BF told me 'on my computer, through FireAnt. I need to be able to comment right then'. Of course it is possible (and likely) that more videobloggers actively used FireAnt, yet it

---

228 The Web Ahead.
229 Joshua Kinberg, Email to Videoblogging list 12 July 2005, https://groups.yahoo.com/neo/groups/ videoblogging/conversations/messages/16 402.

is interesting that even at this point, there wasn't a very vocal support for it.[230] In fact, when Apple released Version 4.9 of iTunes in June 2005, some videobloggers opted for using this as their main video aggregator (Andreas Haugstrup Pedersen, Richard Hall). Another reason for this might also be the release of the 5th generation Apple iPod in 2005, which allowed mobile video playback. Amongst my informants, six (Roxanne Darling, Raymond M. Kristiansen, Gromik Nicholas, Cheryl Colan, Jennifer Proctor, Markus Sandy) reported watching videoblogs on their iPods.[231] The videobloggers were very much ahead of the curve in their use of technologies and the shaping of their cultural artifacts to it.

Figure 9: Badges promoting community sites from freevlog.org

An important website was Freevlog.org, which was created by two videobloggers, Michael Verdi and Ryanne Hodson, in 2005. This site was intended to be a resource for videobloggers, and it hosted tutorials on video-editing, compression, how to take a screenshot, uploading and hosting. Freevlog was one of the main sites around which the community gathered in these early days of videoblogging and provided many services to the community. At the time, small rectangular badges could often be seen on the sidebar of a videoblog, promoting sites

---

230 Fire Ant never made it past its 4th Beta update, but the software is still available for download. In a pertinent moment of nostalgia, perhaps, it still comes with the same twenty preselected channels of Videobloggers, although the links sadly no longer work.

231 The video iPod was a rather odd hybrid device when it launched, not being very suitable for video or film watching, as it had a 4:3 aspect ratio. Of course, with hindsight we see that Apple used this as a means to develop video capacities which were later to emerge in the iPod Touch and the iPhone.

they approved of, such as Blip.tv, Ourmedia.org and FireAnt, and the videobloggers would also have their own badges and display the badges of their 'friends' (figure 9).

These badges were automated and could easily be generated on the Freevlog site. They came in two different styles and sizes, and could be generated using quite simple computer code. Freevlog actually embedded these snippets of code in the sidebar of their front page, so anyone could grab it and put in on their videoblog.[232] Anyone with basic understanding of HTML would be able to take this code, change the content of the <href> (hypertext reference, or web-link) tag to their own webpage, upload a small gif to their website and change the <img src> (image source) tag to their own image link, and thus create their own badges. The videos on Freevlog almost exclusively featured Verdi and Hodson (themselves prominent members of the videoblogging community) and became an important resource for new videobloggers. Freevlog can be seen as a kind of community magazine (zine), similar to those used and developed by previous communities of practice; such as the Raindance corporation's publication, *Radical Software,* with its ties to the Guerrilla TV movement, and the Whole Earth Catalogue, with its links with the web community The Well.[233]

Freevlog would also post weekly tutorials about videoblogging and its practices. For example, Hodson would walk the viewer through how to set up an RSS feed with Feedburner, how to chose the right codec or compression settings before exporting videos or making a screen capture. The site presented videoblogging in '8 easy steps' – talking the new videoblogger through the entire process. The site was even translated into five other languages (Spanish, Portugese, Japanese, Dutch and Italian), with translation freely provided by members of the videoblog community.

I also want to briefly mention the grass root media directory Mefeedia, which launched in January 2005 with 617 videoblogs listed. This was another important site for aggregating information about videoblogging. By January 2007, Mefeedia.com listed 20,913 vlogs, showing that amateur, independent videoblogs (i.e. not vlogs on YouTube) were still gaining in popularity. The site was used by the videoblogging community as a place to look for specific content, and acted as a hub for hashtag campaigns like videoblogging week (#vbweek08, #vbweek09 etc) and videoblogging month (#vlomo), but as the site grew and their business model turned more and more towards advertising and pop up ads and banners, the community began to drift away. Michael Sullivan, who helped name the site back in 2005, wrote to the email list in April 2009 saying that;

I cannot use Mefeedia until at least pop-under ads are deactivated. There was a time that

---

232 The code was quite simple:
    <!-- BEGIN FREEVLOG BADGE -->
    <a href='/web/20051126023358/http://www.freevlog.org/'title='Create A Videoblog For Free'target=_
    blank><img src='/web/20051126023358im_/http://www.archive.org/download/FreevlogBadge80X15/
    freevlog_badge_80x15.gif'title='Create A Videoblog For Free'></a>
    <! -- END FREEVLOG BADGE --> (Freevlog 2005).
233 Fred Turner, *From Counterculture to Cyberculture: Stewart Brand, the Whole Earth Network, and the Rise of Digital Utopianism.*

even promoting a site here with gentle advertising would be an issue. Mefeedia has gone way overboard. I understand you need to capitalize on all your traffic. But it sure makes it difficult to tolerate. Sorry. You know I've been a fan and always interested in a site that I named and I've helped out in some ways, but I have some web browsing standards to uphold.[234]

Today, Mefeedia is an internet media-feed company, aggregating feeds from sites such as Vimeo, Hulu and Vevo, as well as acting as an umbrella company for a range of internet companies. However, instead of being a grassroots site used by amateur video makers, today it is infested with malware – described elsewhere as a 'browser hijacker' – another indication of corporations monopolising distribution and the user experience, and not necessarily for the better.

Video hosting became an integral part of the extended videoblogging platform. Initially, the videobloggers hosted their own content on their own sites – leading to a range of problems, for example, Howe's mention in the *New York Times* as discussed earlier in the book. To work around these problems, the community worked closely with a number of sites and developers to solve them. Among them, OurMedia.org, founded by J.D. Lasica and Marc Canter in 2005 acted as a front-end for Archive.org, where videos were hosted. Similarly, on June 16th 2004, Adrian Miles offered the members of the group 1 GB of free hosting on his basement server (in Australia) to 'kickstart' videoblogging, but even this would have been vastly insufficient at this point. Amongst my informants, Paris Manrashi, Brittany Shoot, Bekah Havens, Andreas Haugstrup Pedersen and Ryanne Hodson indicated that they hosted their videos on blip.tv. Dailymotion, Videobomb and Videosift were sites mentioned by Loiez Deniel, a French videoblogger who used a number of sites based in Europe. Steve Garfield also uploaded videos to Vimeo. Adam Quirk pointed out that he, like many others, were uploading their videos to a 'large number of video-sharing sites' in order to reach wider audiences. Ultimately, however, the battle over video hosting came down to two key players; Blip.tv and YouTube.

I have already introduced YouTube, but Blip.tv was founded in 2005 and worked hard to convince videobloggers to stop paying for their own video hosting and move to the service. After his experience with the *New York Times*, Rupert Howe 'found people using Blip for free, and that solved my billing/bandwidth issue.' Blip.tv was founded by Mike Hudack, Dina Kaplan, Justin Day, Jared Klett, and Charles Hope. The founders were all members of the videoblogging email list and the site was announced there in May 2005 with a short message from Hope, 'here's blip.tv, a beta site that features vlog hosting and aggregation of external RSS feeds. Please take a look and kick it around!'[235] Immediately, and amusingly, there were responses from the community raising technical concerns; 'I'm kinda confused as to what it's doing other than aggregating videos and sticking them on the main page. It appears to pull from certain feeds, but I don't see any place even after logging in to submit a feed URL. You can submit individual videos it appears'.[236] Hope replied within minutes, showing just

---

234 Michael Sullivan, Email to Videoblogging list, 8 April 2009, https://groups.yahoo.com/neo/groups/videoblogging/conversations/messages/74645 (formatting in original).

235 Charles Hope, Email to Videoblogging list 10 May 2005, https://groups.yahoo.com/neo/groups/videoblogging/conversations/messages/10 817.

236 Clint Sharp, Email to Videoblogging list, 10 May 2005, https://groups.yahoo.com/neo/groups/videoblogging/conversations/messages/10 816.

how small these early networks were, 'it is confusing, I'm sorry. You can add stuff with the "Add content" link in your user info, on the right side. It has just been made more prominent'. Through these kinds of exchanges, the community directly influenced design decisions on the blip.tv website. This demonstrates how the *socio-cultural* level (community) could strongly influence the *technical-social* (network) in the early phases of development of a new platform. It also shows how the knowledge and expertise of the videoblog community could be harvested to create digital media products.

Due to its engagement with the videoblog community, Blip.tv became a huge success, but ultimately their business model moved towards advertising – a move strongly condemned by the videoblogging community. After a number of difficult years, Blip.tv rebranded as Blip – an aggregation site featuring paid semi-professional content by new media companies. As a result, the community largely abandoned the site. Blip continued to host many of the early videobloggers videos for years, so for a while these archives remained relatively safe. The latest entry for any of my informants on Blip was in November 2011. In November 2013, however, Blip – recently acquired by Maker Studios – wrote to the members of the videoblogging community and told them they would no longer be hosting their videos. The new owners were looking for content of 'high quality' and most of the videoblogging content didn't fit this definition. They gave the users thirty days to download and back up any content they might want to keep before Blip deleted it, a startling turn around for a company that had worked hard in its early days to make connections with the videoblogging community.

But from the start, Blip had been very secretive about its business decisions. They soon stopped engaging in community conversations on the email list. Dedman told me;

> Blip had a similar experience [to FireAnt]. I don't think any of this is public, but I know the original founders had a huge fight last year. Their shares were all diluted after their last round of funding and they lost control of the company. I think only one of the original guys still works at Blip. I assume the current owners are trying to mainstream it in order to sell it.

Despite trying to sell the site, Blip eventually closed in August 2015. Another part of the videoblogging platform was therefore removed from the internet and along with it any remaining archives it contained.

The videoblogging community had a complex and at times contradictory relationship with YouTube. The community had an intense dislike of YouTube, mentioning the media giant as little as possible in discussions. One of the most interesting aspect of the YouTube debate is how wrong the videobloggers were about the future of the site. One would have thought that the launch of YouTube would have been celebrated in the videoblogging community. Here was a site that finally answered so many of the community's problems. It was easy to use, it was free to use, it seemingly solved some of the technical problems of aggregation and distribution that the videobloggers had been struggling with – if not all of them. However, instead of being conceived of as a solution, YouTube was quickly conceptualised as the enemy.

When YouTube launched in May 2006, one of the three founders, Steve Chen, posted a personal message to the email list. '[We] just launched a new video blogging service at www. YouTube.com,' he wrote

> Many of the same questions being asked here, we had also asked ourselves as this is still a nascent area for technology. Given the state of the technologies that video blogging depends on is still in developing stages, we had to answer the questions within these limitations... currently, we feel that bandwidth and storage is not the problem. The biggest obstacle is getting people to learn how to take videos and getting them onto the site.[237]

Interestingly, Chen's original email didn't get much attention. Perhaps because it was buried in a thread arguing about definitions of videoblogging, or because at this time many new sites offering easy video hosting solutions were launching. The email from Chen had only a few responses and, as had become increasingly common within the community at that time, they were mostly about technical issues. The initial reaction from the community concerned formats, and particularly YouTube's decision to convert video submissions to a flash video file, a proprietary web format owned by Adobe.

The reactions ranged from a disappointed 'everyone is doing Flash...' to the more dismissive; 'Flash gives me hives'. Flash was a mediocre format, providing an inferior image quality. As Cubitt points out, 'like VHS, and so many other victors of previous format wars, they are only good-enough'.[238] YouTube's decision to use interlaced streaming meant that the videobloggers – who valued quality above anything else – were unimpressed. For the average user, however, who just wanted to watch the latest viral video, YouTube was ideal. In an episode of the podcast *The Web Ahead* from 2014, Jen Simmons, Ryanne Hodson and Michael Verdi reflected on the beginning of YouTube and particularly how and why it became such a success;

> When YouTube started... they did everything we didn't want to them to do, sort of. [Laughter] But it all turned out. In the end, it was actually... sometimes I think, "Man, they just saw way further than we did." They had things like... the problem we were trying to solve with the RSS feeds and the downloading the videos, like Jay said, overnight. One of the things that YouTube did at the beginning was, they were like, "We're going to make sure that the videos play automatically right away no matter what." So the "no matter what" meant it had the crappiest quality in the world. It was like, a huge step back in quality and that was one reason why we didn't ever want to use it at first. Because it just made your videos look like crap... All of a sudden, there were all these people who had never even thought to watch a video on the internet. Like, why would you even try to do that? They now had a reason to see video on the internet and they were like, "Oh, I need, whatever, a Flash player. I need a QuickTime plugin. I need a whatever plugin I need to see this stuff".[239]

---

237 Steve Chen, Email to Videoblogging list, 3 May 2005, https://groups.yahoo.com/neo/groups/
videoblogging/conversations/messages/10362.
238 Sean Cubitt, *The Cinema Effect*, Cambridge, Mass.: MIT Press, 2004.
239 *The Web Ahead*, transcript.

One of the technical limitations experienced by the videobloggers early on, was that produc-ing videoblogs took a long time. With YouTube, this problem was streamlined. The fact that non-YouTube videoblogging took a long time and therefore produced a higher quality aesthetic than videos uploaded to YouTube,[240] became one of the defining factors for the videobloggers when attempting to delineate themselves from the rapidly growing community of Youtubers. The videos posted to YouTube were considered to be of a lower standard than the videos produced by the videobloggers. For example, when I first signed up to the email list (in August 2005, six months after the launch of YouTube), I received plenty of encouragement from other videobloggers, but also quite clear warnings about using YouTube (which was where I had initially posted my videos, for the same reasons as 'everyone else': it was really easy). One of my first replies said: 'congrats on the videoblog. I suggest you check YouTube's terms of service. They're pretty oppressive. I would suggest Ourmedia and or Blip.TV. They respect the creative commons[241] (or copyright) you assign to your work.'[242] The videobloggers had a strong sense of in-group/out-group, with the individual videoblogger encouraged to follow community norms and values, which they manifested through this set of technical norms and practices.

Other videobloggers did see the potential of YouTube for reaching a wider audience; 'video can often receive mass attention if it becomes viral and contagious. Thousands or even millions of people will participate in spreading worthy video clips and try to create video clips that can garner such awesome attention on the Internet'.[243] The language and opinions varied, from seeing what YouTube offered the videobloggers in terms of getting their work out to a much wider audience, to a scepticism about control of content. There was also a strong awareness of the economic possibilities in terms of the potential for advertisers to profit from 'the millions of workers who sit in front of computers all day'. A later email referred to 'some of the nutty Youtubers who… were talking of getting several million viewers for their videos. It's nuts', as Jay Dedman wrote in 2007.

The concerns about YouTube within the videoblogging community in 2005 were mainly relat-ed to technical issues, such as quality of videos, formats and codecs. But there were also concerns about ownership and branding, as well as being able to retrieve content back out of YouTube after uploading it. Despite being lauded as one of the most successful Web 2.0 start ups, Uricchio argues that, 'while YouTube's economic model is indeed predicated on participation, it fails the '2.0 test' since users may only upload — and not download — its videos'.[244] The ability to download videos might not seem like a deal breaker for the average user, but within the videoblogging community this was an important issue, especially for those wanting to use FireAnt. This also raised questions of ownership, with Michael Verdi stating

---

240 Other hosting sites, such as Veoh and Dailymotion would soon feature within this discourse too.

241 Although this book does not go into the details surrounding the creative commons licenses in much detail, it might be worth mentioning that these licenses, in particular the 'Attribution-ShareAlike (CC BY-SA)' and the 'Attribution-NonCommercial-ShareAlike (CC BY-NC-SA)' licenses were used by a number of the videobloggers.

242 Personal correspondence with Michael Verdi, August 2005.

243 Michael Sullivan, Email to Videoblogging list, 8 November 2005, https://groups.yahoo.com/neo/groups/videoblogging/conversations/messages/26 271.

244 William Uricchio, 'The Future of a Medium Once Known as Television,' p. 25.

that 'I don't get what people like about [YouTube] with their crazy terms of use where you basically give your work away to them'. The discourse surrounding YouTube is telling, their service is 'crappy', they 'brand' your videos with 'their' logo, they 'lock' your content down, their terms of service are 'crazy' and 'you' end up giving 'them' your work for free. However, the response from Brad Webb perhaps clarifies why YouTube – despite these concerns within the videoblogging community – became as successful as it did. As Webb argued, 'it works, works fast, and users are generally willing to sacrifice quality and freedom for 'just working'... They also remove the "what version of plugin XYZ am I running" headache'.[245]

In trying to explain why YouTube appears so easy to use, Verdi and Webb use a discourse of 'us' versus 'them'. They display an assumed superiority about the videoblogger's technical understanding and aesthetic sensibility, in contrast to the Youtuber, or the 'average user', who would be 'willing to sacrifice quality and freedom', for a user experience that 'just works'. The videoblogger is positioned as up-to-date with technical developments– they 'actually follow these things and care' – and so the apparent problem of rapid changes in codecs and format 'isn't an issue' for them. Here we can see the construction of a discourse that places YouTube on one hand and the videobloggers on the other in terms of different cultural practices distinctive to each. YouTube's focus on content that is low quality (in technical as well as cultural terms), in order to attract audiences, advertisers and corporate sponsorships, whereas the 'craft' of the videoblogging community lay in being able to negotiate a complex technical constellation and produce a distinctive, creative aesthetic.

YouTube was now positioned as the *other* against which the videobloggers defined themselves and their practice. A distinction was drawn between control and freedom, with the videobloggers keen to protect and maximise the autonomy that they had outside of the YouTube platform. Videobloggers tended to host their videos on sites such as archive.org, ourmedia.org and blip.tv, or even pay for their own hosting and domains. In general, these issues related to self-hosting were accepted as part and parcel of retaining ownership of their content. This individualistic and sometimes libertarian-leaning attitude formed an important part of the subject position of the videoblogger and the articulation through which their cultural practice was often expressed. Pierre Bourdieu in his work on the sociology of photography, argues that this type of relationship is 'a mediate relationship, because it always includes the reference to the relationship that the members of the other social classes [in this case, YouTube] have to photography [in this case, videoblogging]'. Bourdieu argues that one class of photographers' relationship to photography is a different relationship, for instance, than that of the *petit bourgeois*. Whereas the peasant 'senses the particularity of his condition', Bourdieu argues, the *petit bourgeois* 'seek to ennoble themselves culturally by attempting to ennoble photography'. He further argues that the *petit bourgeois*, 'find within the disciplines of the sect that body of technical and aesthetic rules of which they deprived themselves when they rejected as vulgar the rules that govern popular practice'.[246] Thus, the rejection by the videobloggers of the low technical and aesthetic standards associated

---

245 Brad Webb, email to Videoblogging email list, 8 November 2005, https://groups.yahoo.com/neo/groups/
     videoblogging/conversations/messages/26280.
246 Pierre Bourdieu, 'Towards a Sociology of Photography,' p. 132.

with posting videos to YouTube becomes part of the very definition of the high technical and aesthetic quality that make videoblogging somehow *better*, or more 'noble'. It also cemented YouTube as videoblogging's *other*.

As with most creative communities, the videobloggers organised a number of events over the years. These aimed to develop the community activities, but also to raise the public profile of videoblogging. For example, in June 2005, the videoblogging community arranged and hosted the first Vloggercon conference.[247] The two-day event was held in New York and included speakers such as email list co-founder Peter van Dijck, Rocketboom-founder Andrew Michael Baron, J.D. Lasica and a number of the core videoblogging community members.[248] On a panel called 'Tools', a group of developers were presenting their various apps to an audience of videobloggers. Josh Kinberg presented FireAnt, which was already a darling of the videoblogging community, Graham Stanley presented the idea hosting/distribution platform *V blog central* and Daniell Krawczyk outlined the premise behind *Digital Bicycle*, a service that compressed videoblogs into a video format with high-enough resolution to be (re)playable through broadcast television.[249]

The videoblogging community also organised *Pixelodeon* in June 2007, the first independent video festival for internet film, held over a weekend at the American Film Institute in Los Angeles. The event combined speakers and presentations, workshops and social gatherings with screenings of videoblogs, all curated by members of the videoblogging community. The *Vloggies* were the videoblogging community's award show, which was first held in San Francisco in 2006. PodTech produced the event, but it was the brainchild of Irina Slutsky and many of the videobloggers were both nominated and won awards at the event (including Casey McKinnon, Roxanne Darling and Ryanne Hodson).[250]

---

247 http://vloggercon.com
248 For a full list of speakers, see http://web.archive.org/web/20060615065257/http://www.vloggercon.
     com/?page_id=10
249 Ryanne Hodson and S. Van Every, *Tools*. Video from Vloggercon 2005, https://archive.org/details/
     VloggerCon05SessionsTOOLStoolsvloggercon05mov. Another speaker on the panel was a young engineer
     from a small start-up called Vimeo. Jacob Lodwick explained how, in 2003, a friend had suggested that
     he start making weekly video updates, which he did. However, as he didn't enjoy talking to the camera,
     so he started making creative videos and staying behind the camera, editing the footage into short films.
     Lodwick developed a program that allowed him to automate the editing process. By adding metadata
     such as dates, location and tags, Lodwick automatically edited clips together, in sequence, with added
     background music. The videos could be spliced together by date (e.g. play all videos from the past
     month), location (play all videos from New York) or tag (play all videos tagged with 'girlfriend') – creating
     an automatically generated, continuous algorithmically generated database narrative in video form. The
     early iteration of Vimeo presented by Lodwick in 2005 never made it out of beta. The company he chose
     to develop instead has become a successful video platform. Although Lodwick is no longer working
     for the company (he now runs Elepath, a company developing iPhone apps), Vimeo is now one of the
     largest video platforms with over 60 million registered users and viewers as of November 2017.
250 There was a big contention in the community in 2007 over trademark rights to the 'Vloggies' brand
     when PodTech claimed ownership over it and subsequently fired Irina Slutsky. Whether the Vloggies
     should 'belong to the community' or be owned by a company were hotly discussed on the videoblogging
     list (see the full discussion thread at https://groups.yahoo.com/neo/groups/videoblogging/conversations/
     topics/62872).

In 2008, the activity on the videoblogging email list started to wane, and by early 2010 the list was receiving fewer than 100 emails per month. By late 2014 the list was receiving less than 100 emails per year (total of 45 emails were sent to the list in 2013). On June 1st 2014 the list's ten year anniversary was marked with a sudden burst of activity. 'Happy anniversary!' Richard Hall wrote, 'this Yahoo group and my video blogging experience was (is) a highlight of my life'. 'It was wonderful to enjoy that brief period of collective excitement,' Rupert Howe wrote, 'I would like it if I could find a similar group of video hackers, experimenting with the new technology that's available to us now'. 'Remember my life in five second increments?' Susan Pitman reflected. Mostly, the comments reflected how far online video has travelled since 2004; 'online video is EASY now. What's video (and tech) going to be like in 10 more years? Yikes!' and how the videoblogging experience had impacted their lives; 'I went on to use my videoblogging skills in several jobs, and have managed to keep most of my archive together on my YouTube channel,' said one videoblogger.

The anniversary was also an opportunity for reflecting on what happened to the community and how and why it dispersed. One member stated that;

> It's interesting as a group of people with the shared common goals of posting video on the Internet in an easy way and in some cases, not all, wanting to monetize that content. We were a very active group. Once uploading video became pretty effortless our activity as a community became less. Coupling that with Twitter and Facebook making it even easier to find and share information about web video the group all but stopped.[251]

I privately emailed Jay Dedman and asked him about the missing details in the history of FireAnt. He told me that what had started as a 'fun project... just a RSS reader for video... Cool for our community but not a big deal',[252] had grown and reached its tipping point, when one of the founders suggested bringing in some 'business guys he knew. It was indeed heady times. YouTube was just bought for $1 billion.' It is interesting that Dedman, a key member of the videoblogging community, someone who had quite an idealistic view of videoblogging, told me he 'never quite understood what happened' with FireAnt. When the project failed to raise money, it became apparent that FireAnt was in financial trouble. Perhaps the different attitudes was part of the problem, but it didn't seem to Dedman as if anything was happening to further the appeal of FireAnt. 'Again, I didn't think we'd get rich, but I didn't have a better plan. Ryanne [Hodson] and I were busy putting on Vloggercon SF, *Pixelodeon* in LA, and having fun in the community. My main job in FireAnt was working with users and helping improve features. I went to only a few meetings with [Venture Capitalists]'.

Dedman told me that 'while it was happening it was very confusing'. After some time, the co-founders worked together to make the project sellable and pay off debts. Dedman had helped Josh [Kinberg] find a buyer for the technology they built, and 'after the sale, we paid off all debts they had incurred. We never did find out exactly how it all was spent.' Despite the

---

251 T. Street, Email to Videoblogging list, 30 May 2014, https://groups.yahoo.com/neo/groups/videoblogging/
       conversations/messages/79 563.
252 Personal email correspondence.

failure of FireAnt, Dedman remains reflexive of his own part in the project. 'If I had to do it all over', he told me over email 'I would have open sourced the project. Have fun until it wasn't fun anymore. I was guilty of falling for the dreams of making it big. Ha ha. Good lesson to learn'.[253]

Here, I think it might be useful to think of FireAnt as 'dead' media, or what Hertz and Parikka call 'zombie' media[254] – 'the forgotten, out-of-use, obsolete and judged dysfunctional technologies' that help us 'understand better the nature of media cultural development'. In other words, FireAnt, though no longer in active use, and perhaps never as widely enjoyed as its developers would have hoped, serves as a 'living dead of media history'. Hertz and Parikka point out how zombie media is never truly dead, but creeps back up in later instantiations of technologies, and thus is 'resurrected to new uses, contexts and adaptations'.[255] Significantly, FireAnt had much of the functionality that was later adopted by other video sharing sites, such as YouTube (for example, the ability to comment on videos directly in the player). Yet, it's biggest problem was that by automatically downloading every video in a user's RSS feed, the user ended up downloading such a large amount of data that it became unmanageable, both in terms of storage space on the user's hard drive and in terms of being able to watch large quantities of media (e.g. Ryanne Hodson having almost 200 feeds in FireAnt meant she always felt 'behind'). This issue of storage was continually a problem, and being a pre Web 2.0 technology, FireAnt and other videoblogging technologies never quite managed to resolve this until YouTube essentially abolished the question of video bandwidth and storage of video. But by then it was too late for the videoblogging community, and so video moved onto a different pathway.

The extended videoblogging platform – as fragmented and unstable as it was – presents a cultural and technical hybrid. The community worked hard to make the platform a reality and displayed a strong sense of loyalty towards the apps and app developers that had been supporting them. Although their rejection of YouTube was tragic in hindsight – after all Youtubers went on to find fame and fortune whereas the videobloggers are mostly forgotten today – their position contributed to a strong sense of community. The platform imaginary of the videoblogging community remained true to its ideals even when the technology was clearly moving in the opposite direction. It also had certain consequences for the development of a videoblog aesthetic, which I discuss in the next chapter.

---

253 Personal email correspondence.
254 Garnet Hertz and Jussi Parikka, 'Five Principles of Zombie Media', *Defunct/Refunct*, (2012) http://ruared.ie/Documents/defunct_refunct_catalogue_web.pdf.
255 Garnet Hertz and Jussi Parikka, 'Zombie Media: Circuit Bending Media Archaeology into an Art Method', *Leonardo*, 45.5 (2012), pp. 424–430.

5. VIDEOBLOGGING AS AESTHETIC FORM

In this chapter I want to shift registers from the sociotechnical to the aesthetic. Here I want to explore the experimentation and associated discourses the videobloggers developed. Videoblogging stood in a complex relationship to notions of quality, beauty, design and aesthetics more generally. They were fully aware of the limited affordances of video, and particularly the digital video form meant certain compromises in terms of technical image quality and aesthetic. Clearly they could not begin to approach either professional television or cinematic levels of quality, but equally they looked with some disdain towards the low quality, stuttering, blocky video of the flash video format, most notably used by YouTube. Under the circumstances it was inevitable that the videoblogger community through their discussions and video-work would begin to theorise their video-practice and thereby develop a justificatory language and new aesthetic practice in relation to these challenges. By sign-posting links to radical film (Vertov, Astruc etc.) but also to theorizations of media (particularly McLuhan) they opened a space within which they created a sense of meaning in relation to their work. This was pragmatically combined with experiments with video practice, and with the affordances of what they saw as a new medium. But videobloggers were always first and foremost makers of video – demonstrating their ideas on the visual, the medium, narrative, form and content through their videoblogs. It was never simply about the audience, products, commercialization or clicks. This aspect of videoblogging, their sense of distinction, and their commitment to experimentation through practice are key markers of the videoblog community at this time.

When the videoblogging community first started making online videos there was no template for how to do it. Both technically and aesthetically, the media form was very much open to experimentation, and there were intense debates on the email list and in their videos about what – if any – shape it should take and which direction it ought to be developed. Over time, as the technical problems were ironed out, solutions were found to things like distribution and consumption of videoblogs, mainly through RSS clients such as Feedburner and media players like FireAnt. Technologies began to improve and issues around storage and band-width became easier to manage. Gradually, the aesthetics developed into what I describe as a digital vernacular, a particular style of video now strongly associated with web or internet video, in terms of the size, length, cinematography, tone and editing. Today, YouTube videos generally have a certain 'look' – an aspect ratio of 16:9, playing a video with a resolution of 360p, 480p, 720p or 1080p, but this has changed over time. Initially, YouTube videos were displayed at a resolution of 320×240, and in March 2008 this was increased to 480×360 pixels. In November 2008, YouTube introduced 720p HD support. The default length for videos uploaded to YouTube was initially set at 10 minutes, although this was increased to 15 minutes in July 2010 and this could be further increased by uploading from a verified account.[256] The production values of YouTube videos are lower than videos produced for

---

256 Formats and resolutions vary across platforms and applications; for instance, Instagram recommends uploading mp4 files using H.264 CODEC and AAC audio at a 3500 kbps bitrate and keeping the file size under 50MB. Snapchat recommends a max size of 32MB using mp4 or .mov files at a bitrate of

television, utilising handheld cameras and regularly feature intimate scenes (as opposed to sweeping landscape or shots) with interiors and people's faces.[257] When put together, these elements form a kind of 'YouTube vernacular' – a language through which a YouTube video can easily be recognised, as opposed to a sitcom, a reality television show or a documentary.

Videoblogging also developed its own video aesthetic, a distinct style found in the vast majority of these early internet videos, and still reflected in much first person user-generated content found online today. This aesthetic developed over time, through discussion and arguments, experimentation and failure. Some of the elements were the result of technical limitations discussed in the previous chapter; others again were methods to get *around* technical constraints such as simple scenes and jump cuts. Videoblogs were influenced by other styles and traditions and owed a great debt to filmmakers and documentary makers of the past, such as Dziga Vertov, Alexandre Astruc and the Guerrilla TV movement. Some also quite consciously drew on television tropes to experiment with intimacy and familiarity using close-ups and fast moving camera shots.

In this chapter, through an analysis of 30 videos from the videoblog community, I explore some of the general elements that make up this videoblogging aesthetic, from title cards to common video shots which make a repeated appearance in videoblogs, such as faces and hands. I also analyse in depth the work of three particular videobloggers who represent different points on the videoblogging spectrum. Their work is at once very different and distinctive, yet, as my analysis shows, the resulting aesthetic has something in common with the majority of videoblogs. By highlighting these commonalities, I hope to draw out and further explore the videoblogging aesthetic and connect the development of this videomaking approach to wider issues of technical affordance and aesthetic experimentation.

I also undertake a close formal analysis of six exemplar videos from these three videoblogs (approximately thirty minutes of video work). I seek to trace what the videobloggers did and how they did it. This will follow a 'traditional' film analysis approach, highlighting the use of techniques such as close-ups, point of view and establishing shots, use of sound (diegetic, ambient etc.), edits and credits. I combine this with a medium-specific analysis, specifically drawing attention to the way in which these formal elements of film production, theory and analysis are re-framed within the particular practice of videoblogs. For instance, a long-take in a movie screened at a cinema is different to a one-take in a video screened in a web browser. By undertaking a formal analysis I can highlight distinctive elements found within the videos, in other words, the ways in which the videobloggers experimented with the medium, or pushed at the boundaries of digital online video. I also supplement this with interview data and discussions in the videoblogging community. The aim here is to see how the discourses of early adoption, experimentation and creative practices are reflected in the videos themselves.

---

192 kbps minimum.

257 I am here referring to user-generated content, not professionally produced or sourced videos such as movie trailers, music videos and clips from TV and film. These videos would obviously fit into a different category of video.

I specifically seek to draw together what the videobloggers do and what the videobloggers say they do, to explore the visual aesthetic. Videoblogging is a context dependent, self-referential cultural form, in which the videoblogger is at once aware of herself as an early adopter of a new public media, and at the same time speaking directly to a particular, identified group of people, perceived to be part of an invested network. Through a detailed formal analysis connected to the way in which these issues are framed and discussed, I highlight the distinctive elements of the videoblog.

The videoblog aesthetic grew directly out of the practices developed in the community of videobloggers. Through their work, the members of the videoblogging community experimented with different styles and genres, and playfully explored a Do-It-Yourself (DIY) or 'good enough' aesthetic.[258] The community shared ideas and methods, from sound and external microphones to editing, which created what I call the videoblog vernacular.

Figure 10: Typical credits showing use of URL as branding, note similarity of form

To start, we might take as an example the title card that most videobloggers used at the end of their videos (figure 10). This would often display the URL on the last few frames of the videos; this was usually done using white type on a black background. The typeface might vary, but as can be seen from a few screenshots below, the result are remarkably similar in form and

---

258 Cubitt, *The Cinema Effect*. See also Caroline Bassett, 'Is this not a Screen', in Marsha Kinder and Tara McPherson, (Eds) *Transmedia Frictions: The Digital, the Arts, and the Humanities*, Berkley and Los Angeles: University of California Press, 2014; Robert Capps, ' The Good Enough Revolution: When Cheap and Simple Is Just Fine', *Wired*, 2009, from http://archive.wired.com/gadgets/miscellaneous/magazine/17- 09/ff_goodenough?currentPage=all.

presentation. The title card grew out of a number of different needs. Firstly, the videobloggers had a strong sense of ownership of their work, and marking it with a name and a URL was a way of signing the work off, perhaps like signing a painting. Secondly, the title card allowed the video to be separated from the videoblog on which it was hosted. Which meant that if the viewer were watching using FireAnt, Mefeedia or iTunes, in a long stream of other videos, they would still be able to identify who the creator was. Thirdly, the title card acted as a signifier that this was a *videoblog*, not just an internet video. It signalled that the producer was part of a community of practitioners following certain technical and aesthetic conventions.

What is striking is the way in which the form of the title card and how it was located within the timeline of the video soon became conventionalised. Through various iterations and experimentations the use of this method of marking videos enabled at least some sense of social status, as members of a distinct community around videoblogging, to be recognised and shared. These social signifiers are important for identification and help maintain a sense of community, or at least some shared practices around which social structures begin to cohere. But just as important is the way in which these practices begin to crystallize a shared sense of an aesthetic appropriate to the form of videoblogging.

The videoblogging vernacular is reflected in a set of stylistic and formal tropes, including narrative decisions and technical equipment, all contributing to the creation of a particular visual result. This shares certain commonalities with what Newman calls a DIY aesthetic, a rather loose concept which he defines as referring to 'a visual or sound style, the modest-means quality summed up by the punk myth that all it takes to start a band is three guitar chords… But DIY can also mean media made using the new tools, themselves the products of professional creators, that allow anyone to set up a blog or a Web photo album.'[259]

The videoblogging vernacular not only refers to how a videoblog *looks*, but also to the wider practices associated with amateur and semi-professional production, which includes a 'shift in taste from an assumption of professionalism as the norm and standard of quality to a position that amateurism has equal or even greater value'.[260] Making do with whatever equipment was available has a long tradition in amateur and semi-professional film and video production, as Patricia Zimmerman showed in her work on amateur film in America's recent past.[261] As such, it is not 'new'. For example, in the 1970s, the term DIY aesthetic was used to describe the video-works of Guerrilla Television. However, the particular constellation of technologies available to these videobloggers was unique. So in contrast, Guerrilla Television had access to portable equipment and editing tools, but access to distribution remained one of their main problems. Whereas Miles argues, networked distribution is where videoblogging is unique in the history of film and video and the videobloggers were aware of this in the way in which they produced the format, but also distributed it.[262]

---

259 Newman, 'Ze Frank and the poetics of Web video'.
260 Newman, 'Ze Frank and the poetics of Web video'.
261 Zimmerman, Reel Families: A social history of Amateur Film.
262 Adrian Miles, 'A Vision for Genuine Rich Media Blogging', in Aksel Bruns and Joanne Jacobs (eds), *The Uses of Blogs,* New York: Peter Lang, 2006.

The videos selected for this formal analysis were recommended by the videobloggers them-selves as key examples of their work. Due to the time that has elapsed since the interviews took place, however, some of these videos, for a variety of reasons, are no longer accessible. As mentioned, Blip.tv – where most of the videos were hosted – deleted old videoblogs in October 2013.[263] Other videos were hosted on a videoblogger's personal server, many of whom are no longer making these files available online. Some have chosen to delete old videos, or have migrated to new web domains and neglected to move the videos to the new site. One videoblogger, Raymond M. Kristiansen, told me his website (he migrated to a Wordpress blog in 2007) got infested with malware, and he can no longer access any of his own videos. At the time I conducted my interviews, I downloaded all the videos that were recommended to me.[264] Some are encoded in old obsolete codec formats, and will no longer play, a frustrating aspect of technical media. Those videos uploaded to the Internet Archive have survived technical upgrades and changes best. It is interesting that so few of the videos survive, considering the community consistently emphasised the desire to use videoblogging as a way of archiving and aiding memory for the future. As Susan Pitman put it, 'I am documenting this for my kids to watch when they're older'.

I chose two videos from each of the three different videobloggers for the close reading from the categories I identified as personal videoblogging, everyday life videoblogging and artistic videoblogging. This was a combined total of 33:47 minutes of video footage. The first set was two videos by Ryanne Hodson, one of the most prolific videobloggers at the time and an early adopter of the practice. Hodson made very personal videos on her blog Ryanedit.blogspot.com, often filming herself as she was getting out of bed, or as she was travelling, hanging out with friends or just videos of her expressing her ideas – often reflections on videoblogging. Hodson worked through a variety of cameras, from a digital camera with a video function, through to the Sanyo Xacti. Hodson's style was deceptively simple, using iMovie to edit her work. Her videos were always more about what she had to say, than how they looked. She was an active and generous member of the videoblogging community whose contributions included the resource site Freevlog, being instrumental in setting up *Have Money Will Vlog*, an early community fundraising site, and volunteering at Apple stores teaching people how to videoblog.

The second set of videoblogs was from Daniel Liss' site Pouringdown. Liss' videos were explorations of the medium of videoblogging through a singular aesthetic that made his work instantly recognisable. Liss was not the most active member of the videoblogging community, and would rarely engage in long discussions on the email list. He did, however, follow the debates closely and often reacted to people through his video-work, as can be seen in the video *Theory:Practice*, explored below. Liss never filmed himself or his family directly, although they often featured in his work indirectly. He relied heavily on voice-overs and narration and would experiment with styles, and effects such as blurring images, long, lingering shots

---

263 Compumavengal, Email to Videoblogging list, 10 October 2013, https://groups.yahoo.com/neo/groups/
      videoblogging/conversations/topics/79534.
264 Some videos, especially those in a flash format, couldn't be downloaded at the time, so some videoblogs
      were never archived.

with minimal movement and editing, but also more rapid cuts and jarring edits that really brought attention to the aesthetic possibilities of the medium. Finally, the third set of videos was gathered from Juan Falla's videoblog, *Viviendo Con Falla*, following Falla and his wife through their everyday lives as they settle in to their new lives in Los Angeles, having recently relocated from Colombia. Falla's videos were playful explorations of the cultural differences between Colombia and the USA, and he usually spoke both English and Spanish in his films. Falla was an aspiring filmmaker, and he often drew on established tropes and styles in his work, caring deeply about the editing process and the finished product.

The videobloggers are quite adept at using established cinematic styles and tropes. There is a diverse mix of styles to be found used in their work. As the practice developed, some videobloggers invested in more professional microphones, but the majority recorded diegetic, ambient sound through the internal microphone of the cameras they used, so generally, the sound in videoblogging was fairly low quality, but its rawness added to the vernacular aesthetic. Some voice-overs were recorded in post-production, resulting in 'better' sound quality, yet neither Daniel Liss or Hodson had these kinds of resources available. Lighting was usually limited to the natural or artificial light that was available where and when the videoblogger was shooting, which meant faces were often 'badly' lit —all of which sharpened the aesthetic of the end product. This aesthetic was increasingly deliberate, as 'according to its own rhetoric, the new participatory online culture needs none of the fancy apparatus of the mainstream media to create something honest and worthwhile, something that communicates citizen to citizen in an authentic and personal mode of expression. It is better off as amateur media than it would be with the means available to professionals'.[265] Certainly, this was seen in videobloggers' work that would rejoice in its alternative and counter-mainstream aesthetic.

Birgit Richard argues that online video, and YouTube in particular, perpetuates an 'ideology of authenticity' linked to the poor-quality recording tools and subsequent poor resolution images produced. This aesthetic, together with the small windows displaying videos 'conspire to create "a look of everyday life"' and far from being a 'substitution or… an exchange for classic media art', YouTube videos are a 'supplement, a marginal but important fresh addition and revitalisation of art', with YouTube bringing to light previously invisible practices. Steyerl likewise conceptualises this in her notion of 'poor images' – or copies in motion – images that travel through culture at an accelerating speed, and lose quality at every iteration, be it through compression, remixing or travelling through low quality digital connections. 'The poor image is no longer about the real thing' she argues, 'instead, it is about its own real conditions of existence: about swarm circulation, digital dispersion, fractured and flexible temporalities. It is about defiance and appropriation just as it is about conformism and exploitation. In short: it is about reality.'[266] As Richard argues, through YouTube, 'the thus far invisible common creative practices —a lot of them may have existed before – are becoming more visible and

---

265 Newman, 'Ze Frank and the poetics of Web video', see also Vito Campanelli, 'The DivX Experience', in Geert Lovink and Sabine Niederer (Eds) *Video Vortex Reader. Responses to YouTube*, Amsterdam: Institute for Networked Cultures, 2011, p. 55-56.

266 Hito Steyerl, 'In Defence of Poor images', *e-flux journal*, 10.11 (2009).

open up the possibility of emerging new art forms'.[267] In contrast, Michael Renov derides this 'lure of authenticity' associated with documentary filmmaking, achieved through a 'cunning appropriation of particular tactics or stylistic traits (the use of 'witnesses'; the low-tech look, shaky camera; grainy, out-of-focus images)', pointing out how some non-fiction also 'displays a number of 'fictive elements' – instances of style, structure, and expositional strategy that draw on pre-existent (fictional) constructs or schemata to establish meanings and effects for audiences'.[268]

In relation to the videoblogs I examined, but also more informally in the wider videoblog community, there was a constant push and pull between a form of grassroots 'authenticity' and a desire for professionalism. Indeed, this would sometimes be observed in a desire for professional ascription, or that some form of recognition was or should be made towards their work. This resulted in a creative tension within the videoblog community as this dual identity, part pre-professional, part authentic artist, would be manifest in various ways in their videos. In fact, I would go further and suggest that the videobloggers identity was in some sense imbricated between two orders of identity. That this tension was never fully worked out into a new synthesis reflects on the shortness of the community's existence, but also in a challenge to their identity which came from an unexpected direction – YouTube. As YouTube's strength and online presence became increasingly hegemonic, the fledgling videoblog community, which was very poorly funded in relation to YouTube, struggled. Nonetheless, we should remember that the aesthetic of videoblogs was largely settled *before* YouTube emerged, and certainly before its full power was realised. So if we look at formal aspects of the videos themselves, such as editing style and technique, a number of recognisable practices emerged early on.

The editing in videoblogs, for example, tended to be circumscribed. For instance, one long-take bracketed each end by a title card and credits, as seen in *Excited* and *V-Blog Conversations*, or feature a number of quick edits, with cuts as short as 1-2 seconds long, for instance *Theory:Practice* and *Greetings*. Videobloggers might chose to approach one video in one way and one in another. For example, 'one video can be really simple,' Juan Falla told me, 'not a lot of editing, but then the next one can be heavy-edited and music... in some videos I feel more like being creative'. Further, the decision about whether a video had a lot of editing might not be planned from the beginning of the shoot. For example, after a weekend visiting Sundance, Falla knew he wanted to make a video about his experiences. It wasn't until he began editing he realised what the video would end up looking like, 'editing it,' he told me, 'I realized that I could tell a story having 10 frame shots only. And it would all be a crescendo for the last shot.'

For me, this comment really highlights how videoblogging differs from conventional film-making practices. This open-ended approach of what we might call elements of 'found-shooting' – that is on the fly video taken in the moment, as life unfolds. I have never come across a videoblogger story-boarding a video, for example, at most they might map out a very rough

---

267 Richard, 'Media Masters and Grassroots Art 2.0 on YouTube' p. 150.
268 Renov, *The Subject of Documentary*, p. 22.

structure. Richard BF liked to experiment with lots of different styles. One week he would do a 'slow motion piece, one in B&W… one upside down, I did one with my camera gaffed to my motorcycle, I did various character voice overdubs, I faked a few "personal" videoblogs, short ones, long ones, art pieces with effects etc.' This playfulness allowed great freedom and personal risk-taking, which was crucial to the way videoblogging was articulated and practiced. This experimentation was not limited to aesthetic choices, but included the technical specifications as well. For example, Hodson told me 'you would play with a number and you go, 'Ok, oh, Q value. What if I put a 60 in here? Let's see what happens. Ok, that didn't work. Let's try 70. Let's see what happens.' Until you got something that worked.' Videoblogging gave her a sense of creative freedom, not just to experiment but to 'post whatever I feel like. It's my outlet.' Jennifer Proctor told me 'I use my site to experiment with new techniques or ways of seeing or storytelling… it's a space that isn't open to me anywhere else. It's kind of a judgment-free zone for me, where I can make work that finds an audience (albeit a small one) but is totally experimental and not necessarily polished. It's a space where I can express myself and connect with others, however imperfectly, and I love that. It's very liberating.' This creativity and space of experimentation also enabled different kinds of gender representation to play out. Without the stifling weight of 'traditional' formats, and a sense of openness towards what a videblog could be, both in terms of form and content, meant that, particularly for the women videobloggers, there was no 'wrong way' to articulate their experiences, affect or arguments. Of course, previous media forms can and did influence the work produced, for example, film, television and video, but there was seldom an attempt to close down experimentation because it didn't conform to a 'norm' established in or through any prior media.

Most informants told me they spent more time on editing than on shooting, this aspect of the practice was important to them. For a videoblogger, editing was highly valued and formed an important part of how they identified the 'craft' of videoblogging. They felt a strong sense of ownership over their content, and in this respect, editing, the shaping of the image, the creation of narrative and affect, was central. The 'power' to create something unique, to manipulate images and sound to create new stories, clearly held a certain appeal; 'in editing, it's only me and nobody else. I love this. I love how from different shots, I end up with something people never imagined,' Juan told me. This emphasis on the importance of the editing process is perhaps best summarised by Richard Hall, who told me that 'editing is like meditation – I'm in a different world,' often spending 4-5 hours editing a video, which ended up being no more than 3-4 minutes long. Falla, equally, highlighted the importance of editing to the videoblogger, saying 'I like to edit a lot. So I take my time. The fastest edit I ever did was like 4 hours. But in other more complicated videos I have spent probably 6 hours per day for 5 days. But that's because I love editing.' Similarly, Charlene Rule told me 'I find shooting to be the most difficult, but again, once I force myself to start, then I'm excited to start editing.'

For Bordwell, the framing of an image shows the 'conscious processes of the film-maker' and he argues that 'whatever its shape, the frame makes the image finite. The film image is bounded, limited. From an implicitly continuous world, the frame selects a sleeve to show us, leaving the rest of the space off-screen.'[269] In contrast, there is a notable absence of particular standard cinematic tropes such as the establishing shot in videoblogging. An establishing shot is intended to give the viewer a full overview of a scene before the action kicks off, establishing boundaries of action and meaning. In some ways, it is one of the main tools used by a director to frame a scene, both symbolically and materially.[270] These alternative and unconventional practices within videoblogging more generally – even for those self-categorising as makers of documentaries – is significant. Movie director Joe Swanberg, who has adopted many 'internet video' elements in his work, and makes movies that operate similarly to some videobloggers (shoe-string budgets, digital cameras, heavily influenced by YouTube and web video), argues the reason he almost never uses the establishing shot is because 'I don't want you to know where people are because it's not important... I like working extremely close because it's all about that moment. When I photograph a body part – a hand or foot – this is what I care about. The little things – tiny details separated from their circumstances.'[271] This wider mainstreaming of the aesthetic practices of videobloggers is something that emerged later but nonetheless showed the creative potentials of these communities.[272]

In videoblogging, consequently, there was a move away from the establishing shot and instead the focus on 'tiny details' such as close-ups of objects; coffee machines (as in Erin Nealey's *Mornings*), hands (Charlene Rule's *Mod,* Daniel Liss' *Prototyping*), and faces (Ryanne Hodson's *V-blog Conversations*, Daniel Liss' *Requiem* and Charlene Rule's *Bump*). Mary Matthews told me that when filming others she focuses on the 'face, eyes, hands. The parts of them that are truly them'. She never elaborated on why these particular parts were 'truly them' but it echoes the notion of partial objects and *faciality* from Deleuze and Guattari. As they argue, the face can be read as a language and 'the close-up in film treats the face primarily as a landscape; that is the definition of film, black hole and white wall, screen and camera'.[273] As such, the face gains an elevated position within film theory and acts as a 'veritable megaphone'. Raymond told me,

> I film myself, mostly... the face, the talking. The conversation... face, head... I don't really see my body as the key of this either. The only reason why I show my body is that it is the carrier of my face, and even though I show my face a LOT less than I used to, I still see the face as being important for the kind of communication I want in my videos.

---

269 David Bordwell and Kristin Thompson *Film art: an introduction*, New York: McGraw- Hill, 2007, p. 197.
270 Bordwell and Thompson further argue that 'whatever its shape, the frame makes the image finite. The film image is bounded, limited. From an implicitly continuous world, the frame selects a sleeve to show us, leaving the rest of the space off-screen. If the camera leaves an object or person and moves elsewhere, we assume that the object or person is still there, outside the frame' (p. 187).
271 Aymar Jean Christian, 'Joe Swanberg, Intimacy, and the Digital Aesthetic', *Cinema Journal*, 50. 4, Summer, (2011) pp. 123.
272 Scottish comedian Brian Limond, who is behind the popular *Limmy's Show* on BBC Scotland, adapted similar elements in his work. The show features many of the aesthetics, structures, and technical choices and limitations seen in the work of the videoblogging community. It is worth noting that Limond started his career posting videos to Vine and YouTube, and returned to YouTube once his show was cancelled. Interestingly, his half hour special from 2018, *Limmy's Homemade Show*, was self-made, using only 'videoblogging' tools and technology.
273 Gilles Deleuze and Felix Guattari, *A Thousand Plateaus*, London: Continuum, 2004, p. 191.

The emphasis on the face was repeated by a number videobloggers. It can also be found across YouTube,[274] where numerous videoblogs show footage of people talking, singing, arguing and laughing into the camera.[275]

This idea that the face plays a vital part in communication is interestingly developed in film theory. For example, Christian argues that 'pushing the camera against the face forces the viewer to contemplate the character's interiority and story expressed through the screen; it defines the film as a mediated, intimate space first, and eventually as a space where something 'real' is possibly but improbably achievable'.[276] Swedish auteur, Ingmar Bergman famously explored the subtleties of the face through his uncomfortably close shots of Ingrid Bergman and Bibi Anderson's faces in *Persona*. In a more recent example, Pablo Larrain's intimate portrayal of Jaqueline Kennedy in the movie *Jackie*, features similar relentless focus on Natalie Portman's face and hands. This mediation of some kind of 'real' is also central to the videoblogging aesthetic, and also to their discourse. Of course, this claim to the real, or to realism, is itself problematic, and even those videobloggers who 'love it', are still reflexive about that fact that what you see is mediated, or somehow manipulated.

There are also technical reasons why the face dominated the videoblogging aesthetic. For example, Juan Falla moved between technical and symbolic reasonings for focusing on the face in videoblogs, thus performing a kind of medium analysis of his own work. He began by giving a symbolic reasoning for his 'directorial choices' telling me that he focuses mainly 'on the face. That's how people watching the video "connect" with it. Because as a viewer we feel compelled and we can understand and accept (or deny) a person's reaction. And the best way is either by an action of the person, like in a movie; or by the person's face.' Falla then moves on to discussing how the medium of videoblogging (though he is really discussing QuickTime here) lends itself to a facial close-up 'in order to connect' with other people. 'We have to understand that videoblogs are 320 x 240, or in our case 480x 280, and *that* is a small screen, so the closer we are to someone's face, the better we can understand and connect with her/him.' Here we can see how the materiality of videoblogging has a structuring influence on the visual it produces, reminiscent of Marshall McLuhan's ideas about close-ups as specific to the medium of television. Falla also points to other material affordances of videoblogging, positioning the practice within a wider cultural frame. He told me that,

> I primarily show the face… because I only have the microphone of the camera, so the closer I am to the person talking, the better sound I get. Another thing is that I love the typical videoblog shot. The one where you shoot yourself holding the camera with your own hand. I think part of the magic of videoblogs is this particular shot. I mean, we have

---

274 For an interesting critique of this, see Adam's *video is fun of this computer website!* which is edited to show various images of his face, from a medium-shot of him walking in the park, to close up of his drooling mouth. The video carries the caption 'I am big fan of Youtbue and Love to make vidoe of me walking in park and my face. The Youtube is for all fun and people to me' (spelling mistakes in the original text, added as a deliberate critique of content on YouTube).

275 The Tumblr-based art project Webcam Tears featuring YouTube videos of people crying is another example.

276 Christian 'Joe Swanberg, Intimacy, and the Digital Aesthetic', p. 123.

medium shots in CNN or BBC News, right? We also have all these incredible shots in the movies where the camera even flies around in a spectacular shot. In videoblogs, we have the camera in 'a person's face', and this is way more personal.

The face in videoblogs has grown to represent a kind of realism, or truth, and some kind of personal connection. However, it is not necessarily the face itself as captured by the video-blogger that suggests an unmediated or authentic record of the event but the fact that the recording exists at an arm's length. Indeed, if we imagine a person holding up their mobile phone in front of them to take a 'selfie' or a snapshot, this makes more sense.

Some videobloggers, made a conscious decision never to show their own faces in their videoblogs. Mica Scalin told me that in her work, 'faces are often secondary because they almost distract too much or allow people to make too quick judgements'. Brittany Shoot told me she didn't 'want to talk to my camera anymore, and I also am not really convinced that's effective. In the sense of putting myself into the video in heart, yes, they are person-al. But do I show my face as much, talk about my life, how I feel? No. I let people draw assumptions from whatever I make'. Shoot talked at length about how she 'used to show emotion when I talked to the camera, but it backfired when I got too angry on film', and this affected her relationship with the videoblogging community. Equally, Daniel Liss never showed his face in his videos. Liss and Shoot's positions echoes Patricia Lange's notion of a 'privately public' videoblogger. [277] Lange argues that despite having a group of followers/subscribers/fans/friends, some videobloggers, particularly those she calls 'privately public' videobloggers, are fiercely protective of their friends and family. For Shoot, her honesty on film left her vulnerable to personal attacks – perhaps not surprising to anyone following the debates surrounding Gamergate and more recent 'hashtag events' like #metoo and #notokay – detailing the kinds of abuse, sexual and otherwise, women experience, especially on digital media. In Liss' case, his daughter, who featured quite heavily in his videos, was only ever referred to as 'Mookie' and her face is never fully shown in his work. Liss himself only ever revealed snippets about his own identity in his videos, beyond the fact he is male and lives in New York. Hiding became a way of squaring the contradiction of living a private life in a public medium. I think this dichotomy between the 'real' represented by an 'arms-length' selfie video, and the desire by some videobloggers to withhold their faces is interesting in thinking about what a videoblog is. We might term these different approaches 'selfie-real' versus 'talking-real' to bring out the different ways in which the documentary-mode, which was often gestured towards through the aesthetic and practice, was presented. This idea of the face as real as opposed to the voice as real (as in the voice-over) is offered to explore and highlight different ways of thinking about what the practice of videoblogging brought forward or foregrounded in its practice. Nonetheless, the 'selfie-real' certainly emphasised a stronger dimension, or representation, of the personal.

Now I want to change register to consider close readings of a number of videoblogs, starting with what I term 'personal videoblogs'. The aim here is to give a stronger sense of the way in

---

277 Patricia Lange, 'Publicly Private and Privately Public: Social Networking on YouTube', *Journal of Computer-Mediated Communication,* 13, (2008): p. 372.

which different videobloggers might work in a specific mode whilst nonetheless conforming to the general principles of the videoblogging aesthetic. In this case, a personal mode was reflected in the content of the videoblog, but also in specific moments in the form of the videos. This section will explore Ryanne Hodson's videoblog. Hodson started videoblogging in November 2004 and was one of the most active videobloggers in the core community. She had been working as a video editor at WGBH, a virtual channel part of a PBS television station in Boston when she started feeling disillusioned with the constrains under which she worked. She saw videoblogging as a medium that would allow ordinary people to transform themselves from media consumers to media producers. She self-defined as a 'personal videoblogger' documenting her everyday life, and had a number of 'talking head' videos in which she mostly speaks to the camera from her room in her apartment in New York. She was heavily involved in promoting videoblogging, including co-writing a book on videoblogging, speaking at conferences, organising workshops and running freevlog.org.[278] Hodson had a natural way of being on camera. She was at ease with both herself and her audience, creating a sense of intimacy with the viewer as she invited them into her life. Her enthusiasm for videoblogging was also palpable in her work. For instance, she would sometimes turn the camera on upon waking up in the morning, giving a long, rambling monologue about a subject she was passionate about with sleepy eyes and messy hair. This made her videos compelling. What she had to 'say' was the focus of her posts, and she was never short of an opinion, controversial or otherwise. One of her first videos, *Excited* (00:50 min, 240x180) was the first video in which Hodson turned the camera on herself. Her previous work had featured her mother and time-lapse videos from Boston. After turning the camera on her own face, manifesting what I am calling 'selfie-realism,' we might say Hodson found her 'thing' and she also found her audience.

In *Excited*, Hodson started creating her particular style of videoblogging, which she develops further in *V-Blog Conversation* (03:32 min, 160x120). The videos use the selfie-realism videoblogging head shot, the talking head, which Hodson also highlighted as one of her most used devices. '[I film] the face mostly, talking head, talking at ya!' In *Excited*, her face fills almost the entire screen (figure 11), which is framed slightly off centre and slightly blurred. She is often poorly lit, in fact, it looks as if her face is being lit by the light emanating from her computer or laptop, which means she either filmed this video using the recording video function in iMovie, on a webcam or on a digital camera with video function perched on the desk in front of her. Later, Hodson would go on to use the new Xacti camera for most of her videos, but until the Xacti was launched (in January 2006), she relied on one of these three methods of filming. With the move to the Xacti, the quality of the image improved dramatically, but her style remained similar. Hodson's first mention of the Xacti is in 2006 (on the videoblogging list, where she posted a review). Like many videobloggers, using the video function on a digital camera was their preferred method of capturing film, and Hodson soon moved to use this technique.

---

278 Ryanne Hodson and Michael Verdi, *Secrets of Videoblogging*, Berkeley: PeachPit Press, 2006.

Figure 11: *Excited* (Hodson, 2004)

In *V-Blog Conversations*, it is clear that she is holding the camera in her hand. The shot isn't nearly as steady as in *Excited*, and it moves around as she does. In their book, Hodson and Verdi call this the 'classic 'talking to the camera' videoblogger shot'. Dedman and Paul also refer to as the 'classic videoblogger shot'[279] and Will Luers describes it as 'the most pervasive vlogging camera position... the arm-extended, camera-turned-on-oneself method of address'.[280] I prefer the term 'selfie-realism' which more strongly brings out the connotations of the real and the personal that this technique foregrounds. At one point in her video, Hodson also pans it around the room to show where she lives. Again, the lighting is poor, this time her face is half-lit by what looks like a light source off-screen to the left, which means half of her face is hidden in shadows for most of the duration of the video.

Figure 12: *V-blog Conversation* (Hodson, 2004)

Hodson's face fills the screen in a close-up and only towards the end, when she is showing the viewer her room, does the camera pan away from her face (figure 12). The framing of her face echoes the way our faces are framed in Skype chats or other kinds of instant video-communication. In other words, the look of the videoblog is reflected in its content, and Hodson is chatting, literally, to whoever wants to listen. As she says in the video,

---

279 Jay Dedman and Joshua Paul, *Videoblogging*, Indianapolis: Wiley Publishing, 2006, p. 46.
280 Will Luers, 'Cinema Without Show Business: a Poetics of Vlogging', *Post Identity* 5.1 (2007).

Hello… hello videobloggers. Um, I… just watched Jay's video of him sitting with like a purple curtain behind him, talking, um, and saying, wait, why shouldn't I just type this, it's a blog, so [laughs] I was inspired to just sit in front of my camera and talk about videoblogging, because, um, I am so excited about it.[281]

She goes on to describe some of the things she loves about videoblogging, which are linked to the kinds of intimate relationships the medium is facilitating with a new audience,

On the Internet, you just make it. And you post it. And people laugh. In California. [smiles] And they write you and they say 'oh my god, I laughed so hard when I saw that' [laughs with entire face] It's so great! It's just the best thing…. you know, the internet, it's a five minute thing I want to do, ok I'm gonna do it and people can watch it and I feel great, oh my god, that's the best thing in the world. So, it's 3 am, right now, and I just played poker all night, and I couldn't get to sleep, cos I just saw Jay's video and I was like I'm totally going to get my camera and talk to people.[282]

Both *Excited* and *V-Blog Conversations* are notable for being filmed in one take, they have no cuts or edits in the main body of the video, which is a common trait in this particular type of videoblog; the personal, confessional, diary-style videoblog. This is for two reasons. Firstly, from a purely technical perspective, having long single-take video makes the production process much quicker and easier; the videoblogger simply adds a title card at the beginning and credits at the end, before compressing and uploading. Secondly, it creates a sense of intimacy and realism. By showing herself in one take, Hodson gives the viewer the impression that she is 'able to put [herself] out there and be so vulnerable with people' – rather than present an edited version of herself. This echoes André Bazin's notion that 'cinema is objectivity in time'.[283] Bazin argued for the 'use of long, continuous shots in order to preserve spatial and temporal continuity' and believed that 'editing serves to falsify reality by breaking up space and time'.[284] Bazin also argued that the screen is 'putting us 'in the presence of' the actor. It does so,' he claimed, 'in the same way as a mirror – one must agree that the mirror relays the presence of the person reflected in it – but it is a mirror with a delayed reflection, the tin foil of which retains the image'.[285] Similarly, in an online setting, these kinds of long, or one-take videos are part of creating an air of authenticity surrounding the videoblogger. Her success is related to her ability to communicate her sincerity to her viewers. As Vanderbeeken points out, 'what is special about web video documents is that their credibility depends on the viewer's willingness to accept their authenticity, as there is no guarantee that they are not staged or manipulated'[286]. Clearly, the selfie-real forms of

281 *V-blog conversation*, transcript.
282 *V-blog conversation*, transcript.
283 André Bazin, 'The Ontology of the Photographic Image', in *What is cinema?* Vol 1, Berkley and Los Angeles: University of California Press, 1967.
284 Richard Brody, *Everything is Cinema. The Working Life of Jean-Luc Godard*, London: Faber and Faber, 2008, p. 14.
285 Bazin, 'The Ontology of the Photographic Image' p. 409.
286 Robrecht Vanderbeeken, 'Web Video and the Screen as a Mediator and Generator of Reality', in Geert Lovink and Rachel Somers Miles, (Eds) *Video Vortex Reader II: Moving Images Beyond YouTube*,

video are as open to manipulation as other mediated forms. But nonetheless, it still seems to contain a kind of aura of realism.

Interestingly, when Hodson started working with Jay Dedman on the project *Ryan is Hungry*, a funded web series about sustainable living and ecological farming, their videos were much 'snappier' – featuring sharp edits, professional-looking logos and following much more traditional documentary-style tropes (interviews, commentary, narrative). The personal videoblog, then, was, for Hodson at least, a personal space in which she could narrate stories from her own life and share experiences with her other vlogger friends, 'this has been the greatest gift of videoblogging. Having people say 'me too!' Isn't that what we're all looking for? I think so'. She also filmed inside her own bedroom, inviting the viewer into her private sphere, even giving the viewer a tour of her personal space highlighting the sense of intimacy.

In her work, Hodson also explores the idea of videoblogging as a new platform for expression and free speech, a medium in which videobloggers express themselves – 'I am so excited about videoblogging. Because I can say whatever I want and the FCC can't do [BLEEP]'. This freedom of expression, both artistic and political, was very important to her; 'it's like complete freedom, I post whatever I feel like. It's like an open diary to the world.' At the time, Hodson was working in television, and was frustrated with how making content was laborious, expensive and censored. In her interview she said her videoblog is 'something really different than TV'. However, it is very clear from her video that Hodson is also censoring herself, choosing to bleep out not only her swear words, but even the surname of George W. Bush, whom she clearly dislikes,

> Hodson: Hmm. *Looks away from camera as if she is thinking what to say next. Faces camera* BLEEP you, George W BLEEP BLEEP BLEEP BLEEP [mouths 'Bush, you fucking asshole']. You BLEEP [mouths 'suck'].[287]

In other words, there is a tension in Hodson's video between the perceived potential for artistic and political freedom, and the self-censorship of bleeping out 'bad words' as if she is on a public network channel. This could be seen in contrast to her video *V-Blog Conversation*, in which she speaks much more frankly to a much more specific audience, even referring to other videobloggers by name. She mentions particular videobloggers in other videos too, an example of how the videoboggers were creating a sense of community; referencing each other's work, commenting and engaging one another in conversations across videos and across videoblogs. *V-Blog Conversation* was only posted a month after *Excited*, but the tone and style had changed quite dramatically. In *Excited*, Hodson was creating a fairly stylised piece – the tone, tempo and combination of words, image and music work together to form a polished piece. In *V-Blog Conversation*, however, she is notably more relaxed and you get a sense that she is talking directly at a specific audience. I believe this is a testament to how quickly the community was forming at the time as Hodson had shifted from addressing a generic (and unknown) audience to speaking directly to a network of people she knew

---

Amsterdam: Institute for Networked Cultures, 2011, p. 40.
287 *Excited*, transcript.

(probably by name) and felt part of, from small imagined audience to a small but intensive real community. These videos have roughly the same amount of comments (10 comments on *V-Blog Conversation* versus 9 comments for *Excited*), but as Hodson starts to learn not just that people *are* watching, but *who* are watching, her tone changes, and her style becomes more conversational and less of a performance.

Stylistically, *Excited* feels entirely self-contained; it has a clear narrative arc, and, although it shares a theme with many of Hodson's other videos (the theme being videoblogging itself), it can be seen as a stand-alone video that can be viewed in isolation and still make sense. *V-Blog Conversation*, on the other hand, lacks the visual clues of a narrative arc, there's no title card, no credits, and, although she starts with 'hello' and ends on 'goodnight', there is no real narrative progression. *Excited* is clearly scripted, whereas *V-Blog Conversation* feels like a complete improvisation, she saw a video online she really liked, she was inspired to join the conversation and she just started talking. The transcript reveals a kind of stream-of-consciousness in which Ryanne is seemingly just talking to herself or the audience, about whatever pops into her mind at any given moment. In this sense, despite looking quite similar, the two videos are in fact quite different. They also show that for a lot of videobloggers at this time, videoblogging was very much about experimenting, not just technically, but in terms of genre, style, technique and 'finding a voice'.

In contrast to personal videoblogs, I now want to turn to look at what I am calling artistic videoblogging. These videoblogs, I loosely group due to their focus on aesthetic practice in terms of both form and content, I am particularly interested in the way in which the videoblog is treated as a medium of expression, but not in the sense of the selfie-realism I referred to earlier. In contrast, here the explorations tend to be in terms of representational tropes, visual effects, montage and collage and it is interesting to look at the work of Daniel Liss, whose artistic practice and video work creates a critical case study of the artistic videoblog.

Daniel Liss lived in New York with his wife and daughter when he discovered videoblogging. Whilst home with his new-born child, and as an outlet for his creative impulses, videoblogging became a way to explore the city around him. Liss self-defined his practice as 'experimental personal film(?)making' [sic]. When asked if his videos had any kind of narrative, he was quite clear that he does not create 'any linear stories. But visual stories. Textural stories. Tone poems'. His work explores a number of potentialities for videoblogging; *Theory: Practice* explores the much-debated question of what videblogging *is*, whereas *World Maps* is a video playing with the idea of videoblogging as a medium for exploring concepts and ideas. The videos can be seen as a reflection of Liss' own practice, as well as a commentary on videoblogging more generally.

Theory: Practice is a visual polemic, just short of 4 minutes long, in which Daniel Liss presents his contribution to the community debate around what a videoblog. For him, the video is an attempt to distance himself from those in the community who had a tendency to lock down any debate around definitions, demarcate and control a specific definition of videoblogging that everyone should adhere to. As he told me, looking back;

I remember being (disproportionately?) incensed by a segment of the dialogue happening [on the videoblogging email list]. Specifically this: I felt that we were like a bloodthirsty horde marauding happily across the plains (what were we bloodthirsty for? maybe every perceived revolution is bloodthirsty?) and then suddenly some in our group: maybe some stragglers, or self-appointed generals even, were saying Guys Guys, you're not marauding right! That's not proper marauding! THIS is proper marauding. There were suddenly rules about which chunk of online video was eligible, and which wasn't. And I was riled up. And that specific video, *theory : practice*, was certainly a response to that.

Theory: Practice (3:54 min, 400x300) is a tone poem on the relationship between the city, art and practice. The video features footage from New York; an apartment block filmed through the window of a car and, later, the botanical gardens, interspersed with close-ups of objects that drive the story; scraps of paper, a mechanical pen, a baby's hand, and views of objects through windows (figure 13). Liss' voice-over is used in conjunction with the images. *World Maps* (03:38 min, 400x300) is a reflection on the capriciousness of memory and is structured much in the same way, hand-held footage of a baby exploring maps, books and other travel memorabilia set to Liss' self-composed music and voice. Here, however, the narrative is more linear than in *Theory: Practice* – as the video progresses, the objects become more and more scattered, and the baby is more and more intimate with them, putting them in her mouth, touching, feeling. The voice-over in *World Maps* follows a narrative path, whereas in contrast, the footage and narrative in *Theory: Practice* is cut in a non-linear way.

Figure 13: *Theory: Practice* (Liss, 2004)

In contrast to Ryanne's videos, Liss never makes talking-head videos,[288] something he discusses in *Theory: Practice*, saying he doesn't 'point the camera at myself and explain' what is going on in his videos. 'It's probably shyness but I think it's something more than that. I don't see the world that way and I don't tend to listen that well when information approaches head on.'

Instead of selfie-realism, Liss uses the point-of-view shot as his main form of expression. Always looking out at the world from his eye level and almost always hand-held, the camera,

---

288 Not once in his archive could I find a video of him pointing the camera at himself. Additionally, when footage emerged from the videoblogging film festival *Pixelodeon*, he either shied away from being filmed, or requested that his face be blurred out. Amusingly, within the community, a cut out photo of the American actor Yul Brynner was often pasted over Liss' face in photos as a joke.

which 'roams freely', acts like an extension of his eye, seeing the world as he sees it. Like Dziga Vertov's *kino-eye*, or Alexandre Astruc's idea of the *camera stylo*, Liss writes his story through images, matching words and images, cuts and words, visual movement with rhetorical movement. In *World Maps* this is evident, as the camera pans around at floor level, panning around the baby, as she is experiencing the map, zooming in and out to focus on her hands, then feet, and finally a full shot of her as she is sitting on the map (see figure 14).

Figure 14: *World Maps* (Liss, 2004)

By situating the camera in the middle of the action, the viewer feels part of the story as it unfolds. Like hand-held camera footage from a concert or a demonstration, where the camera travels between bodies, the present-ness of Liss' camera connects the viewer to the world he's creating. The effect is twofold. Firstly, as the camera is situated literally in the action, the viewer feels quite close to it. Secondly, the hand-held camera is close to the floor and not able to capture a perfect image at all times, and so the quality of the image is variable, in and out of focus. This acts as a reflection on the limitations of memory – as the baby is discovering memorabilia from past travels, Liss is also remembering them, but poorly, as a faint (blurred) memory.

In *Theory: Practice,* similar blurred images and 'half-captured' scenes – objects seen through car windows obscured by rain drops – contributes to Liss' theory of videoblogging, an art form which he argues isn't *supposed* to be perfect. Campanelli calls these artifacts 'disturbed aesthetic experiences' and presents the hypotheses that 'the use of digital tools in relation to cinema, and the consequent lowering of product quality, are not necessarily a consequence of the small budgets of young independent directors. Rather… we are in the midst of a new aesthetic positioning – one which, as usual, is picked up by the antennae of artists before becoming obvious to all… these are all conscious aesthetic choices, which have nothing to do with finances available to the production'.[289]

This can be seen as a deliberate stylistic choice, as much as a result of the constraints on the videoblogger due to equipment and bandwidth, especially in the case of *Theory: Practice.* As well as bringing the viewer closer to the action, creating a sense of intimacy, Liss is making the point that this is videoblogging as he sees it, because this is how he sees the world; 'I am showing you a part of my world and telling you a little something about it…. This is my world. This is how I see it, how I think it'. As Newman argues,

---

[289] Campanelli, 'The DivX Experience', p. 52.

Rare is the videoblog that has anything resembling the look or sound of a local news program or network sitcom. Just as punk is opposed to the polish of pop, Web video is opposed to the gloss and sheen of Hollywood entertainment. That sense of opposition is the spirit and ethos of DIY production whether in music, publishing, or audio-visual media. As Frank describes it, videoblogging is "a cheap and fast alternative to making media — that looks cheap and fast".[290]

Throughout his work, Liss plays with form and narrative. He skips back and forth in time, for example, a sheet of paper is initially shown with writing, scribbles all over it, and later in the video the same sheet of paper is shown blank. Sometimes he displays the same image repeatedly. For example, the image of the New York building is shown twice before he uses it a third time with an inverted image of a hand layered over it. He manipulates the image by using double exposure on the images of the hand and the building, to highlight the mediated nature of videoblogs, pointing out that, even when someone simply shoots-and-posts, their videos are still mediated. 'To pretend that's something unmediated in itself is I think a little naïve', he explains. He also manipulates the sound, bringing in music at dramatic moments in the narrative, to create emotional effect often in conjunction with sharp cuts or swift camera movement.

Like Ryanne Hodson, Liss speaks directly to the viewer, although his style is very different. Whereas Hodson is talking to the viewer, sitting down in front of and facing the camera and speaking into it in a conversational tone, Liss' interactions are more subtle. Here, I am not thinking of the way he communicates through sound and image, rather by the way in which he occasionally comments 'I vlog it for you' or 'I wanted to bring you something' and, at the end of *World Maps*; 'I never thought of the possibility of someone else going through it, not the baby leafing backwards through her dads adventures. And not you.' I asked Liss about his particular use of 'you' in his videos. He replied, 'if I had to speculate – and really why do you make the choices you make artistically? – I'd say that there is/was a somewhat heartening immediacy to it all, an inexorable feeling of conversation, a presumed someone looking back at you. And maybe at the best of times an intimacy to the proceedings. And so you address it directly'. This notion of an 'imagined community' of others to whom one speaks is a fascinating aspect of the videoblogging form. Even in notionally subjectless, perhaps aesthetic oriented work, there remains the perceived or imagined other to whom one addresses the work. Not as an audience, but rather as a colleague, an equal, a member of one's community.

Looking through his archives, I noted that initially, Liss' videos were cut with sound, image and text only, very little narration, but that at some point he started talking directly to the viewer. I asked him why this was. 'I remember being somewhat dismayed by this at points,' he told me 'people responded much more... if I spoke in my videos. Like, they weren't my favourites but they were relative crowd pleasers (where crowd equals something like 30 visitors)'. In

---

290 Newman, 'Ze Frank and the poetics of Web video'. 'Frank' here refers to American comedian and 'videoblogging pioneer' Ze Frank, who ran a videoblog *The Show with Ze Frank* every day for a year, between March 2006 and March 2007. Frank is a professional comedian who was not a member of the videoblogging community. Consequently, he does not feature heavily as part of this book.

other words, Liss started adding more voice-over narrations because his viewers seemed to respond. The feedback from the community – the recognition from the invested network perhaps – was important to the videobloggers, even to someone focussing on or trying to create a different aesthetic.

Pettman argues that in the age of digital sound, 'the subject is increasingly vulnerable to being lost in an aural version of Fredric Jameson's Bonaventure Hotel. The cues for recognizing individuality via the ear become something other than the timbre of the voice: the melody, the beat, or a catch phrase, for instance'.[291] Liss' voice certainly contains some of these qualities. Contrary to the visuality of his videos 'images are *out there*, on the screen, and framed by it', the sonic - and particularly his voice – 'does not appear to stand before us but rather to come to us or at us'.[292] His narration is melodic and rhythmic, clearly scripted, and yet, because it is repeated over the narrative arc of his entire body of work, becomes synonymous with the videoblog itself. I would probably not recognise Liss if I walked past him on the street, but I would have no trouble picking his voice out. His voice is part of what makes his videoblogs unique, which emphasises that videoblogs are not just visual objects, but aural.

Newman argues that videoblogging 'might usefully be considered as self-taught art, a term art historians use to refer to artworks by individuals "who have no academic artistic training and little connection to the mainstream traditions of Western art history."' The self-taught artist is someone who lacks the skills considered the standard within a particular art world and 'connotes an absence of rules for the artist to follow, a lack of familiarity with 'proper' ways of solving certain aesthetic problems.'[293] Although he had no formal training, Liss was clearly familiar with both cinematic rules and how to apply them to develop his work and increase viewership. For example, at the end of *Theory: Practice*, Liss uses denouement to conclude his polemical defence of his right to videoblog expression. A denouement is defined as either the final scenes after the dramatic climax of a story, where the author/film maker ties up all the lose ends or the brief period of calm at the end of a film where a state of equilibrium returns. As the music gets louder, the video cuts back to the park scene, and zooms in on the piece of cardboard, now shown to be filled with tiny scribbles. 'While the baby was out,' he narrates, as if to summarize, 'I filled first the cardboard and now this wrapper with these scribbles, it's all in here.' Then,

> [*Cut to park bench, with (white) wrapper and cardboard, both filled with writing*] Voice-over: But let me show you one last thing, and I feel a lot better already doing this. [*Camera pans to baby, who is smiling, Cut to image of spring flowers peeking up through the grass*] Voice-over: Here in the garden, there's the first sign of the spring thaw. [*Cut to black screen*].[294]

---

291 Dominic Pettman, 'Pavlov's Podcast: The Acousmatic Voice in the Age of MP3s', in Rey Chow and James Steintrager (Eds) *Differences. A Journal of Feminist Cultural Studies*, 22. 2&3 (2011).

292 Ray Chow and James A. Steintrager, 'In Pursuit of the Object of Sound' *Differences. A Journal of Feminist Cultural Studies*, 2.2/3 (2011), p. 2.

293 Newman, 'Ze Frank and the poetics of Web video' p. 142.

294 *Theory: Practice*, transcript.

By returning to the park scene, where his theorizing about videoblogging began, Liss captures a glimpse of the baby, now awake, who is smiling, reminding us that 'naptime' is when Liss gets most of his videoblogging done. Showing us the 'first sign of spring', Liss shows the viewer his life, symbolic both of the aesthetic aspect of his videoblogging practice, and a reminder that videoblogging can be a crystallisation of a collection of scattered moments.

With the last videos, I want to spend some time exploring the notion of what I call everyday life videoblogging. In contrast to the previous forms of videoblogs, in this section I want to examine videoblogs that celebrate and document the everyday, the commonplace and the quotidian. This form of videoblog tends towards the documentary, toward the exploration with the camera as the 'eye' and in the recording of the quiet and transient moments of life as lived experience. Again, I attempt to explore this type of videoblog through a set of exemplar videos, which I subject to a close reading.

The spectacle of the everyday and the intimate view of private life has always been of interest to the film and television industries, 'what is different about videoblogs (or vlogs) is the spectacle of the un-commodified everyday'.[295] Although there are examples of videoblogs attempting to monetise their practice, there is something new about videoblogging in that it exists within a social context that is not explicitly consumerist. Luers recognises that although the technologies available to the videobloggers (be it 'RSS feeds, video compression codecs, and tagging systems') can be seen as technical extension of advertising strategies, aimed at allowing the videoblogger maximum exposure and reach of her videoblogs, 'rather than compete for attention in the marketplace, most vloggers look to their peers for feedback and conversation. For perhaps the first time, we have a somewhat organized public arena for a cinema without show business'. It might be argued that people videoblog to make their life cinematic, prompting the question of why dramatic conflict is a necessary filter for understanding the stories we occupy in our everyday? Further, he asks what we are missing in our private lives that can be rediscovered and shared with others through the medium of video. For Luers, it is the idea of living cinematically that lies at the heart of videoblogging, a need to aestheticise the everyday through the process of framing, editing and (re)-presenting the personal. Digital production tools and online distribution systems make us into a kind of global citizen with new forms of visual vocabulary and grammar. But as an example of a nascent global cinema culture, videoblogging has been part of rediscovering a collective value in the local and the personal. Not the bland universals offered by the entertainment industries, but the depth and texture of everyday experience. But unlike personal videoblogs, here what I am calling everyday life videoblogs eschew the single take shot dominated by selfie-realism, and instead use cuts and other techniques to change the experience of watching dramatically.

To explore these ideas I look at the videoblogs of Juan Falla and his wife Ximena, who made videoblogs because they wanted to stay in touch with friends and family.[296] Falla described his videoblog as a reality show of their life in Los Angeles. Originally from Colombia, Falla

---

295 Luers, 'Cinema Without Show Business: a Poetics of Vlogging.'
296 Although Falla and Ximena made their videos together, Falla did most of the shooting and editing, so unless indicated otherwise, it is his voice that is heard here.

told me they 'wanted to show [their] families how [their] life is [in LA]… So we began shoot-ing our selves doing normal things like, going to the grocery store, going to the beach, in our apartment cooking, if we made a trip we would shoot it, etc.' Stylistically, Falla's videos draw on televisual aesthetics, rooted in the visual style of situation comedy. Mainly featuring himself and Ximena, Falla's videos are on average between 4 and 5 minutes long, and have relatively high production values especially when seen in comparison to some of the earlier videoblogging videos (like Ryanne Hodson). Falla told me he 'want[ed] each video to feel 'real'. Just as 'real life' is. This meant he made a deliberate choice to, for instance, not use any effects on the image, filters etc., and keep transitions to a minimum; 'from the moment we decided to make our videoblog, we decided that we wanted each video to be entertaining, to have a beginning, middle and end. So we edit and add music to each video. This way, it's exciting, and not boring'. Falla attempted to edit and add music to make it more 'enjoyable'. He told me 'nobody wants to see "boring moments", not even our own family (not even me!), so I edit out those boring moments… instead of having a half hour video, we have a 3 or 5 minute "really nice video"'. Here, it would seem that Falla's decision to make videoblogs of a certain length, which other videobloggers argued were made for technical reasons, such as restrictions on bandwidth, were in fact made for deliberate, stylistic, reasons. Later, he elaborated on this, telling me that 'between you and me, I prefer the short video, instead of a long one. Our attention span is getting shorter every year, we want things to happen fast. So having short videos, things begin and end in a blink of an eye.' In essence, the everyday life videoblog, in trying to conform to the 4-5 minute videoblog norm, reconstitutes life as a series of sharp cuts and highlights. Life remediated and reedited, but life nonetheless.

Figure 15: *Greetings* (Falla, 2005)

Greetings (4:07 min, 384x288), is Falla's first video, and acts as an introduction to the cou-ple's videoblog practice. The video has only a short fade-in from black, and is shot with Juan and Ximena both directly facing the camera. Throughout the video, the Fallas are sitting next to each other on a sofa with the camera resting either on a table or on a tripod about a meter in front of them. They speak either directly to the camera or to each other. As the image fades in from black, Falla is seen moving away from the camera to the sofa behind him, in other words, showing the viewer that he has just turned the camera on (figure 15). This is a tech-nique often used in documentaries and films to show that the protagonist is filming herself on a small, usually hand held device. It is often followed by a monologue directed at the camera, the moving image's version of the selfie, but here not the selfie-realism represented by the extended arm. It is a visual representation of the way the camera doesn't simply observe events, but becomes an active participant in the film.

Greetings features a quick succession of short cuts, all edited together. Usually, cuts and edits are made in a video to remove content, but what is interesting here, is that what is usually discarded has been left in. Apart from the sequence between 02:47 and 03:58 in which Juan and Ximena introduce their videoblog (in both English and Spanish), the video is basically a collection of out-takes, showing Ximena and Juan joking and laughing as they repeatedly forget what they are supposed to say ('where is the SCRIPT!'), speak over each other, feel silly on camera ('That sounded so bad!!!' 'Why is it that people get nervous when they're in front of a camera'), or one of them starts talking about something unrelated ('We don't have any fights… or sex'). These out-but-in-takes are reminiscent of gag-reels from television or films, where actors are shown breaking character, or what is called corpsing or breaking, through fits of giggles. Gag-reels are often presented to the viewer to create a human connection between the performer and the audience, showing that even the successful actor is 'only human' and makes errors just like the rest of us. However, this material is rarely or never left in the original footage, but instead assigned to the external gag-reel. In some videoblogs, this material is often brought to the forefront and instead of being cut, it is shown to the viewer. This is often done to assure the audience that what they are seeing is the full story, a gesture towards authenticity and seeing behind the curtain, perhaps in some sense, breaking the fourth wall of video as a mediated form.[297]

In a similar way Daniel Liss and Ryanne Hodson both discussed videoblogging within the videoblog itself, Falla and Ximena at one point digress into the same topic,

> Ximena: This is so stupid. Stop the camera! [*laughing.*] *Cut* Falla: That's what a videoblog is [*points to himself*] We don't have to act. We don't have to be another person Ximena: ok ok [*She starts counting down (in Spanish) to another take.*] Cinco, Quatro, tres, dos, uno, action. *Cut* Ximena: I need a script. This doesn't work without one. [*Both laugh*] *Cut.*[298]

It is interesting how videoblogging becomes the subject of the videoblog itself. However, where Hodson projects excitement at the 'new' medium she is about to start exploring, and Liss is vehemently opposed to being put in a pre-defined box, Falla – who came to videoblogging slightly later – seems to have accepted some kind of idea of what a videoblog is or should be. Falla described his videoblog as a 'reality show' and looking at the various stylistic and editing decisions he repeatedly made, as well as the structure and narrative of the videos produced, this description is revealing. His videos of himself and his wife on various trips, events and domestic settings might fall into the category of everyday life videoblogging, yet as both *Greetings* and *Sancocho* show, Falla's editing practice echoes those of reality TV shows in terms

---

297 Newman, 'Ze Frank and the poetics of Web video'. This style was adapted by Amanga Congdon, anchor of the internet news videoblog Rocketboom (2004 – 2006), but it was also used by Ze Frank and others (like Juan and Ximena) for comic effect.

298 *Greetings*, transcript.

of cuts, focus and narrative development. Here, perhaps, is the key to understanding Juan and Ximena's practice – they were influenced greatly by what they loved, television, stating 'we watch a lot of TV. I'd say minimum 3 hours a day'.

'What I like about videoblogs' Falla told me 'is that they are done by 'normal people'. He also liked the non-commercial aspect of videoblogging at the time, explaining,

> If I want to see a good mystery story, I might go to the movies or watch a TV show; but both these mediums don't deliver the raw footage that a videoblog does. When you have a housewife, or an architect, or a truck driver (people who don't work in the TV or Movie business) telling you how they see life, the things they do, there's something there that commercial TV and the Movies can't give us... Both TV and the Movies are a business which needs to give profits; instead videoblogs are done by people who just want to express themselves. They're doing it because they like to, because they want to. They are not doing it for the money. So this makes all the difference.

Sancocho (5:52 min, 480x270), another of their videoblogs, features Juan and Ximena in their kitchen, making Sancocho, a Colombian dish. It was first uploaded on 15th September 2006, so we can see that in the year after uploading *Greetings* (4:07min, 320x240), Falla was already improving his production values and experimenting with the quality of his videos. In *Sancocho*, Falla films using a combination of the PoV shot ('everything we show is based on our point of view') and the talking head shot. Here, he holds the camera stretched out and slightly up above himself, in order to capture not just his face but his wife in the background. At some point he also places the camera on the kitchen counter, which allows him to help with the preparation, whilst carrying on recording. The result is a slightly odd image, sometimes cutting off the top of his head, whilst at other times, they lean down towards the camera to chat (figure 16).

Figure 16: *Sancocho* (Falla, 2005)

Videoblogs are sometimes criticised for their poor quality, and if one downloads any of the videos today, what will stand out is not just the poor compressions, but the limited lighting, sound, editing and the mundanity of the subject matter. However, as Lange argues in relation to her work on YouTube, what people often fail to understand about videoblogging, is that the quality of the videos is not necessarily the deciding factor in terms of how these videos affect the social networks they interact with.[299] For Lange, the videos have value because the

---

299 Lange, 'Publicly Private and Privately Public: Social Networking on YouTube', p. 368.

creation and circulation of video endorses social relationships between those who create and those who watch the videos. Regular and frequent interaction between video bloggers and viewers is a core component of this participation. The social network on YouTube is created, not merely through profile pages, linkages and so forth, but through the videos produced and the interaction between users watching, commenting on and sharing videos. I argue the same can be said for the videoblogging community at an earlier period in digital media history.

The videobloggers understanding of cinematic tropes shows how they utilise them to create their stories. Through their work, they employ cinematic elements to drive narrative, draw the viewer in and try to keep their attention right through to the end credits. But videoblogging is a medium-specific practice, which utilizes and experiments with its own technical restrictions, in order to push the boundaries of what (at the time) was possible to achieve within the online production of moving images. In October 2006, Will Luers, videoblogger, artist and frequent poster on the videoblogging email list made the following observation about the videoblog aesthetic as a reticular aesthetic,

> The other day I screened, that is projected on a screen, a little bit of pouringdown and 29fragiledays. I expected that, as art students, they would see creative possibilities. Not so. There was more of an appreciative shrug. What's the point? One student asked. Then it hit me. These were shown completely out of context. There is the context of the vlogger's serialized posts, the ongoing layering of ideas, the sense of a living person picking up the camera or finding images elsewhere. The excitement, the suspense, of what they will come up with next. There is also, of course, the text introducing the post and the comments etc. But here is the other part that is so intangible. The context of seeing the work along with other vloggers. To see Duncan [Speakman]'s work next to Daniel [Liss]'s and Jay [Dedman]'s and [Michael] Verdi's etc. This is the context of the network and it is very different from a screening of shorts at a festival, where each work is made and presented without awareness of the other work. The social part is central to the activity.[300]

In contrast, Newman sees the videoblogs as an 'interstitial form' of media, due to the fact that it 'fills gaps between other activities'.[301] He argues that by design, web video is only meant to fill the gaps in the daily schedule of the viewer. In other words, the fact it is rarely more than 3 minutes long, with no necessary links to other videos, users or narratives, indicates that the videoblog is only meant to be viewed in gaps in the viewers' daily schedule. Where Newman sees Web video as an 'in-between', I argue that actually the videoblogging community was always very much *an invested network*. The participants actively sought out other videoblogs to watch, creating meaning for its members through the very shared context in which it existed, the collective experiences of making and watching videoblogs together. Not in the same place, or at the same time, but rather in the same network.[302]

---

300 Will Luers, Email to Vlog Theory List, 4 Octover 2006, https://groups.yahoo.com/neo/groups/vlogtheory/conversations/messages/840.
301 Newman, 'Ze Frank and the poetics of Web video'.
302 Newman's point is well observed in relation to recent videos on Instagram where videos are often

This is a cultural-technical community of videoblogging – the videobloggers and the videos, the blogs, the emerging platforms, networked together through links that are both material (http, blip, archive.org) and symbolic (friendships, work relationships, shared aesthetics). Adrian Miles' argues that videoblogs differ from (text-based) blogs in that their content (the videos) are not tied to the blog itself, but can float free from it. In 2000, he argued that 'currently you can place the video content of your videoblog onto DVD and project it in a gallery or cinema, and it is for all intents and purposes the same content as appears in the videoblog'.[303] Further, he argues that once video (or audio) have been published online (regardless of the efforts to produce it) it becomes a 'closed and whole object that is deaf to the network that it ostensibly participates within'. I disagree. For me, the videoblog can only truly be understood contextually, within its specificity as a digital and networked cultural object. The videoblog itself, within the community, forms an invested network and a community of interest around a shared set off practices, norms and aesthetics that are historically specific.

In the next chapter I want to develop some of these ideas by thinking about the more cross-cutting issues around the practice of videoblogging. In particular, I want to develop a theoretical response to some of the questions I have explored in this and previous chapters, and start to look at what the videobloggers do.

---

accompanied by subtitles making it possible to watch them with the audio turned off. This indicates that the videos are being watched (or specifically designed to be viewed) in (social) situations where silence is required or desired, in other words, in between other activities, for example at work or whilst on public transport.

303 Miles, 'A Vision for Genuine Rich Media Blogging'.

6. DOING VIDEOBLOGGING

> This is why good videoblogs are so personal, because superficially they look like they're
> about a subject, but in reality, they're about the videoblogger (Richard BF).

Crucial to the question of what people *do* with media, is what people *say* they do with media,
and what it means to them. De Certeau famously theorized the practice of everyday life,
exploring the relation between the spatial and signifying practices that make up our everyday experience of the world.[304] His notion of the practice of everyday life strongly influenced
theories of media consumption, particularly the way it 'reaches beyond individual experience
and action towards the (transcendental) ground of everyday practice and includes a defence
of 'ordinary' language'.[305]

In this chapter, I want to use some of de Certeau's insights to engage with videoblogging as
a media practice. I seek to explore the embodied practices the videobloggers performed
routinely. The focus on media as practice has intensified in scholarly writing in recent years[306]
but here I am also drawing particular attention to Nick Couldry's notion of media as practice
as a starting point for thinking about what videobloggers do with media.[307] The emphasis on
practice in the study of media does not start with Couldry, nor is it unique to the study of media,
but I think Couldry's work is very helpful for thinking through the way in which videobloggers'
practices were organised and actualised.

I also draw on Roger Silverstone's notion of the 'double articulation' of media in my analysis
of videoblogging as a technical-cultural hybrid, with a specific aesthetic vernacular. By taking into account the material social practice and cultural content of the media, as well as its
technological conditions and visual output, we can think about cultural production as a 'field
of embodied, materially interwoven practices centrally organized around shared practical
understandings'.[308]

Couldry argues that a theory of media as practice is concerned with analysing two publicly
observable processes, namely practices and discourse.[309] Here, practices are understood
as routine activities that are unconscious and 'un-thought' in character, as opposed to consciously chosen actions.[310] Discourse is understood not only as the things people say, but

---

304 Michel De Certeau, *The Practice of Everyday Life: Living and cooking,* (Trans. Steven Rendall),
     Berkeley and Los Angeles: University of California Press, 1984, p. 105.
305 Helga Wild, 'Practice and the Theory of Practice. Rereading Certeau's "Practice of Everyday Life"',
     Journal of Business Anthropology, Spring (2012) p. 3.
306 John Postill and Birgit Bräuchler, 'Introduction: Theorising Media and Practice.' In John Postill and
     Birgit Bräuchler (eds) *Theorising Media and Practice*, New York: Berghahn Books, 2010, p. 1-32.
307 Nick Couldry, 'Theorising Media as Practice', *Social Semiotics,* 14.2 (2004).
308 Elisenda Ardèvol, Antoni Roig, Gemma San Cornelio, Ruth Pagès, and Pau Alsina. 'Playful Practices:
     Theorising 'New Media' Cultural Production.' In Birgit Bräuchler and John Postill (Eds) *Theorising
     Media and Practice*, New York: Berghahn Books, 2010, p. 259-80.
309 Here he draws on the work of Ann Swindler.
310 Couldry, 'Theorising Media as Practice', p. 121.

the system of meanings that makes it possible for them to say anything in the first place. So we can examine *videoblogging as practice* as un-thought in character and how the practice of videoblogging is part of the everyday life of the videoblogger. By observing their practices, and by listening to how they articulate their practices, we are able to gain a more complete picture of videoblogging. In her exploration of amateur home-movies in the bourgeois family, Patricia Zimmermann discusses the complicated relationship between discourse and practice. She argues 'the complexities of the relationship between discourse, which often presents itself as even, uninterrupted, and organized, and practice, which is much more unruly, and contradictory, erupt when we consider the myriad of relations between amateur-film discourse and actual amateur filmmaking. While these theoretical issues are tempting to analyse, their empirical answer is bound by the availability of amateur film'.[311] Equally, this investigation into the practice of videoblogging is bound by the amount of material available to me.

I am interested in the following questions; what types of things do the videobloggers do in relation to videoblogging, and what types of things do the videobloggers say in relation to their practice? We can look at the activities of the videobloggers, and how they use videoblogs in and around their everyday activities, for example how they shape space and time. It is also crucial to analyse the content of the videoblogs.

There is a tension here, between the 'un-thought' in relation to everyday life practices – which in some sense is centred around the achievement of the everyday in itself – and the way I use 'un-thought' to refer to the videobloggers creative practices. There is also a question related to how one gets at individuals' un-thought practices – if they are un-thought they are also possibly not self-reflexive – and when asked to describe them, they are by definition no longer un-thought. But by undertaking a long period of participant observation I was able to draw on both what the individuals were saying they did and my own experience of doing it, thus gaining a richer understanding of the practices of videoblogging. I do not claim that this process of reflexivity lies only within the expert domain of academia, rather I argue that videobloggers themselves are also continuously reflecting on their own practice. Indeed, observing the high volume of posts on the Vlog Theory email lists, one can see discussions and reflections on videoblogging were regular occurrences at a high level of theoretical and technical fluency.

The perspective of practice helps us understand how media are embedded in the interlocking fabric of social and cultural life. It allows us to get an understanding of how media practices are 'differentially ordered for those with ready access to media resources… and for those without'.[312] In other words, doing things with media isn't 'one thing' to 'all people': it is a different thing depending on the context in which you do them. So, for instance, although Jenkin's concept of participatory culture acts as an anchoring term for a variety of activities and practices performed by individuals across the world, participatory culture isn't one thing to everyone. Participatory culture is a diverse practice, with a variety of practices that inform and illuminate it, be it blogging, videoblogging, tagging content on Flickr, Instagram or Tumblr,

---

311 Zimmermann, *Reel Families*, p. xiv.
312 Couldry, 'Theorising Media as Practice', p. 129.

or actively or occasionally contributing to the constantly evolving content of Wikipedia. Further, participatory culture also provides a structure under which people can create discourses for understanding and articulating what they do. The subject position of the videoblogger, is discursively constructed through the email list, and more concretely asserted as an identity and a set of practices in the interviews. Videobloggers use space and place in their practice, and attempt to mediate these notions. Questions of time and temporality are crucial in relation to understanding videoblogging by exploring how ritual and habit are both lived and mediated by videoblogs.

As previously discussed, my analysis involved a formal coding of the videos submitted, as well as a discursive analysis of the interviews. Despite many self-defining as artistic or experimental film/video-makers, in terms of a more formal theory of aesthetics, most fit in a category of autobiographical, or personal video-making. This resonates with the idea of videoblogging as a personal practice, drawing on influences such as home-movies and scrapbooking,[313] which also use creative and artistic tropes. Few, if any, videobloggers have any institutional support or links with the traditional art world, galleries or such like. However, later there was a move towards film-inspired screenings and short-film festivals, such as *Pixelodeon* (2007) in Los Angeles and award-type events, like the Vloggies (2007).[314]

As previously discussed, one of the main distinctions between someone posting videos to YouTube and a videoblogger in the sense that is used in this book, is that the videoblogger maintains her own (video)blog, usually individually designed, with custom blog-rolls (or vlog-rolls), archives and about pages, where they might post videos between three times a week to once a month. Compared to the relative ease with which people adopted blogging in the early 2000s, videoblogging required quite a high level of technical competence and knowledge. In contrast, someone who posts videos on YouTube, will often define him/herself as a Youtuber or 'Tuber. Amongst the videobloggers I interviewed, they generally felt they were part of a videoblogging community. Indeed, all were subscribers to the videoblogging email list around which the community was mainly situated. The videoblogging list was also followed by a number of people who were not formally videobloggers, but who would occasionally post to the list. In contrast, Youtubers have much less of a sense of community and shared practice, being dispersed, but also more hierarchically structured with celebrity Youtubers at the top – often earning millions in sponsorships – and amateur Youtubers at the bottom.[315] Nonetheless, there has been a shift in vocabulary with some Youtubers beginning to prefer the term 'videoblogger' to define themselves. For the original self-defined videobloggers,

---

313 Karina Hof, 'Something you can actually pick up: Scrapbooking as a form and forum of cultural citizenship', *European Journal of Cultural Studies*, 9. 3 (2006); p. 364.

314 The uncertain register of videoblogs was a constant source of debate within the videoblogging community during its early phase. Whether the videoblog was a documentary, reportage, short-film, artwork or as Richard BF put it, a genre in itself, was never really decided upon until YouTube created its own notion of a 'YouTube video' which is now a commonplace form. However, at the time this was far from settled.

315 Instead, one can perhaps talk of YouTube communities, dispersed groups centered around interests or subject areas, in contrast to the videoblogging community which was centered around videoblogging itself.

the videoblogging identity was an important aspect of their self-definition and constitutive of their practice and community, something that perhaps Youtubers don't share even today.

Videoblogging is both a private practice, carried out, mostly from within the confines of the home, and at the same time a public practice, both in terms of the availability of the videoblog to the internet as a whole and as a practice existing within a public community of users. Here we might consider the way in which videoblogging was creating practices around what we might call intimate technologies, long before the arrival of smartphones that capture life through phone cameras. It is also interesting to think about the way in which they also functioned as 'domesticated' technologies, in the sense of Roger Silverstone, which is that they are brought into the home and make an important contribution to the everyday life of the users of technology. But also in contrast to Silverstone's conceptualisation, they are able to reverse the valence – not only bringing the outside world into the home, but also taking the inside of the home outside into the world. Although the sharable nature of videoblogging and sharing practices often took place within a self-referential community of interest, rather than shared as a public or wider community public practice, the majority of my informants emphasized the way in which videoblogging was a personal, quotidian practice, a way to narrativise their lives and archive experiences for the future.[316] There were of course other, different discussions going on in the community at the time, about copyright, remix culture and the relationship between amateur and professionally produced content. In the videos themselves, however, the representation of the everyday and the much-celebrated intimacy between videobloggers helped forge deep emotional bonds and friendships reinforced by the intimate form of the videoblog. Some videobloggers even formed strong real-world relationships and at least one couple who met through videoblogging actually married.

From the very beginning, the videoblogging community showed clear resistance against creating a unified definition of what videoblogging was or should be. I think it is helpful to think about videoblogging starting as an *empty signifier* which helped enroll video and film makers into a shared set of practices and which slowly began to coalesce around practices, technologies and aesthetics. There were no unambiguous *types* emerging at the end of my interviews, so instead it was more fruitful to focus on *how* they described their practices, as well as examining the videos themselves.

From a total of thirty-three informants, fourteen described their practice as 'art' (Sam Reinsew, Mica Scalin, David Howell, Adam Quirk, Brittany Shoot, Andreas Haugstrup Pedersen, Daniel Liss, Jay Dedman, Jen Proctor, Markus Sandy, Loiez Deniel, Charlene Rule, Paris Marashi, Bekah Havens) or artistic (Charlene Rule) videos (see figure 17). Brittany Shoot called it 'arty junk'. Paris Marashi told me 'I consider my vlog a studio space or workshop, I use the blog mechanism to help me apply some order to the ideas that come tumbling from my head'. Daniel Liss called his practice 'experimental personal film(?)making' [original formatting] and Jennifer Proctor told me she makes 'short experimental nonfiction videos… about everyday life that attempt to shift the ordinary into something novel or to make the

---

316 Roger Silverstone, *Media and Morality: On the Rise of the Mediapolis,* Cambridge: Polity Press, 2006, p. 91.

unnoticed bigger or more profound'. Rule said her work was 'generally more artistic and it contains pieces that are from my daily life and pieces of little art ideas or sketches'. Mica Scalin, Jen Gouvea and Gromik Nicholas identified as making documentaries. Erik Nelson and Enric Teller both called their videoblogs 'short films for the internet' whereas Cheryl Colan preferred 'short personal documentaries'.

Self-defined type	Videoblogger
Personal	Zadi Diaz, Steve Garfield, Raymond M. Kristiansen, Brittany Shoot, Bekah Havens, Cheryl Cole, Gena Hackett, Juan Falla, Richard Hall, Susan Pitman, Ryanne Hodson, Rupert Howe, Richard BF, Mary Matthews, Adam Quirk
Art	Sam Reinsew, Mica Scalin, David Howell, Adam Quirk, Brittany Shoot, Andreas Haugstrup Pedersen, Daniel Liss, Jay Dedman, Jennifer Proctor, Markus Sandy, Loiez Deniel, Charlene Rule, Paris Marashi, Bekah Havens
Everyday life	Andreas Haugstrup Pedersen, Erin Nealey, Jay Dedman, Jen Gouvea, Juan Falla, Mary Matthews, Richard BF, Charlene Rule, Gena Hackett, Paris Marashi
Documentary	Mica Scalin, Jen Gouvea, Gromik Nicholas
Internet TV	Erik Nelson, Enric Teller, Juan Falla
Comedy	Adam Quirk, Casey McKinnon

Figure 17: Videobloggers' self-definitions

Among the videobloggers, ten told me their videoblogs were about their 'daily' or 'everyday life', Marashi told me her videos were 'everyday moments that make up your life, that can give a western audience some perspective into Iranian life'. Haugstup Pedersen told me his videoblogs were 'video snapshots on my daily life'. Interestingly, the term most commonly used by the informants to describe their videoblogs, was 'personal'. Sixteen videobloggers said their videos fell into this category, meaning, as Bekah Havens told me, they 'fit under the giant umbrella of personal videoblogging'. Havens further added that she saw 'each video… like a little arts & crafts project that I get attached to, because they are usually personal in terms of subject matter'.

To illustrate what was meant by 'personal', Susan Pittman added her videoblog acted as a 'diary' or as Mary Matthews put it, as 'intimate, personal experiences of my life, my work, my relationships, my spirit, all captured in moments'. Erin Nealey likened the practice of videoblogging to 'home videos' with the added element of being 'edited and a little more polished and hopefully more pleasant to watch. These are moments from our family life and I like to think of them as a video scrapbook of our memories and times together.' As seems clear, there was quite a lot of overlap between these categories, with fewer defining themselves within just one type. Further, it seems that many of these descriptions, although consistent, could easily be grouped together – where describing a videoblog as 'personal' might just be another way of saying that their videoblogs were stories from their 'everyday life'. Equally, terms such as 'home movies' and 'scrapbooking' have been shown by others to be terms used quite frequently when describing social and personal activities online. As Hof explains, 'scrapbooking exemplifies how an everyday cultural practice can magnetize and mobilize people through a community of practice'.[317] Indeed, the majority of the videobloggers fell within the category of producing 'personal' videoblogs, in other words, *not* producing content for wider public circulation as such, 'artistic' and 'everyday life' were the second largest groups.[318]

Even those, like Jennifer Proctor, who initially told me their videos were not 'personal,' and that their videos 'don't often feature people at all' and instead featured 'objects or shapes or landscapes or movement', admitted that even these videos were on some level personal to them. 'Sure, almost all of them, on some level,' she elaborated. 'It's all an on-going process of watching, incorporating, chewing up, spitting back out'. Haugstrup Pedersen further problematized the category of personal media by stating that his videos 'are personal because they are all me (created by me, dealing with my life) but they are not personal because they don't deal with personal matters'.

Nonetheless, many of the videobloggers defined their practice as falling into the category of a kind of personal media: 'these are windows into my life,' Kristiansen told me 'small windows into a mood I might be in, or it may be the result of me playing around with the computer'. Kristiansen explained that he usually was the protagonist of his videosblogs. Adam Quirk told me the '12" nude plastic doll' that features in his videoblogs, was in fact 'my thinly veiled doppelganger'. A few users expanded on this idea of themselves as protagonists in their own videoblogs, for instance, Cheryl Colan told me that she saw herself as the protagonist of her videos. 'Why me? Well, because I'm making videos about my life, so I'm the natural choice. If I switch to someone else, it would be because I want to highlight them or am making a tribute to them. Or because I want to try to see/show the world through someone else's eyes.' Similarly, Juan Falla told me he and his wife were the protagonists of their show, *Viviendo con Falla* (Living with the Fallas), 'Everything we show is based on our point of view,' he told me. 'Although, I have to say that we don't touch political or religious themes. Our videos are of 'normal moments of life'. And we are the protagonist because we want to show our families (and friends) the things we do here in Los Angeles.'

Richard BF conceptualised videoblogging as a genre in itself, and attempted to outline this for me, arguing that he considered 'videoblogging a genre, so I guess they fit themself. I would describe what I do as "I carry my video camera with me wherever I go, and if I see something interesting, I'll shoot it and put it on the web. It's like what people do with a camera phone, but I also talk into the camera. It's like a video diary, but the whole world can see it".' Other videobloggers were less interested in any kind of definition, as Markus Sandy wrote, 'I don't have an interest in defining videoblogging. I don't want to define it. It's like writing'. Indeed, Erik Nelson explained he 'intentionally attempts to avoid getting pinned into something that is

---

317 Karina Hof, 'Something you can actually pick up: Scrapbooking as a form and forum of cultural citizenship', p. 364.
318 One notable counter-example was Casey McKinnon, who told me she produces a 'sci-fi comedy show' aimed at earning her and her partner a living.

easily describable' and Kristiansen told me he tried to 'avoid the boxes, putting my work into this or that narrative tradition'. This resistance to being 'put in a box' was further elaborated by Markus Sandy, who told me that 'the quest to define videoblogging has been going on since it started and it's the videos themselves that define it, not people, not critics, academics or anyone else. Just the videos. And even then, people still want to describe it, box it, corner it and catch some of it, maybe. I don't know. Is this how it was for the early days of television? I think we are still discovering what television can do and be.' Sometimes they would describe their narrative practices in ways that could be said to *automate* their identities. This raised questions of how their life stories are archived, edited, and reassembled in forms 'influenced and constrained by the architecture of the system, by users who may in the end narrate or refuse the tale'.[319] Videoblogging as a media form constantly engaged with archival practices – it should be noted that informants were extremely cognizant of the problems of digital storage and backup and the dangers of losing their archival material.

We might consider why people take photographs. They do so for a number of reasons, including 'to construct personal and group memory; in order to create and maintain social relationships; and for the purposes of self-expression and self-presentation'.[320] Indeed, the idea of 'self-expression' and 'self-presentation' is reflected in videoblogging practice and demonstrated by Cheryl Colan, who explained her motivations for videoblogging. 'Videoblogs,' she told me, 'are a means of productive self-reflection. A way for me to live an examined life and have something to show for it. And a way to re-story my life… It's a valuable record too.' Here, then, Colan actively uses her videoblog to 'live an examined life', to reflect on her actions and learn something from her experiences. This notion is deeply philosophical in construction and is reminiscent of Socrates, who thought 'the unexamined life is not worth living'.[321] Colan also gestured towards memory as a technical effect of media, arguing that her videoblog gives her 'something to show for it'; a 'valuable record' of her lived experiences.

It has been argued that one of the motivating forces behind amateur photography has been the desire to create a record of one's own life. Drawing on Bourdieu, Gye argues that 'the *desire* to photograph is not a given—it is socially constructed and culturally specific' and that 'the rise in its popularity can be directly attributable to the emergence of a correlation in the public imagination between photographic practice and private memorialization'.[322] Bourdieu, too, argued that as 'a private technique, photography manufactures private images of private life… Apart from a tiny minority of aesthetes, photographers see the recording of family life as the primary function of photography'.[323] This is echoed from the videobloggers such as Erin Nealey who said that her videoblog explores 'moments from our family life and I like to think

319 Bassett, *The Arc and the Machine*, p.110.

320 Lisa Gye, 'Picture This: the Impact of Mobile Camera Phones on Personal Photographic Practices', *Continuum: Journal of Media & Cultural Studies*, 21.2 (2007): pp. 280.

321 Plato, *Plato in Twelve Volumes*, Vol. 1 (Trans. Harold North Fowler; Introduction by W.R.M. Lamb), Cambridge, MA: Harvard University Press, 1966, 5-6.

322 Gye, 'Picture This: the Impact of Mobile Camera Phones on Personal Photographic Practices', p. 280, itallics in original.

323 Pierre Bourdieu, 'Towards a Sociology of Photography', *Visual Anthropology Review*, 7.1, Spring, ([1965] 1991): pp. 130.

of them as a video scrapbook of our memories and times together. This will be something I'm sure I will cherish in years to come (and hopefully my children will too!)".

Dedman also conceived of videoblogging as a way of archiving life, but he argued that it also provides a sense of narrative connections and meaning to what would otherwise be random and disconnected moments. He told me 'my videos are really just an exploration of moments I live through. You know, most of life could be said to be very mundane, while it could also be said that every moment is full of meaning'. Videoblogging was Dedman's way of noticing moments of meaning, remembering them and sharing them with others. Like many of the artistic videobloggers, Jan McLoughlin, a freelance sound designer with a particular interest in audio (she submitted her interview to me as an audio file rather than as text), used more creative language in her description of what a videoblog is, saying, 'videoblogging is anything I want it to be' and 'it's making something of beauty and sharing it with the world'.

Similarly, Falla said he was creating a 'visual archive of my life', taking a camera with him everywhere 'because I like to keep track of my life on video. I want to be able to 'see' my life how it was, and not only have a memory of the moment'. Colan also described a similar experience. 'I would say that the videos are short, personal documentaries that I use to share my life experiences,' she told me, 'together they make a longer documentary of the journey of my life, from the silly or mundane to more profound experiences'.

Some videobloggers argued that videoblogging was actually a sub-genre of blogging, and utilised quite technical language to describe it. For instance, Richard Hall, a university professor of Information Science and Technology at an American University, gave a rather technical definition. 'It's like a web page,' he said, 'but it's a log where people have a linear list of posts. A video blog is a variation on that where you have a linear list of videos and they are usually associated with some text and a traditional thing with video blogs is that they have syndication so that you can use an RSS reader so you can use RSS with enclosures.' Enric Teller equally defined his practice in quite technical terms. A videoblog, he told me, is basically 'video in a blog format with entries in reverse chronological order that can be syndicated for distribution. The creation and distribution of the videoblog is personally controlled by the videoblogger(s) without approval required from any media gatekeeper.' Control over content, both the production process and the distribution across media platforms, was clearly as important to Teller as the content of the videos or how they were displayed in the blogs, as he explained, 'most people define videoblogging as having control over the production and distribution of their rich media work. Having no gatekeepers for making and distributing vlogs. This is not explicitly defined, but through their actions of talking about the process of making vlogs on their own, where it gets distributed to, how to control and get information on syndication (distribution), concern and action on unauthorized distribution by others.'[324] This definition of videoblogging as 'control over production and distribution' and 'having no gatekeepers' was clearly influenced by strands running through the open-source and free culture movement. Many articles from the same time on sites such as Techcrunch, Digg and Gawker were very influential on

---

324 Enric Teller, Email to Videoblogging list, 7 July 2006, https://groups.yahoo.com/neo/groups/
     videoblogging/conversations/messages/44493.

the videoblogging community, and a lot of discourses written at this time were influenced by the work of Lawrence Lessig, on copyright, code and law, and Tim O'Reilly on Web 2.0.[325]

In contemporary society, we tend to think of user-generated media as being produced 'on-the-go'. New technologies such as smartphones and software platforms such as Snapchat and Instagram make mobile media engagement through video easy and quick. It is important to remember that the practices we now take for granted were once slow, meticulous, negotiated and invented processes that took considerable time to produce. These practices – now at the tip of our fingers – required a different kind of labour and commitment. The technical equipment and necessary bandwidth meant that most videobloggers produced their work at home, using quite crude technologies compared to the software available post-Instagram or post-Snapchat.

We might therefore describe the videoblogging practice as an early instance of *everywhere computing*. The ubiquitousness of mobile computing which today allows us to interact with each other anywhere and any time, via our devices, was quite avant-garde when the video-bloggers were experimenting with mobile devices such as the Nokia N95 (which looked like the Sanyo Xacti, but provided a lower technical standard, made up for by having access to the internet). Yet, there were many videobloggers who still preferred to work from within the home, and whose videos reflect the domestic use of desktop computers and keyboards and mouse video-editing. Silverstone emphasised the important and contradictory nature of the home in relation to media. At once a secure space, the home also acts as a protection against the world outside; 'the home, as the shell around the body [...] and as the walls around the family, articulates this defensiveness even as it offers security. The domestic space is thus forged dialectically, as a contradiction'.[326] With this in mind, and remembering both that Silverstone would have envisaged the media as entering into the home, as opposed to being projected from the home, and Couldry's notion of 'un-thought' practice, the *videoblogger at home* is an interesting way to explore the videoblogger's relationship to the 'domestic', in Silverstone's terms.

Of the 33 videobloggers I interviewed, 17 said they recorded their videos either at home or a variant of the home, 'home office' (Zadi Diaz, Markus Sandy), 'home studio' (David Howell), 'home/ on location' (Enric Teller, Jennifer Proctor) or the more general 'home/out' (Mica Scalin, Raymond M. Kristansen). When it came to editing the videos, the overwhelming majority (all but one) revealed they worked from home. When asked to expand, they told me they edited (and uploaded) their videoblogs at home, usually from the bedroom, or a space characterised as a 'studio' or 'home office'. An example of this was illustrated by Haugstrup Pedersen, a 25 year old student from Denmark, who, when describing to me 'where his main work computer was located in relation to the rest of the room it was in,'[327] gave me the following, detailed

325 O'Reilly, 'What is Web 2.0. Design Patterns and Business Models for the Next Generation of Software'.
326 Caroline Bassett, 'Of distance and closeness: the work of Roger Silverstone', *New Media & Society,* 9.1 (2007): pp. 45.
327 The detailed description asked for in the interview was an attempt to bridge the gap created in the shift from a 'standard' to a virtual ethnography. I didn't want to ask the participants to send me photos of their home, as this may have seemed intrusive, which is why I asked them to describe it instead.

description, 'It's on my work desk. The desk itself is filled with various papers and trinkets. When working I'm staring into the wall, but one of two windows in the room are on the immediate right. Directly behind me is my bed and to the right after the window my bookcase is sitting (I need to buy a new one, this one is overflowing – I even placed a smaller bookcase on top of the actual bookcase). To the left of the desk I have my tv and behind that the kitchen area begins. Behind me and to the left I have a small table with some chairs. Usually the table has either more papers or laundry sitting on it.'

What struck me immediately about his description was how the space he uses for working had invaded (or was invaded by) domesticity, most notably his laundry and his bed. Further questions revealed that 'I do everything from my apartment' and that 'everything is jumbled together on the same desk and the same computer'. The fact that Haugstrup Pedersen (at the time of the interview) was a student and working freelance perhaps explains this feeling of living in one room from where everything necessarily needs to be done, but he was not the only videoblogger describing this to me. Quirk, a self-employed 28 year old from New York, stated that 'my bedroom doubles as my office', and Brittany Shoot, 24, from Boston, explained; 'my desk is in my room, which sort of doubles as my office at home'. Jennifer Proctor, a 33 year old professor of arts, told me she, too, works from 'a converted bedroom'. Amongst those videobloggers who self-identified as 'artistic', the demarcation of a space to videoblog was more prominent than amongst those who self- identified as making 'personal' videoblogs. David stated he works from a 'modified attic space' and Erik Nelson, a 31-year-old American based in the Netherlands, divulged 'I have the entire attic space to myself, along with the washer and dryer.'

The lack of a separate space within the home from where they recorded or edited the videoblog was a very prominent outcome of the interviews. Facilitated by laptops and small, portable equipment, those who didn't indicate that they had a dedicated 'office-space' or 'studio-space' in which they worked, told me that one of their reasons for videoblogging was that it was something they could do 'anywhere'. For instance, Colan said she videoblogged 'in the house, classroom, office, car, restaurant, grocery store, wilderness – everywhere!' Dedman revealed he produces videos 'wherever I am. I have a camera right in my pocket'. He also told me he 'record[s] everywhere.. and then edit on my laptop. Usually at home, but could be anywhere'. Similarly, when asked where his computer was located in the house, Daniel Liss described how 'it roams freely'. Shoot stated that 'sometimes I bring my computer – a laptop – into the living room and do work out there.' She indicated she worked mainly from her bedroom, so explained that 'mostly, especially for editing, which requires external hard drives, I'm in my room'. In other words, it was the technical requirements of an external hard drive, not as mobile as a laptop, which caused Shoot to work mainly in one space.

Female videobloggers described the importance of being 'comfortable' whilst videoblogging. This was illustrated by Pitman, who described how videoblogging, 'forms part of my every day life, because when I get home from work, I recline back in my lazy boy chair, and there's my laptop waiting for me beside the chair.' Similarly, Colan stated that she had 'strategic power

---

However, two of the informants did in fact send me photographs, two others referred me to photos on their Flickr accounts in which their offices were depicted.

strips located around the house - in the dining room and near the comfy LazyBoy chair' which allowed her to 'move to where I'm comfortable'.

Charlene Rule, a 37 year old film editor living in New York, revealed how she usually edits videos on the kitchen table. 'If I'm at the kitchen table, I'm facing a wall with two windows on either side,' she told me. 'Fridge to my right (it's a very tiny kitchen). Stove behind me. The living room is also behind me'. From her own description, Rule was working in a domestic space, surrounded by everyday things, like the fridge and the stove. Rule's video, *Dear Tesla* (1:08, 320x240) illustrates this domestic space mediated through her videoblog. The video shows her sitting in her kitchen eating spaghetti, talking, with her face reflected in her toaster. This mediation of household objects and domestic space is also the theme of some of her other videos, for instance *Quarterplus* (0:51, 320x240), which features her attempts to kill a cockroach that had hidden in a cupboard (figure 18).

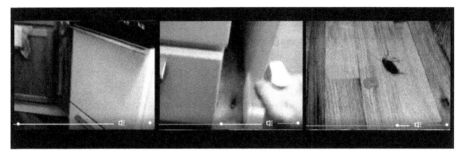

Figure 18: *Quarterplus* (Rule, 2005)

Rule's extensive use of lighting and sound effects contributes to an attempt to defamiliarise her home – much like the space she has created on her videoblog, a space where 'the boundaries are crossed between what is real and what is not...' She elaborated,'I am able to jump into playful ways of looking at my own reality and that is what seems to be a given in terms of the vernacular for the audience'. Nonetheless, even at this moment, as the home becomes uncanny, it remains central to the form and content of the videoblog.

As this example shows, the home has a dual significance to the videoblogger. It is both the space from where she videoblogs, but is also often represented in the videos, for example, Erin Nealey's video *Mornings* (3:05, 320x240), which is a fast-paced video montage of her morning ritual – making coffee and breakfast for her kids – in which short sharp edits are cut together to create a vibrant montage of the everyday rituals of life. In *Mornings*, the video creates 'the intimate space of the home at once the site for mundane transactions and a constituent part of this other vaster space which might have both psychical and mythical dimensions'.[328] Nealey's video is cut to the diegetic sounds of getting ready in the morning, with the coffee grinder providing the acoustic rhythm and cups and spoons providing the beat.

---

328 Bassett, ' Of distance and closeness: the work of Roger Silverstone' p. 45.

Similarly, Hodson told me her videoblog was 'a document of my life. Me, observing the world and translating it. It's like complete freedom.' This sense of freedom is reflected in a number of her videos, 'this is like the reason I vlog. I've showed myself crying, laughing, ranting, thinking, anything. I just want to relate to other people, not feel like I'm alone and crazy'. Howe also reflected on this aspect of videoblogging, telling me how amazed he was when he first found the videoblogging community. The videos were like nothing he had ever seen before, a mix of 'intimate and mundane parts of their lives. Stuff you still didn't see anywhere... Back then it was extraordinary to see someone making a video about taking their child to the park and talking to you about it... For me, the more mundane it was, the more excited I was by the newness of it.'

As one of the most outspoken of the videobloggers, Dedman mused that 'if done well, something is really shared in these moments. The visual artform is just so rich. The fact that videoblogs are archived also allows me to go and watch a person's past creations and life'. The idea of sharing the spaces of their lives, of creating archives and repositories of memory, of narrativising their lives and being able to draw on the videos at a later time, was clearly important to the videobloggers. 'I think most of my videos are simply sharing moments rather than telling a story,' Erin Nealey told me. Jen Gouvea described videoblogging as 'my way of sharing of myself personally and processing my experiences'. 'I would describe my videos as moments,' was how Mary Matthews put it, 'intimate, personal experiences of my life, my work, my relationships, my spirit, all captured in moments'. Paris Marashi, who made videos about Iran and being an Iranian in America, revealed to me that 'sharing' was one of her main goals through videoblogging. 'Initially, it was about cultural expression and sharing' she elaborated. However, as she got deeper into the community, she found that videoblogging spoke to her on a more personal level; 'through this experience of videoblogging,' she said 'I have been learning about how it can facilitate my own personal self-expression. Sharing my cultural identity with others, so that others can identify with it, I began to experiment with emotion and feeling.'

Many videobloggers saw videoblogging as a way of sharing stories and personal experiences, as well as their, perhaps unrealistic, notion that the videos they produced in 2004 would remain as an archive for future generations. Dedman speculated, 'imagine what it'll be like in 50 years when people's lives are all in video in different ways! It'll be gold to our ancestors.' Ironically, writing in 2018, due to technical changes, shuttered web sites and general link breaking, only a handful of Dedman's videos are still available on the internet, and only to those who know where to look. The unstable nature of the technologies that made up the original techno-social foundation of the practice, as well as unexpected things, such as hosting companies changing owners, or changing terms of service etc., caused the videoblogging community to slowly fracture. When videoblogging fell out of favour with hosting sites such as Blip in November 2013, a company ironically started by videobloggers and which used to be intimately linked with the community, a large set of archival videoblogs was mostly deleted.

I now want to turn to briefly think about how time and temporality are manifested in the practices of the videobloggers I interviewed, but also consider how this is demonstrated in their rituals, habits and repetitions. To Silverstone, the 'veritable dailiness' of everyday life, the routinized practices that make up the fabric of the everyday, exists through a sense of order and ritual.[329] Couldry also describes media practices, understood as 'routine activities' as opposed to 'consciously chosen actions'.[330] How we make sense of these quotidian practices, Silverstone argues, is through 'an order manifested in our various traditions, rituals, routines and taken for granted activities – in which we, paradoxically, invest so much energy, effort and so many cognitive and emotional resources.'[331] I want to note how these are mediated through the videoblogs, both consciously and unconsciously. Videoblogging was a practice that required technical expertise and was very time consuming. Thus, I wanted to explore the amount of time, in general, the videoblogger spent videoblogging; was it a daily occurrence, weekly, monthly? Did they videoblog all day, for a couple of hours or five minutes? How long would it take to produce an entry on a videoblog, how often would the videoblogger produce content, what time of day (or night) would she work? Many videobloggers talked about sharing stories and developing visual archives for the future, thus I was interested in the idea of videoblogs as repositories of memory, working archives of lived experiences and how the videobloggers articulated this both discursively and in their work.

Having to *make* time for videoblogging was highlighted by a number of respondents. To illustrate, Gromik Nicholas told me it would take him on average '1 day or more' to record a video, 'a day to edit and up to half a day to upload'. Erik Nelson said he spent 1-2 hours recording, up to 20 hours editing and 30 minutes to an hour uploading a videoblog. Zadi Diaz revealed her videos took her, on average, 1-2 hours to record, 6-8 hours to edit and 2 hours to upload. There were, of course, those who spent '3 minutes' recording, and only '15 minutes' editing (Steve Garfield) or 'a few minutes' shooting (Markus Sandy) but 'anything up to an hour' to edit (Richard BF), but the majority of respondents reported spending at least an hour recording, editing and uploading videos to their videoblogs.

Mary Matthews told me that, 'vlogging is routine… though [it] does fall behind if other work gets busy, but I video blog every day – be it shooting, editing, writing. I look forward to it. I am always thinking about it'. Mica Scalin's answer was an ambiguous 'whenever,' but when asked to elaborate, she revealed that, 'artmaking is a daily process for me. I have always made myself do something every day. I started working with digital video and vlogging simultaneously so it was about making a process that was simple and something that could be incorporated into daily life. When it feels like a chore I take a break. I have taken periodic breaks to work on specific projects.' Mica's answer represented a more general attitude to videoblogging – that it shouldn't be a chore. For Jennifer Proctor, the incorporation of videoblogging into her everyday life was part of her routine, but for others, like Susan Pitman, a mother of two, videoblogging could be a guilty pleasure as well; 'sometimes (guilty) I have to make myself wait until after the kids go to bed, so I can spend some time with them instead of editing videos when we could be playing together'. Erin Nealey, 33 year old mother, expressed a similar mix of guilt and pleasure when she described her perfect night in. 'I absolutely LOVE to edit video that I have captured,' she said. 'There have been times where I've let that overtake my day, but since I have two children I am trying to be careful about that […] there is nothing better than

---

329 Silverstone, *Television and Everyday Life*, p. 3.
330 Couldry, 'Theorising Media as Practice', p. 121.
331 Silverstone, *Television and Everyday Life*, p. 1.

the feeling of the kids sleeping peacefully in their beds, me at my desk with a coffee in hand and working on my latest project.'

Many of the respondents highlighted that one of the main obstacles to videoblogging was that the process took a long time. In general, the editing was by far the most laborious part of the creation of videoblogs, with recording mostly completed in around an hour and uploading generally completed within 15 minutes. With upload times being fairly slow, creating shorter videos, no more than 5 minutes in length and compressed to as small a file as possible made a lot of sense technically. Jennifer Proctor told me she makes videos, 'really randomly. I have no schedule. I usually take 1-6 months recording moments, and then actually sit down and put them together. I really see it like making a photography book.' Similarly, when I pressed on whether taking more time over videos allows for greater reflection, she answered, 'oh yeah.... I got to let things sit. Usually I'll record a moment and know its good. You just know. But I have no idea how to use it. I have to collect these good moments over time...and then let them fall into place. Allowing time to pass between recording moments and publishing moments allows me to understand why I happen to record it at the time. To be clear, there are no answers here. Time just helps me see how 'cool' life can be. That's all recording a moment is. Trying to make the mundane...special.'

Amongst those self-identifying as 'artistic' videobloggers, there was a clear trend towards working at night. 'I reserve the hours 9:00PM-3:00AM for video work, after the kids are put down for the night,' Nelson revealed. Quirk was convinced his 'best work happens between the hours of 9pm and 4am.' Equally, Loiez Deniel, who defines videoblogging as a form of poetry, said he works 'during the night generally.' For some, like Richard BF, working at night wasn't a necessity, i.e. to work around children, work or other commitments, but merely out of choice. '[I work] all over the place,' he told me. 'Sometimes I'll edit straight after shooting, which could be any time of the day or night. I guess generally it's at night, but that's just because I like to work at night, not because I'm busy during the day'. These were also the participants who were most likely to tell me they worked from a 'studio' (Adam Quirk and Jennifer Proctor, see above) – most notably from a converted attic space (David Howell and Erik Nelson, again, see above). This recalls images of the romantic artist and, interestingly, these were the participants whose explanations of their videoblogging practices were also quite ambiguous. By this, I mean that they were more likely to talk about their videos in 'artistic' terms. Interestingly, media theorists Kember and Zylinska argue that in the age of the digital, with the distributed networks of users and potential collaboration across time and space, the creative subject is now collaborative rather than individualistic, yet she is still 'driven by the very same desires, motivations, and fantasies that had shaped the Romantic creative: those of artistic freedom, self-worth, and individual fulfilment'.[332] So a comparison between the answers of Erin Nealey, who mainly videoblogged about her family and children, and David Howell, who self-identified as an artist, is interesting. Nealey usually allocated '10-30 minutes' recording her videos, whereas Howell told me he spent 'as long as is required' to complete the process of capturing video. Additionally, Nealey told me she used 'anywhere from 6-12 hours' to edit a video, whereas Howell would work 'until it is finished'. Lastly, when explaining the length

---

332 Sarah Kember and Joanna Zylinska, *Life After New Media*, Cambridge, MA: MIT Press, 2012, p. 175.

of an individual video, Nealey articulated a clear and rational reasoning for the length of her videos (her videos range from 3 to 5 minutes). 'I just feel like people don't have the attention span to watch anything much longer than that sitting at their computers,' she stated. 'Every now and then, I'll throw a longer video in there that maybe I didn't create specifically for the videoblog. But generally if I'm creating something that is especially for my site, I will try and keep it under 5 mins.' In comparison, although his videos tended to be within the same range, (mostly between 1 and 5 minutes) Howell couldn't (or wouldn't) give me a reason, 'no rhyme or reason to the length. I am currently trying to make them shorter than 1 minute and tell a longer more complex story. It doesn't always work out that way though. My videos generally dictate to me how long they wish to be'. He did add, however, that the pleasure he experienced in relation to videoblogging was linked to spending hours alone creating something, a bit like a craftsman at work; 'I fit it in when I have time to sit locked away for an extended time. I very much look forward to making them and wish I could do it all the time'.

This difference in terms of gender and the time and space available are reflective of external pressures such as family or domestic labour, so for Nealey, consideration for kids, family and the everyday demands of being a mother came first. Nealey's notions of videoblogging were shaped by these external (or rather, domestic) demands on her time. She knew exactly how long she had to videoblog, and exactly when she could take the time to do so.

A few of the 'everyday life videobloggers' have had periods of reduced videoblogging and even complete withdrawal from the 'vlogosphere'. Raymond M. Kristiansen, who whilst the interview was taking place was on a self-imposed hiatus from videoblogging, showed signs of burn-out when he talked to me; 'in the beginning of "my videoblogging career" I structured my days around producing videos, watching videos, interacting with other videobloggers. I would wake up, and watch videos before eating breakfast. I might make a movie after breakfast. I might spend an evening after work talking with other videobloggers on AIM or Skype. Especially between October 05 and June 06 I spent a LOT of time… videoblogging'. Others showed a pragmatic approach to videoblogging. Jennifer Proctor maintained her own personal site where she posted 'short experimental non-fiction videos'. She worked full time as a professor at a university in America and tried to 'fit my videos in when I can.' Her attitude, similar to Mica Scalin's, is that videoblogging is an organic process and that she usually does it 'when the video calls for it, rather than forcing myself to do a video… But I do put some pressure on myself to keep producing. If it's been a while since I've posted anything, then I more actively seek stuff to shoot, or find stuff to edit, or try to come up with something interesting to post. It's something that's always on my mind, in the back of my head, but I really just fit the process in where I can, like another piece of my weekly life puzzle.'

In relation to whether she had to *make* time for videoblogging, she stated categorically 'I would say no – it's simply on-going, like another part of life. It's just another thing I do during the week, like going for a walk or making a nice dinner'. Proctor was drawn to the contingency of videoblogging, and described how it allowed her to react to events in her life in a more spontaneous way. As a professor of film studies, videoblogging presented an alternative approach to creating moving images that she found 'liberating'. She told me 'I think part of the great power in videoblogging is related to its spontaneity, to its now-ness, and to its capturing of those beautiful, fleeting life moments that we all experience but rarely have an opportunity to document. So for me, those random events are often the more uncanny or moving or interesting, the being-there-at-the-right-time kind of moments, that don't as often occur when you capture life in more of a planned or scripted way.'

Videobloggers have a number of different motivations for videoblogging, from Richard BF's 'there's something exciting about the immediacy and global audience that makes it fairly unique as a hobby', to the self-fulfilment Juan Falla felt from being a content producer with an audience; 'it's great to be with the camera shooting stuff. I feel like a movie director doing short films'. Kristiansen told me, 'I felt as if my head was about to explode every few hours, when I realized just how much [videoblogging] could change everything... To me, videoblogging... was the missing link. It was what would allow people from regions like sub-Saharan Africa to communicate with the world... Videoblogging, if done with a low-key approach to it, could really change how we communicate.'

Hall, a university professor of information science and technology and 'early adopter' of videoblogging, told me he preferred videoblogging to his 'real' work. With some irony (he is an academic) he told me that '... many more people have watched my most popular videos, than have read my most prestigious journal publication'. Hall described videoblogging 'like meditation – I'm in a different world [...] several hours goes by and it feels like I just started and my concentration is such that little sounds and stuff really bug me if they get my attention ... very much a feeling of "flow"'. It also became clear that the practice of videoblogging was conceptualised and experienced by the videobloggers as inherently *social*. For some, it also became a way of meeting people, like Quirk, who told me that 'when I found videoblogging I realized that I could have conversations with these other people online and experience some kind of socializing without having to resort to going to bars and meeting strangers face to face.'

So, videoblogging is an everyday media practice, defined in many ways by where and when the videoblogger was able to produce her work. In this chapter I have explored some of the social dimensions related to videoblogging and how it created a means for the videoblogger to mediate her life, whilst creating a personal archive of lived experiences. For the majority of the videobloggers interviewed for this project, videoblogging engendered an intense personal relation with mediated time and space, one in which social relations were explored and engaged with, where ideas were exchanged and life experiences were shared. Videoblogging practice, mediated through the channels of communication available to and utilized by the videobloggers, shaped the contours of a community of users forming what I have been calling an invested network. By invested network I point toward the notion of a self-referential community of interest around a shared object of focus, in this case the videoblog and related technologies, email lists and video artifacts. I now turn to the final chapter in the book to bring many of these strands together.

7. THE ENDS OF VIDEOBLOGGING

> That's what's cool about video on a blog. Francis Ford Coppola, his quote that one day
> the next Hollywood masterpiece would be made by a 10 year old girl with her dad's
> video camera, right? I think we all know [laughs] that she's a videoblogger.[333]

Understanding the close entanglement of culture and technology in the area of digital media
production in the early 2000s – most notably in the self-definition and development of a
community based around video objects and technologies – has been crucial in the development of this book. Through an ethnographically-informed approach to cultural history, which
maintains an interest in materials as well as discourses, the book has explored the practices
and technologies of videoblogging, a new form of cultural-technical hybrid that emerged in
our increasingly digital age. The book traced the discourses and technological infrastructures
that were developed simultaneously within and around the community of videobloggers that
created the important pre-conditions for the video artifacts they produced and their associated practices.

This research has focussed on the ends of the videoblog as described, practiced and lived by
the videoblogger cohort who made up my sample. Whilst individual interviewees may have
personal ends and goals for their own videoblog, there are also the collective ends of the videoblog community, which should not be ignored. The ends have included notions of sharing,
of collectivity, and of a lived community mediated through a new, innovative and mediated
internet experience. Sharing their ideas freely, their thoughts, their practices, experiences
and hence their culture, they created something extraordinary for too short a period of time.
But we are in danger of forgetting these achievements altogether, in a situation whereby their
archives are incomplete if not absent.

The fragility of digital artifacts, and the status of the videoblog as a historically located object,
has had a number of implications for this book, both methodological and epistemological. It
became apparent, particularly as the book evolved from a contemporary critique to an historical project, that as digital material objects, videoblogs are subject to the same conditions
of temporality as other non-digital objects – over time, if not archived, catalogued and cared
for, they can become difficult to locate and impossible to play-back and watch. As explored
above, the identity of the videoblogger was closely tied to a videoblogging platform, fuelled
by a desire to capture the personal and create visual archives of their everyday life. However,
as there is currently no central functioning archive of early videoblogs, the videoblogger
memory is in some sense under threat, especially its memories and archives as a community. Methodologically, this meant that creating a representative corpus was difficult for me,
and in many instances I have had to rely on the kindness of the videobloggers to share their
personal copies with me. Changing technical standards have also meant that even where
video files could be located, they would not necessarily play. All digital media systems might
be archival in nature, but although they act as organisers of different kinds of data, be it per-

---

333 Verdi, *Vlog Anarchy*, transcript.

sonal, scientific, social or cultural, the kinds of data that help us constitute the self through time and space, no digital system – however well-designed – is guaranteed to last forever. As Parikka argues, the archive might be a central concept for digital culture, but what are the consequences when the archive is missing or broken, as it so often is.[334] In terms of this book it is critical that greater efforts are made to store the videobloggers' 'archiving of the self' through an institutional repository for online video culture. All digital media systems may be archiving systems or memory banks, but although they store information for a time, they don't necessarily do it well or reliably. We might add to that that the *collectivity* of the videoblogging comments should also be persevered by archiving and without media storage they are lost to history. The archiving of digital video does present particular challenges in terms of technical storage but also copyright issues, distribution and access.

The emergence of the videoblog as a short-form digital film is strongly tied to the technical constraints under which it was developed. It is also linked to a set of perceived socio-technical assumptions about how much data could successfully be uploaded to the internet, how fast the video would download from the internet, how much content a perceived possible audience would want to watch and so on. It also develops, in its early stages, as a strong sense of the need to adhere to a kind of videoblogging standard; a set of practices that, within the video-blogging community, were defined as *videoblogging*. As such, the videos I explored tended to follow certain stylistic and technical norms, developed within a core community of users, and subsequently adopted by the wider community. The media-form aesthetic sustained itself, with the community acting as both guide and regulator of its standards, informing users if they were 'doing it wrong' but also acting as a technical and social support system, through which expertise was shared, experiences publically debated, and feedback given. The community also sustained its radical edge through constant debate and contestation, which meant that, despite its concern with a 'videoblogging vernacular', it never quite settled for a fixed definition of what videoblogging was, and thus remained open to ideas and new possibilities. This openness, what I also refer to as its contingency, would ultimately lead to the gradual decline in the community activities, as the members moved on to newer networks, new technologies and different platforms.

The early communities of practice and related cultural forms that crystallised around digital video on the internet between 2004-2009, moved from a nascent and developing techni-cal-cultural assemblage to a videoblogging platform. This emerged as a specific instance of the short-form digital film around which a community of users emerged who through contestation and debate were able to sustain a shared conceptualisation of video-work. The videoblog-gers' sophisticated understanding of their own practice, combined with the awareness of wider cultural norms and aesthetic influences and specific technical expertise, created the conditions of possibility for videoblogging as practice. Although the central work of this book has been to present a cultural history and ethnographic analysis of the early developments of 'online' video, and to begin to trace the history of videoblogging before YouTube and the rise of social media, a key argument of this book is that early internet video cultures are a forgotten but important aspect of the rise of video online. As such, the book examines the

---

334 Parikka, *What is Media Archaeology?* p. 160.

interaction between the technical conditions of possibility and the everyday practices undertaken by videobloggers, understanding the emerging videoblogging platform through both Langlois et al's platform-based research and through Couldry's theory of media as practice. This framework contributed to my analysis of the videobloggers practice, together with the aim of exploring what can be called a videoblogging aesthetic – which I also call the short-form digital film. This is a cultural form that, as I have shown throughout the book, is 'sharable' in Silverstone's terms, but also is 'shared', or has the potential to be so. It points towards a public culture that increasingly uses video as part of its aesthetic repertoire, whilst also – and also increasingly – integrating it, so this history helps inform the vernacular of a digital everyday life. We might think about this change in the status of video (and film), as it moves away from its complex, difficult and technical beginnings towards a more 'democratic' everyday medium. This reflects a videofication of culture – particularly in relation to the way in which personal memory is increasingly held in video form, especially short-form versions between 6 seconds and 3 minutes. We are living in an increasingly videoed and video-centric age.

Throughout the book, I have argued for the importance of an historically informed approach to studying digital culture. Following the nascent writings on media archaeology, the book subscribes to the view that 'dead-ends' and 'failed' media forms are perhaps more useful and revealing about the shape of our contemporary media landscape than the more obvious historical narratives often assigned to events retrospectively. The materialist influence on this book is informed by the field of media archaeology, which itself draws on the writings of the German Media School, and provides a key part of the theoretical foundation to the original ethnographic research I have undertaken, and has allowed me to frame the critical engagement I have made with the material technologies and practices of videoblogging.

Despite being involved in what became a 'failed' project, the videoblogging community developed and in some cases remediated some of the key aesthetic and technical practices that were taken up by subsequent online video users. For example, the visual effect created by using the tip of your finger in the now extinct video application Vine, for instance, is remarkably similar to the editing styles used by many early videobloggers. Although some videoblogs may appear to confirm claims that videoblogging merely reproduced televisual aesthetics, in contrast, by combining an historical contextualisation with an analysis of the videobloggers' self-definitions of their practice with a close visual analysis of their videos, I argue that videoblogging draws on a much wider range of influences, and which contributed to a new and distinctive form of video creativity. In relation to this, it has been instructive that the informants in this study constantly demonstrated their reflexivity in relation to their videoblogging practices and in the multiple forms in which it was deployed.

Videoblogs are an invested network, and their cultural value is best appreciated within the context of the videoblog and a videoblogging community. Therefore it is time for the establishment of a videoblogging archive aimed at cataloguing and preserving these disorganised and dispersed objects - and it is crucial that they are archived, with appropriate means for preservation and possible future playback. I argue that it is important to build and maintain this archive with consultation with the former members of the videoblogging community, in order to acknowledge what has been established here; that the videos are far more than simply video files. They are crystallisations of the embodied practices, technical and aesthetic experimentations and personal narratives of a closely knit community of interest.

It is ironic to note that, despite their investment in community, and the fact it was sustained in part by demands of investing in/sharing technological expertise, the videoblogging community was constantly looking for ways to make the practice of videoblogging more widespread, accessible and 'easier' in terms of technical expertise, seen for example in the excitement and passion within the community at the emergence of Web 2.0. This promised many solutions to technical issues that the videoblogging community struggled with in its early days. The ease of use, the seamless integration of video publishing and consumption, as well as the potentials for hosting and distribution, really resonated with the members of the community – despite their antagonistic attitude towards YouTube.

In the end, the very technologies that were meant to assist and improve the practice of videoblogging, and I would argue in many ways fulfilled that, also signalled the end of the early-adopter community and the beginning of a 'new generation' of online video. By removing the technical obstacles that had fostered such intense communication and discussions on the list, the community saw itself grow larger in actual numbers, but arguably smaller in terms of personal communication and sharing. Many users who had been very active in the beginning, faded away, or moved to new social networks and video services. A sense remained, however, that these new services lacked something that the original videoblogging community had provided, 'I have tried Vine a little bit,' Dedman told me in 2013 'its cool. I love how simple videoblogging has gotten.' With the ease of at first YouTube, and later, video applications such as Vine, Snapchat and Instagram, which allows professional looking video-editing at the tip of your fingers, the need for a specialised community space in which to discuss the technical, social and aesthetic intricacies of laboured and time-consuming video-production, was made less compelling for videobloggers and other interested parties. In other words, technical communities were very much a reflection, not just of shared values and practices, but also of a shared sense of esprit de corps towards a difficult and challenging environment.

The videoblogging community was formed not just with a concern for making these short-form digital films, although these remained important, but also the technical *a priori* and the complexities and contestations that crystallised around it, where they were able to develop and strengthen the community and its self-identity. The cultural-technical hybrid that I am gesturing towards here is unique in that it demanded its members to be both culturally *and* technically proficient as well as keen to control and manage both its cultural production *and* the means of production themselves. However, this remained a fragile network based around a generally non-commercial sharing orientation drawn from open-source software and principles from open culture, and thus remained susceptible to co-option by corporate capital and funded alternatives like YouTube.

The videobloggers' early digital works have been presented here as original case studies of material digital culture on the internet. Traces of the practices, technologies and aesthetics of videoblogging have since been drawn on and amplified in network culture, mainstream media, and contemporary media and cultural production. I argue that the discourses and technological infrastructures that were developed both within and around the community of videobloggers created important pre-conditions for the video artifacts they produced. Early online video did not start with the launch of YouTube, but rather the practices and technologies were already being debated, experimented with and utilised since the early 2000s. In 2004, videoblogging as it is conceptualised here, started to take shape. The constellation of technologies that were made available around this time, the stability of QuickTime in this period played a part here, as did the rise of open-source software, the web platform, Blogger (which was bought by Google in 2003). Blip.tv and OurMedia were also important, and the Sanyo Xacti digital camera, which was launched in 2005, was widely loved for its functionality and aesthetic. We might also link the openness of media to its reusability, particularly in terms of a lack of strong proprietary platform control.[335]

This book has sought to fill a gap in previous studies of online video that generally haven't engaged with videoblogs and their materiality. This book is thus somewhat distanced from previous, screenic studies of videoblogging, which also tended to avoid issues of materiality. My concern has been with an approach to videoblogging which analyses it through not only the screen image but also through the embodied practices of the videobloggers, and its medium-specific cultural-technical practices. Treating the videoblogs as material digital objects meant analysing their content but also their technical a priori. In this respect it is interesting that the videoblogging platform, or the technical systems enabling videoblogging as practice experienced a period of relative calm in the years between 2004 and 2009, which is when the community was at its most active. The calm came about partly because during this period Apple slowed releases of QuickTime while concentrating on moving between microprocessor platforms. At this time other components of the videoblogging platform also fell into place, and for a while a constellation of compatible technologies co-existed in digital harmony, allowing the media form to develop. Some technical stability may in fact have been a key condition of possibility in the emergence of the videoblogging community, allowing it to focus on developing practices and processes, and to negotiate technical complexity, rather than expending its energy constantly learning about and updating video codecs. Technical effects of the media, such as the one outlined above, intervene in interesting ways as a cultural formation develops. Silverstone's notion of the 'double articulation' of media, which argues that 'through its double articulation, the medium does become the message, though that message is not pre-given by the technology. It is worked and reworked within the social circumstances under which it is both produced and received' is very apt for describing this process.[336]

Throughout this book I have attempted to remain reflexive of the videoblog as an historically located cultural practice. In relation to questions of materiality, here I would like to return to the issue of the importance of archives and the lack of institutional repositories in relation to some aspects of popular culture in digital contexts. Indeed, it is impossible to quantify just how much digital culture has already been lost. For example, Geocities was very nearly destroyed as an archive, and the British Library only started archiving the UK portion of the

335 Parikka, What is Media Archaeology? p. 149.
336 Silverstone, Television and Everyday Life, p. 83.

internet in 2013. As a comparison, the Norwegian *Nasjonalbiblioteket* started archiving the Norwegian web as early as 2006.

In this book, I have presented a cartography of the cultural/technical structures, created and maintained by the videoblogging community and I like to think we can see the outlines of the trajectories of future media and cultural production. Indeed, this is demonstrated by the kinds of networked cultural-technical hybrids I have highlighted. In this work I have been keen to draw attention to the tendency within digital and new media cultures to *forget*. The desire to embrace new technologies, as seen with the increasing focus on YouTube developing in conjunction with tools and technologies that allow for the adoption of videoblog-like practices, sometimes means that earlier iterations are side-lined or dismissed as irrelevant or out-dated. I argue that in order to maintain critical understandings of the media practices and theories we observe around us today, it is essential to remember the media practices of the past, especially those that – even only 10 years after – may on the surface seem out-dated, or even irrelevant. I agree with Parikka who argues that researchers need to 'look at media… in terms of their long-term relations that radically steps out of the short-term use value that is promoted in capitalist media industries'.[337]

Public discourse around the new media landscape is arguably not so utopian today as in the 2000s (although Morozov shows that this utopianism is still operative in some sense in the technical industries of Silicon Valley).[338] YouTube is big business now, with a class of YouTube 'stars' making a living off either highly polished brands or the reviews/commentary of games and gameplay such as Twitch.tv. Although YouTube takes a large cut, content creators are perhaps not making as much money as the media has reported.[339] Today, it is rare to watch a video on YouTube without first having to sit through (or skip) an ad, and a large proportion of content consumed online is now corporate content, television programmes, music videos or news. The millennials may be watching more digital video than TV, but the question should be not just what are they watching, but also how are they creating and changing this new video age? One of the interesting aspects of writing about early internet culture today, is to look back on the discourses of optimism and excitement that prevailed in the early days of the videoblogging community, with a perhaps more nuanced and critical take on how events transpired. The early videoblogging community was excited about video, about community and about the possibility of making media, sharing it with the world and being part of the 'new media' landscape. This excitement was reflected in the debates on the list, which could be heated and antagonistic, but also caring and supportive. Jen Simmons, an early videoblogger, summarised videoblogging; 'One of the things that… felt so fresh and weird and new 10 years ago is that, you know, I would watch that video, it's, whatever, 5 minutes. I spent 5 minutes of my life watching something that didn't matter… That was not a hit NBC television show in a primetime slot on Thursday night. It was not designed to get 40 million people to watch it. It was, like, you were going to show it to your 4 friends. Today, in 2014, it's like, 'So

---

337 Parikka, *What is Media Archaeology?*, p. 147.
338 Morozov, 'The Meme Hustler'.
339 J. Edwards, 'Yes, You Can Make Six Figures As A YouTube Star... And Still End Up Poor', 2014, http://www.businessinsider.com/how- much-money-youtube-stars-actually-make-2014-2.

what? Duh.' But back then, that felt so radical and weird... It did mean something. It was a kind of conversation on a small level that was intimate, that mattered.'[340] Instead of being a one-way communication from creator to consumer, videoblogging was arguably about creating conversations among members of a community.[341] This gestures towards something new and interesting about digital culture.[342]

Companies such as Google and Facebook are hoovering up content, scraping data and storing infinite amount of information about all of us on their servers. As the events surrounding Edward Snowden have made painfully clear, even our own governments are monitoring and collecting data on an unprecedented scale. This, it goes without saying, includes video and audio – which has created a new terrain for thinking about the growth of vernacular video and its growing penetration of everyday life, facilitated by the distribution through social media platforms like Facebook and Twitter. I leave the implications of this new and dangerous potential for monitoring and surveillance to others as it lies outside the scope of my book. Nonetheless, I think I have demonstrated the importance of understanding new forms of digital video practices in both private and public contexts. It also points toward new ways of reading and writing culture, and the dissemination of ideas and arguments in *public* through new forms of digital media.[343]

The complexity of studying new cultural practices entangled with new media technologies requires a new constellation of methods and approaches. This book has redoubled my feeling that it is crucial that at important junctures in digital culture we take the time to study even the most ephemeral of cultural practices, and also to seek to archive them in a responsible way that enables future historians and cultural theorists to use them. There is little doubt that as media merge in new forms through the pressure of digitalisation and the growth in the power and versatility of digital technology, rethinking method will be an on-going process. As Burgess and Green argue, rather than explaining amateur video as 'video about nothing' or celebrity without talent, it might be more helpful to situate the practice in the much longer history of 'vernacular creativity – the wide range of everyday practices (from scrapbooking to family photography to the storytelling that forms part of a casual chat) practiced outside the cultural value system of either high culture or commercial creative practice'.[344] The practices associated with videoblogging, serve as an important example of how amateur and semi-professional video artists were working, creating and distributing video across the internet in the mid-2000s. Unfortunately, most of these videoblogging archives are currently residing 'offline' on individual hard drives and in a variety of unstable video hosting sites. They hold narratives and memories of friends, family, lived experiences, and of a community that

---

340 The Web Ahead, 'Videoblogging with Jay Dedman, Ryanne Hodson and Michael Verdi.'

341 Hodson and Verdi, *Secrets of Videoblogging*, p. 189.

342 See for instance Christian Fuchs, 'Against Henry Jenkins. Remarks on Henry Jenkins' ICA Talk "Spreadable Media"' 30 May 2011, http://fuchs.uti.at/570/.

343 The issue of public culture and the way in which videoblogging and practices of video reading and writing can contribute to it lie beyond the scope of this book, but remain suggestive of new means for politics to reconnect with younger citizens who increasingly connect to public life through *video* in the first instance through platforms like YouTube, Facebook, Vine and Vimeo.

344 Burgess and Green, *YouTube*, p. 25.

helped introduce a large number of people to posting video on the internet. As such, it is strange that videoblogging has remained little explored in relation to internet history. But as a cultural form, some aspects of videoblogging lives on, in some sense remediated through a constellation of new technologies and adapted practices, from YouTube to Instagram, Snapchat and Facebook, perhaps as a form of reconstituted dead or zombie media.[345]

Videoblogging is a cultural practice that, although somewhat changed in relation to the form that was prevalent in 2004-2007, is now expanding, as mobile phones and other technical devices incorporate new video cameras, software and technologies that enable the sharing and storing of moving image materials. Many of the commonplace practices we see on YouTube, Instagram, Snapchat and other video sites were first developed for a digital environment by the early community of videobloggers. As such, the rich cultural history of videoblogging explored here has tried to do justice to the contradictions and complexities of a living, evolving and above all creative community of technologists, artists, video-makers and designers in light of these later developments.

I believe the videoblogging community raises important questions about the trajectories and failures of what was once called 'new media'. The videoblog has silently contributed toward the growing penetration of digital video as a vernacular medium, but also a medium that increasingly documents the present in a form that captures a 'rough draft of history'. This is a partial history to be sure, but one that is mediated by new techniques of storing the moving image, and new and remediated narrative structures and aesthetics. In many ways videoblogs are an answer to the call for a democratized form of vernacular media but crucially they also suture the film of yesterday with the film of tomorrow. This is a reticular medium that can be sharable and shared, private and public, individual and collective. In some senses, then, videoblogging is not so much the film of tomorrow, envisaged by Francois Truffaut in 1957, but rather the film of today.

---

345 Hertz and Parikka, 'Zombie Media: Circuit Bending Media Archaeology into an Art Method'.

TABLES AND FIGURES

BIBLIOGRAPHY

Abbate, Janet. *Inventing the Internet*, Cambridge, MA: MIT press, 2000.

_____. *Recoding gender: Women's changing participation in computing*. MIT Press, 2012.

Agre, Phil. 'Toward a critical technical practice: Lessons learned in trying to reform AI', *Bridging the Great Divide: Social Science, Technical Systems, and Cooperative Work, Mahwah, NJ: Erlbaum* (1997).

Austin, Thomas. '"…to leave the confinements of his humanness": Authorial voice, death and constructions of nature in Werner Herzog's' Grizzly Man'. In Thomas Austin and Wilma de Jong, (eds.) *Rethinking documentary: new perspectives, new practices*. Open University Press, Maidenhead, 2008: pp. 51-66.

Bazin, André. *What is cinema?*. Vol. 2. Univ of California Press, 2004.

Anderson, Benedict. *Imagined communities: Reflections on the origin and spread of nationalism*. London: Verso Books, 2006.

Apple. Thoughts on Flash, 2010, http://www.apple.com/hotnews/thoughts-on-flash/.

Astruc, Alexander. 'The Birth of a New Avant-Garde: La Caméra-Stylo', in Timothy Corrigan (ed) *Film and Literature: An Introduction and Reader*, NJ: Prentice-Hall, 1999 (1948).

Ardèvol, Elisenda, Roig, Antoni, San Cornelio, Gemma, Pagès, Ruth, and Alsina, Pau. 'Playful Practices: Theorising 'New Media' Cultural Production.' In Birgit Bräuchler and John Postill (eds) *Theorising Media and Practice*, New York: Berghahn Books, 2010.

Bakardjieva, Maria and Feenberg, Andrew. 'Involving the Virtual Subject: Conceptual, Methodological and Ethical Dimensions', *Journal of Ethics and Information Technology*, 2.4 (2004): pp. 233-240.

Ballard, James G. 'Interview with JGB by Andrea Juno and Vale', *RE/Search*, no. 8/9, 1984.

Barbrook, Richard and Cameron, Andy. 'The Californian Ideology', 1996, http://www.hrc.wmin.ac.uk/theory-californianideology-main.html.

Barlow, John P. 'A Cyberspace Independence Declaration', 1996, http://w2.eff.org/Censorship/Internet_censorship_bills/barlow_0296.declaration.

Barlow, Melinda M.. 'Feminism 101: The New York Women's Video Festival, 1972–1980', *Camera Obscura*, 18.3 (2003): p. 2-39.

Bassett, Caroline. 'Of distance and closeness: the work of Roger Silverstone', *New Media & Society,* 9.1 (2007).

_____. *The Ark and the Machine: Narrative and New Media*, Manchester University Press, 2007.

_____. 'Is this not a Screen', in Marsha Kinder and Tara McPherson, (eds) *Transmedia Frictions: The Digital, the Arts, and the Humanities*, Berkley and Los Angeles: University of California Press, 2014.

Bassett, Caroline, Hartmann, Maren and O'Riordan, Kathleen. 'After convergence: what connects?', *The Fiberculture Journal*, 2008, http://thirteen.fibreculturejournal.org.

Bazin, André. 'The Ontology of the Photographic Image', in *What is cinema?* Vol 1, Berkley and Los Angeles: University of California Press, 1967.

BBC Press office. 'BBC enters strategic relationship with Adobe to enhance BBC iPlayer and bbc.co.uk', *BBC Press Office*, 2007, http://www.bbc.co.uk/pressoffice/pressreleases/stories/2007/10_october/16/adobe.shtml.

Benkler, Yochai. *The Wealth of Networks: How Social Production Transforms Markets and Freedom,* London: Yale, 2006.

Berners-Lee, Tim. 'The World Wide Web: A very short personal history', 1998, http://www.w3.org/People/Berners-Lee/ShortHistory.html.

Berry, David M. *Copy, Rip, Burn: The Politics of Copyleft and Open Source,* London: Pluto Press, 2008.

_____. *The Philosophy of Software: Code and Mediation in the Digital Age*, London: Palgrave, 2011.

_____. *Understanding Digital Humanities*, London: Palgrave Macmillan, 2012.

Blom, Ina. 'The Autobiography of Video: Outline for a Revisionist Account of Early Video Art', *Critical Inquiry*, 39. 2 (2013): pp. 276-295.

Blood, Rebecca. 'Weblogs: A History and Perspective', *Rebecca's Pocket*, 7 September 2000, www.rebeccablood.net/essays/weblog_history.html.

Bogost, Ian. *Alien Phenomenology, or What It's Like to Be a Thing*, Minneapolis: University of Minnesota Press, 2012.

Bordwell, David and Thompson, Kristin. *Film art: an introduction*, New York: McGraw- Hill, 2007.

Bourdieu, Pierre. 'Towards a Sociology of Photography', *Visual Anthropology Review*, 7.1, Spring, ([1965] 1991).

boyd, danah. 'A Blogger's Blog: Exploring the Definition of a Medium', *Reconstruction*, 6. 4 (2006).

Boyle, Deidre. 'Subject to Change', *Art Journal*, (1985): p. 229-230, http://www.experimentaltvcenter.org/sites/default/files/history/pdf/boylesubjectt ochange_182.pdf.

Brody, Richard. *Everything is Cinema. The Working Life of Jean-Luc Godard*, London: Faber and Faber, 2008.

Brügger, Niels. 'Web history and social media', in *The SAGE Handbook of Social Media*, Jean Burgess, Alice Marwick and Thomas Poell (eds) London : Sage Publications, Incorporated, 2018, pp. 196-212.

Bucher, Taina. 'Want to be on the top? Algorithmic power and the threat of invisibility on Facebook', *New Media & Society*, 14. 7 (2012): pp. 1164- 1180.

Burgess, Jean. 'Re-mediating Vernacular Creativity: Digital Storytelling', Paper Presented at *First Person: International Digital Storytelling Conference*, Australian Centre for the Moving Image, Melbourne, Australia, February 2006, 15 June 2014, from http://eprints.qut.edu.au/3776/1/3376.pdf.

_____. *Vernacular Creativity and New Media,* PhD Diss. Creative Industries Faculty, University of Technology, Queensland, 2007.

Burgess, Jean and Green, Joshua. *YouTube*, Digital Media and Society Series, London: Polity, 2009.

Campanelli, Vito. 'The DivX Experience', in Geert Lovink and Sabine Niederer (eds) *Video Vortex Reader. Responses to YouTube*, Amsterdam: Institute for Networked Cultures, 2011, p. 55-56.

Campbell-Kelly, Martin and Garcia-Swartz, Daniel D.. 'The history of the internet: the missing narratives'. *Journal of Information Technology*, 28.1 (2013): p. 18-33.

Capps, Robert. ' The Good Enough Revolution: When Cheap and Simple Is Just Fine', *Wired*, 2009, from http://archive.wired.com/gadgets/miscellaneous/magazine/17-09/ff_goodenough?currentPage=al.l

Carr, Nicholas. *The shallows: What the Internet is doing to our brains*. WW Norton & Company, 2011.

Castells, Michel. *The Information Age. Vol. I: The Rise Of The Network Society*, Oxford/

Cambridge: Blackwell, 1996.

_____. *The Information Age. Vol. II: The Power Of Identity,* Oxford/Cambridge: Blackwell, 2000.

_____. *The Internet Galaxy*, Oxford/Cambridge: Blackwell, 2001.

Cavell, Stanley. *The world viewed: Reflections on the ontology of film.* London: Harvard University Press, 1979.

Chanan, Michael. 'Tales of a Video Blogger', *Reframe*, 2012, http://reframe.sussex.ac.uk/activistmedia/2013/03/free-e-book-tales-of-a-video- blogger-by-michael-chanan/.

Chapman, Sara. 'Guerrilla Television in the Digital Age', *Journal of Film and Video*, 64.1-2 (2012).

Chen, Steve. Email to Videoblogging list, 3 May 2005, https://groups.yahoo.com/neo/groups/videoblogging/conversations/messages/10362.

Chow, Ray and Steintrager, James A. 'In Pursuit of the Object of Sound' *Differences. A Journal of Feminist Cultural Studies,* 2.2/3 (2011): pp. 1-9.

Christian, Aymar J. 'Joe Swanberg, Intimacy, and the Digital Aesthetic', *Cinema Journal,* 50. 4, Summer, (2011).

Cerf, Vinton G., Leiner, Barry M., Clark, David D., Kahn, Robert E., Kleinrock, Leonard, Lynch, Daniel C., Postel, Jon, Roberts, Larry G., and Wolff, Stephen. 'A Brief History of the Internet', *InternetSociety.org*, https://www.internetsociety.org/internet/history-internet/brief-history-internet/.

Collingwood, Robin G. *The Idea of History*, Oxford: Oxford University Press, 1961.

Compumavengal. Email to Videoblogging list, 10 October 2013, https://groups.yahoo.com/neo/groups/videoblogging/conversations/topics/79534.

Coppola, Francis F. *Hearts of Darkness: A Filmmaker's Apocalypse, Fax* Barh, George Hickenlooper and Eleanor Coppola (Dir) USA: Paramount, 1991.

Corrigan, Timothy , *The Essay Film: From Montaigne, After Marker*, New York: Oxford University Press, 2011.

Couldry, Nick. 'Theorising Media as Practice', *Social Semiotics,* 14. 2 (2004): pp. 117-128.

_____. *Media, society, world: Social theory and digital media practice.* London: Polity, 2012.

Cubitt, Sean. 'Codecs and Capability', in Geert Lovink and Sabine Niederer (eds) *Video Vortex*

Reader. Responses to YouTube, Amsterdam: Institute for Networked Cultures, 2008.

_____. *The Cinema Effect*, Cambridge, Mass.: MIT Press, 2004.

Dawson, Jonathan. 'Dziga Vertov', *Senses of Cinema,* issue 23 (2003).

De Certeau, Manuel. *The Practice of Everyday Life: Living and cooking,* (Trans. Steven Rendall), Berkeley and Los Angeles: University of California Press, 1984.

Dedman, Jay. Email to Videoblogging list, 1 June 2004, https://groups.yahoo.com/neo/groups/videoblogging/conversations/messages/2.

_____. Email to Videoblogging list, 16 Decenber 2005, accessed 18 July 2014 from email digest.

_____. Email to Videoblogging list, 27 January 2009, https://groups.yahoo.com/neo/groups/videoblogging/conversations/topics/73905.

Dedman, Jay and Paul, Joshua. *Videoblogging*, Indianapolis: Wiley Publishing, 2006.

Deleuze, Gilles and Guattari, Felix. *A Thousand Plateaus*, London: Continuum, 2004.

The Economist. 'New Tube', *The Economist*, May 3-9 (2014).

Edwards, Jim. 'Yes, You Can Make Six Figures As A YouTube Star... And Still End Up Poor', 2014, http://www.businessinsider.com/how- much-money-youtube-stars-actually-make-2014-2.

Elsaesser, Thomas. 'Early Film History and Multi-Media: An Archaeology of Possible Futures?' in Wendy H. K. Chun and Thomas Keenan, (eds) *New media, old media: a history and theory reader*, London: Routledge, 2006.

Feldman, Seth. 'Vertov after Manovich', *Canadian Journal of Film Studies*, 16.1, (2007); pp. 39-50.

Fox, Broderick. 'Rethinking the Amateur, Acts of Media Production in the Digital Age', *Spectator*, 24:1 (2004): pp. 5-16.

Franklin, Ursula. *The Real World of Technology,* Ontario: Anansi, 1990.

Fuchs, Christian. 'Against Henry Jenkins. Remarks on Henry Jenkins' ICA Talk "Spreadable Media"' 30 May 2011, http://fuchs.uti.at/570/.

Fuller, Matthew. *Software Studies: A Lexicon*, Cambridge: MIT Press: 2008.

Galloway, Alexander R.. *Protocol: How Control Exists After Decentralization*; MIT Press, 2004.

Gansing, Kristoffer, Bazzichelli, Tatiana, Lillemose, Jacob and Schwierin, Marcel. BWPWAP CURATIORIAL STATEMENT, *Transmediale 2013*, Amsterdam, http://www.transmediale.de/content/bwpwap-curatiorial- statement.

Garcia, David. '(Un)Real-Time Media: 'Got Live if you Want It'', in Geert Lovink and Sabine Niederer, (eds) *Video Vortex Reader: Responses to YouTube*, Amsterdam: The Institute for Network Cultures, 2008.

Garcia, David and Lovink, Geert. The ABC of Tactical Media, *Nettime*, 1997, http://www.nettime.org/Lists-Archives/nettime-l-9705/msg00096.html.

Garfield, Steve. *Year of the Videoblog*, 2004, https://web.archive.org/web/20041231011613/http://homepage.mac.com/st evegarfield/videoblog/year_of.html.

Geoghegan, Bernard D. 'After Kittler: On the Cultural Techniques of Recent German Media Theory', *Theory, Culture & Society*, 30. 6 (2013): pp. 66-82.

Gillette, Felix. 'Hollywood's Big-Money YouTube Hit Factory', Blooberg Businessweek, accessed 08 September 2014 from http://www.businessweek.com/articles/2014-08-28/youtube-hollywoods-hit-factory-for-teen-entertainment.

Goode, Luke. 'Social news, citizen journalism and democracy', *New Media & Society,* 11.8 (2009): pp. 1287-1305.

Grant, Catherine. 'The audiovisual essay as performative research', NECSUS: European Journal of Media Studies, Autumn 2016, http://www.necsus-ejms.org/the-audiovisual-essay-as-performative-research/.

Grossman, Lev. 'You — Yes, You — Are TIME's Person of the Year, *Time Magazine'*, 2006 http://content.time.com/time/magazine/article/0,9171,1570810,00.html.

Gunning, Tom. 'Systematizing the Electric Message', in Charlie Keil and Shelley Stamp (eds) *American Cinema's Transitional Era: Audiences, Institutions, Practices,* Berkeley: University of California Press, 2004.

Gerlitz, Carolin and Helmond, Anne. 'The Like economy: Social buttons and the data-intensive web', *New Media & Society*, 15. 8 (2013): pp. 1348-1365.

Gye, Lisa. 'Picture This: the Impact of Mobile Camera Phones on Personal Photographic Practices', *Continuum: Journal of Media & Cultural Studies*, 21. 2 (2007).

Hall, Laura E. 'What Happens When Digital Cities Are Abandoned?', *The Atlantic*, 2014, http://www.theatlantic.com/technology/archive/2014/07/what-happens-when-digital-cities-are-abandoned/373941/.

Hardt, Michael and Negri, Antonio. *Multitude*, London: Hamish Hamilton, 2005.

Harraway, Donna. 'A cyborg manifesto: Science, technology, and socialist-feminism in the late 20th century.' *The international handbook of virtual learning environments* (2006).

Hayles, N. Katherine. 'Print is flat, code is deep: The importance of media-specific analysis', *Poetics Today*, 25.1 (2004): pp. 67-90.

Heffernan, Virginia. 'Uploading the Avant-Garde', *The New York Times*, 3 September 2009, http://www.nytimes.com/2009/09/06/magazine/06FOB-medium- t.html?_r=0.

Herring, Susan C., Scheidt, Lois Ann, Bonus, Sabrina and Wright, Elijah. 'Bridging the Gap: A Genre Analysis of Weblogs', *System Sciences*, 2004.

Hertz, Garnet and Parikka, Jussi. 'Five Principles of Zombie Media', *Defunct/Refunct*, (2012) http://ruared.ie/Documents/defunct_refunct_catalogue_web.pdf.

_____. 'Zombie Media: Circuit Bending Media Archaeology into an Art Method', *Leonardo*, 45.5 (2012): pp. 424–430.

Hicks, Jeremy. *Dziga Vertov: defining documentary film*, London: IB Tauris, 2006.

Hoby, Hermione and Lamont, Tom. 'How YouTube made superstars out of everyday people', The Guardian, 11 April 2010, http://www.theguardian.com/technology/2010/apr/11/youtube-web-video-stars.

Hodson, Ryanne and Verdi, Michael. *Secrets of Videoblogging*, Berkeley: PeachPit Press, 2006.

Hodson, Ryanne and Van Every, S. *Tools*. Video from Vloggercon 2005, https://archive.org/details/VloggerCon05SessionsTOOLStoolsvloggercon05mov.

Hof, Karina. 'Something you can actually pick up: Scrapbooking as a form and forum of cultural citizenship', E*uropean Journal of Cultural Studies*, 9. 3 (2006); pp. 363-384.

Hondros, John. *Ecologies of Internet Video: Beyond YouTube*. New York: Routledge, 2018.

Hope, Charles. Email to Videoblogging list 10 May 2005, https://groups.yahoo.com/neo/groups/videoblogging/conversations/messages/10 817.

Howe, Rupert. Email to Videoblogging List 30 May 2014, https://groups.yahoo.com/neo/groups/videoblogging/conversations/messages/79 558.

Huhtamo, Erkki. 'From Kaleidoscomaniac to Cybernerd. Towards an Archeology of the Media' 19 June 2014, 1997, from http://www.stanford.edu/class/history34q/readings/MediaArchae-ology/HuhtamoArchaeologyOfMedia.html.

Huhtamo, Erkki and Parikka, Jussi. *Media Archaeology: Approaches, Applications, and Impli-ations*, London: University of California Press, 2011.

Jenkins, Henry. *Convergence Culture. Where Old and New Media Collide*, New York: New York University Press, 2006.

_____. 'What happened before YouTube?', in Jean Burgess and Joshua Green (eds) *YouTube. Digital Media and Society Series,* Cambridge: Polity, 2009.

Jimroglou, Krissi M. 'A Camera with a view JenniCAM: visual representation, and cyborg subjectivity', *Information, Communication & Society*, 2. 4 (1999): pp. 439 – 453.

Juhasz, Alexandra. 'Learning from YouTube [Video Book].' *MIT Press (BK)* (2011).

Kattelle, Alan. 'A Brief History of Amateur Film Gauges and Related Equipment, 1899-2001', 17 July 2014, http://oldfilm.org/content/brief-history- amateur-film-gauges-and-related-equip-ment-1899-2001.

Keen, Andrew. *The Cult of the Amateur: How blogs, MySpace, YouTube, and the rest of today's user-generated media are destroying our economy, our culture, and our values*, Ran-dom House, 2007.

Kember, Sarah and Zylinska, Joanna. *Life After New Media,* Cambridge, MA: MIT Press, 2012.

Kinberg, Joshua, Email to Yahoo Email List, 12 July 2005, https://groups.yahoo.com/neo/groups/videoblogging/conversations/messages/16 402.

Kinder, Marsha. 'The Conceptual Power of On-Line Video: 5 Easy Piece', in Geert Lovink and Sabine Niederer, (eds) *Video Vortex Reader: Responses to YouTube*, Amsterdam: The Institute for Network Cultures, 2008.

Kirschenbaum, Matthew. 'Extreme Inscription: The Grammatology of the Hard Drive', *Text Technology,* 13. 2 (2004): pp. 91-125.

Siegfried Kracauer, *Theory of film: The redemption of physical reality*. Princeton University Press, 1960.

Lange, Patricia. 'The Vulnerable Video Blogger: Promoting Social Change through Intimacy', *The Scholar and Feminist Online*, 5. 2 (2007) www.barnard.edu/sfonline, 2007.

_____. '(Mis)Conceptions about YouTube', in Geert Lovink and Sabine Niederer (eds) *Video*

Vortex Reader. Responses to YouTube, Amsterdam: Institute for Networked Cultures, 2008.

_____. 'Publicly Private and Privately Public: Social Networking on YouTube', *Journal of Computer-Mediated Communication,* 13, (2008): pp. 361-380.

Langlois, Ganaele, McKelvey, Fenwick, Elmer, Greg, and Werbin, Kenneth. 'Mapping Commercial Web 2.0 Worlds: Towards a New Critical Ontogenesis'. *Fibreculture* 14 (2009): p. 1-14.

Lanier, Jaron. 'DIGITAL MAOISM: The Hazards of the New Online Collectivism', *Edge*, 2006, http://edge.org/conversation/digital-maoism- the-hazards-of-the-new-online-collectivism.

Lessig, Lawrence. *Free Culture*, London: Penguin Press, 2003.

Lialina, Olia. 'A Vernacular Web, The Indigenous and The Barbarians', talk at the Decade of Web Design Conference in Amsterdam, January 2005, http://art.teleportacia.org/observation/vernacular/.

Livingstone, Sonia. 'Media literacy and the challenge of new information and communication technologies'. *Communication Review*, 7.3-14 (2004): p. 3-14.

Lovejoy, Margot. *Digital Currents; Art in the Electronic Age,* London: Routledge, 2004.

Lovink, Geert. 'Tactical Media, the Second Decade', 2005, http://geertlovink.org/texts/tactical-media-the-second-decade/.

_____. 'The Art of Watching Databases', in Geert Lovink and Sabine Niederer (eds) *Video Vortex Reader. Responses to YouTube*, Amsterdam: Institute for Networked Cultures, 2008.

_____. 'Engage in Destiny Design: Online Video beyond Hypergrowth', in Geert Lovink and Rachel Somers Miles (eds) *Video Vortex Reader II: Moving Images Beyond YouTube*, Amsterdam: Institute for Networked Cultures, 2011.

_____. 'Engage in Destiny Design: Online Video beyond Hypergrowth', in Geert Lovink and Racheal Somers Miles, (Eds) *Video Vortex Reader II: Moving Images Beyond YouTube*, Amsterdam: Institute for Networked Cultures, 2011.

_____. 'What Is the Social in Social Media?', *E-flux,* accessed 19 March 2013 from http://www.e-flux.com/journal/what-is-the-social-in-social-media/ (December 2012).

Luers, Will. Email to Vlog Theory List, 4 Octover 2006, https://groups.yahoo.com/neo/groups/vlogtheory/conversations/messages/840.

_____. 'Cinema Without Show Business: a Poetics of Vlogging', *Post Identity* 5.1 (2007).

Manovich, Lev. *The Language of New Media*, London: MIT Press, 2001.

_____. *Software Takes Command*, London: Bloomsbury Academic, 2013.

_____. 'Visualizing Vertov', *Russian Journal of Communication,* 5. 1, (2013) pp. 44-55.

Marker, Chris. 'Marker Direct', *Film Comment,* 39.3 (2003).

Matthews, Nicole. 'Confessions to a new public: Video Nation Shorts', *Media Culture & Society,* 29. 3 (2007): pp. 435-448.

McLaughlin, Jan. Email to Videoblogging list, 21 August 2005, https://groups.yahoo.com/neo/groups/videoblogging/conversations/messages/20517.

_____. Email to Videoblogging list, 15 June 2015, https://groups.yahoo.com/neo/groups/videoblogging/conversations/messages/14072.

McLuhan, Marshall. *Understandig media. The Extensions of Man.* New York: Routledge, 1964.

Merrin, William. 'Still fighting "the Beast": Guerrilla television and the limits of YouTube.' *Cultural Politics,* 8.1 (2012): p 97-119.

Metz, Christian. *Film Language: A Semiotics of the Cinema,* University Of Chicago Press, 1990.

Mitchem, Matthew. 'Video Social: Complex Parasitical Media', in Geert Lovink and Sabine Niederer (eds) *Video Vortex Reader. Responses to YouTube,* Amsterdam: Institute for Networked Cultures, 2008.

Miles, Adrian. *Vogma, a Manifesto,* http://hypertext.rmit.edu.au/vog/manifesto/, 2000.

_____. Email to Videoblogging list, 18 June 2004, https://groups.yahoo.com/neo/groups/videoblogging/conversations/messages/44.

_____. Email to Videoblogging list, 22 July 2004, https://groups.yahoo.com/neo/groups/videoblogging/conversations/messages/38 7

_____. Email to Videoblogging list, 26 May 2005, https://groups.yahoo.com/neo/groups/videoblogging/conversations/messages/12 165.

_____. 'A Vision for Genuine Rich Media Blogging', in Aksel Bruns and Joanne Jacobs (eds), *The Uses of Blogs,* New York: Peter Lang, 2006.

_____. 'Softvideography: Digital Video as Postliterate Practice', in Byron Hawk, David M. Rieder and Ollie Oviedo (eds) *Small Tech: The Culture of Digital Tools,* Minneapolis: University of Minnesota Press, 2008.

_____. 'Vine and Light (a poetics of the sublime ordinary)', 29 Janary 2013 from http://vogmae.

net.au/vlog/2013/01/vine-and-lightt-a-poetics- of-the-sublime-ordinary/.

Moglen, Eben. 'The DotCommunist Manifesto: How Culture Became Property and What We're Going to Do About It', 2001, http://moglen.law.columbia.edu.

Morozov, Evgeny. The Meme Hustler, *The Baffler,* 2013, http://www.thebaffler.com/salvos/the-meme-hustler.

Morrison, Aimee H. 'An impossible future: John Perry Barlow's "Declaration of the Independence of Cyberspace"', *New Media & Society*, 11.1-2, (2009): p. 53-71.

Morse, Margaret. 'Virtually Female: Body and Code', in Jennifer Terry and Melodie Calvert (eds) *Processed Lives; Gender and Technology in Everyday Life*, London: Routledge, 1997.

Nagle, Angela. *Kill all normies: Online culture wars from 4chan and Tumblr to Trump and the alt-right.* John Hunt Publishing, 2017.

Naughton, John. *A Brief History of the Future*, London: Phoenix Press, 1999.

Neale, Steve. *Cinema and Technology: Image, Sound, Colour*, London: Macmillan Education, 1985.

Negroponte, Nicholas. *Being Digital*, New York: Vintage, 1996.

Nelson, Ted. Branching presentational systems-Hypermedia, *Dream Machines*, 1974.

Newman, Michael Z. 'Ze Frank and the poetics of Web video', *First Monday,* 13.5. 2008.

Nicholson, Heather N. 'In amateur hands: framing time and space in home-movies', *History Workshop Journal*, 43 (1997): p. 198-213.

Noble, Safiya U. *Algorithms of Oppression: How search engines reinforce racism.* NYU Press, 2018.

O'Reilly, Tim. 'What is Web 2.0. Design Patterns and Business Models for the Next Generation of Software', 2005, from http://oreilly.com/web2/archive/what-is-web-20.html.

Pasternack, Alex. 'The Other Shooter: The Saddest and Most Expensive 26 Seconds of Amateur Film Ever Made', *Motherboard*, 15 July 2014, http://motherboard.vice.com/en_uk/blog/the-other-shooter-the-saddest-and- most-expensive-26-seconds-of-amateur-film-ever-made.

Parikka, Jussi. *What is Media Archaeology?* Cambridge: Polity, 2012.

_____. 'Friedrich Kittler - a media anthropology without the Man?' (2011), http://www.media-anthropology.net/ file/parikka_kittler.pdf.

Pariser, Eli. *The filter bubble: What the Internet is hiding from you*. Penguin UK, 2011.

Pettman, Dominic. 'Pavlov's Podcast: The Acousmatic Voice in the Age of MP3s', in Rey Chow and James Steintrager (Eds) *Differences. A Journal of Feminist Cultural Studies*, 22. 2&3 (2011).

Plato. *Plato in Twelve Volumes*, Vol. 1 (Trans. Harold North Fowler; Introduction by W.R.M. Lamb), Cambridge, MA: Harvard University Press, 1966.

Poe, Marshall T. *A History of Communications: Media and Society from the Evolution of Speech to the Internet*, Cambridge: Cambridge University Press, 2011.

Postill, John and Bräuchler, Birgit. 'Introduction: Theorising Media and Practice.' In John Postill and Birgit Bräuchler (eds) *Theorising Media and Practice*, New York: Berghahn Books, 2010.

Quirk, Adam. Email to Videoblogging list, 15 June 2015, https://groups.yahoo.com/neo/groups/videoblogging/conversations/messages/14050.

Rascaroli, Laura. 'The essay film: Problems, definitions, textual commitments.' *Framework: The Journal of Cinema and Media* 49, 2 (2008): p. 24-47.

Raymond, Eric S. *The Cathedral & the Bazaar*, Beijing: O'Reilly Media, 2001.

Renov, Michael. *The Subject of Documentary*, London: University of Minneapolis Press, 2004.

Rheingold, Howard. *The virtual community: Homesteading on the electronic frontier*. Harvard: MIT press, 2000.

Richard, Brigit. 'Media Masters and Grassroots Art 2.0 on YouTube', in Geert Lovink and Sabine Niederer, (eds) *Video Vortex Reader: Responses to YouTube*, Amsterdam: The Institute for Network Cultures, 2008.

Rieder, Bernard. 'Studying Facebook via data extraction: the Netvizz application', in *Proceedings of the 5th Annual ACM Web Science Conference,* (2013): pp. 346-355).

Rodowick, David N. *The virtual life of film*, Cambridge, MA: Harvard University Press, 2007.

Scalin, Mica. Email list, 2004, https://groups.yahoo.com/neo/groups/videoblogging/conversations/topics/3.

Scholz, Trebor. The Participatory Turn in Social Life Online, 2007, http://www.slideshare.net/trebor/the-participatory-turn.

Shamberg, Michael. *Guerilla Television,* New York, NY: Holt, Rinehart and Winston, 1971.

Sharp, Clint. Email to Videoblogging list, 10 May 2005, https://groups.yahoo.com/neo/groups/videoblogging/conversations/messages/10 816.

_____. Email to videoblogging list, 14 July 2005, https://groups.yahoo.com/neo/groups/video-blogging/conversations/messag es/16789.

Sherman, Tom. 'The Nine Lives of Video Art: Technological evolution, the repeated near-death of video art, and the life force of vernacular video...' Lecture held during the conference 'Video Vortex - Responses to YouTube', Amsterdam, 18 January 2008.

Silverstone, Roger. *Television and Everyday Life,* London: Routledge, 1994.

_____. *Why Study The Media?,* London: Sage, 1999.

_____. *Media and Morality: On the Rise of the Mediapolis,* Cambridge: Polity Press, 2006.

Snickars, Pelle and Vonderau, Patrick. *The YouTube Reader*, Stockholm: Mediehistorisk arkiv, 2009.

Stark, Trevor. 'Cinema in the Hands of the People': Chris Marker, the Medvedkin Group, and the Potential of Militant Film, *October Magazine*, 139 (2010): p. 117-150.

Sterne, Jonathan. *MP3: The meaning of a format.* Duke University Press, 2012.

Sterne, Jonathan, Morris, Jeremy, Baker, Michael Brendan, and Moscote, Ariana. 'The Politics of Podcasting', *Fibreculture*, issue 13 (2008).

Steyerl, Hito. 'In Defence of Poor images', *e-flux journal,* 10.11 (2009).

Street, T. Email to Videoblogging list, 30 May 2014, https://groups.yahoo.com/neo/groups/videoblogging/conversations/messages/79 563.

Sullivan, Michael. Email to Videoblogging list, 8 November 2005, https://groups.yahoo.com/neo/groups/videoblogging/conversations/messages/26 271.

_____. Email to Videoblogging list, 8 April 2009, https://groups.yahoo.com/neo/groups/video-blogging/conversations/messages/74645.

Taylor, Astra. *The people's platform: Taking back power and culture in the digital age.* Metropolitan books, 2014.

Teller, Enric. Email to Videoblogging list, 7 July 2006, https://groups.yahoo.com/neo/groups/videoblogging/conversations/messages/44493.

Terranova, Tiziana. 'Free Labour: Producing Culture in the Digital Economy', *Social Text,* 18.

2 (2000): 33–58.

Treske, Andreas. *The Inner Lives of Video Spheres*, Amsterdam: Institute for Network Cultures, 2013.

Turkle, Sherry. *Life On the Screen: Identity in the Age of the Internet*, London: Simon & Schuster, 1995.

_____. *Alone together: Why we expect more from technology and less from each other.* Hachette UK, 2017.

Turner, Fred. *From counterculture to cyberculture: Stewart Brand, the Whole Earth Network, and the rise of digital utopianism.* University of Chicago Press, 2010.

Uricchio, William. 'The Future of a Medium Once Known as Television', in Pelle Snickars and Patrick Vanderau (eds) *The YouTube Reader*, Mediehistorisk arkiv, 2009.

Vanderbeeken, Robrecht. Web Video and the Screen as a Mediator and Generator of Reality, in Geert Lovink and Rachel Somers Miles (eds) *Video Vortex Reader II: Moving Images Beyond YouTube*, Amsterdam: Institute for Networked Cultures, 2011.

van Dijck, José. 'Users like you? Theorizing agency in user-generated content', *Media, Culture & Society,* 31.1 (2009): pp. 41-58.

_____. 'Television 2.0: YouTube and the emergence of homecasting.' *Creativity, Ownership and Collaboration in the Digital Age, Cambridge, Massachusetts Institute of Technology* (2007): p. 27-29.

Verhoeff, Nanna. *Mobile screens: The visual regime of navigation,* Amsterdam University Press, 2012.

Wardrip-Fruin, Noah and Montfort, Nick. *The NewMediaReader*, Cambridge, MA: MIT Press, 2003.

Watkins, Steve. Email to Videoblogging list, 15 July 2005, https://groups.yahoo.com/neo/groups/videoblogging/conversations/messages/16 975.

_____. Email to Videoblogging list, 6 December 2006, https://groups.yahoo.com/neo/groups/videoblogging/conversations/messages/53080.

The Web Ahead. 'Videoblogging with Jay Dedman, Ryanne Hodson and Michael Verdi' [transcript], accessed 16 September 2014 from http://5by5.tv/webahead/76.

Wild, Helga. 'Practice and the Theory of Practice. Rereading Certeau's "Practice of Everyday Life"', *Journal of Business Anthropology*, Spring (2012).

Willett, Rebekah. 'Always on: Camera Phones, Video Production and Identity', in David Buckingham and Rebekah Willett (eds) *Video cultures,* London: Palgrave McMillan, 2009.

Williams, Raymond. *Television: technology and cultural form*, London: Routledge, 1990 (1974).

Zimmerman, Patricia. *Reel Families: A social history of Amateur Film*, Indiana University Press, 1995.

FILM/VIDEOGRAPHY

Baron, Andrew. *Rocketboom*, Episode 2, 2004, http://cdn.rocketboom.com/video/rb_04_oct_28.mov.

Coppola, Francis Ford. *Hearts of Darkness: A Filmmaker's Apocalypse,* Barh, F., Hickenlooper, G. and Coppola, E., (Dir) USA: Paramount, 1991.

Falla, Juan. *Greetings*, 19 August 2005, http://viviendoconfallas.blogspot.com/2005/08/vlog-01-our-first-vlog-nuestro-primer.htm.l

____. *Sancocho*, 15 Septebmer 2006 http://viviendoconfallas.blogspot.com/2006/09/vlog-47-e33-sancocho.html.

Garfield, Steve. *Year of the Videoblog*, 1 January 2004, https://web.archive.org/web/20041231011613/http://homepage.mac.com/stevegarfield/videoblog/year_of.html.

Hodson, Ryanne. *Excited*, 1 December 2004, http://www.archive.org/download/excitedmov/excited.mov.

____. *V-blog conversations*, 4 December 2004, http://www.archive.org/download/V-blogConversation_494/conversation3001.mov.

Hodson, Ryanne, and Van Every, S. *Tools*. Video from Vloggercon, 7 February 2005, https://archive.org/details/VloggerCon05SessionsTOOLStoolsvloggercon05mov.

Howe, Rupert. *London Bombings – should I stay or should I go*, 2006, http://www.momma-radio.com/fatgirlinohio/2007/03/re-vlog-london-bombings-should-i-stay.html.

_____. *Anarchy in the UK,* 2007, http://twittervlog.tv/2007/05/15/my-music-video-for-vlog-deathmatch/.

Liss, Daniel. *Pouringdown: Seven Maps*, 30 June 2006, http://pouringdown.tv/sevenmaps/.

_____. *Theory: Practice*, 3 February 2006, http://pouringdown.tv/?p=21.

_____. *World Maps*, 8 March 2006, http://pouringdown.tv/?p=28.

Lumière, Auguste, and Lumière, Louis. *L'Arrivée d'un train en gare de La Ciotat,*1895, Société Lumière.

Marker, Chris. *A bientot j'espere*, United States of America: Iskra Societe pour le Lancement des Oeuvres Nouvelles (SLON), 1968.

Miles, Adrian. *Welcome*, 6 December 2000, http://hypertext.rmit.edu.au/vog/vog_archive/000082.html.

Nealy, Erin. *Mornings*, 2006, https://www.youtube.com/watch?v=db4TaJ1xExE&list=PLXem-bWNMLs6BMZxSETpnhvILAre4uOEKl&index=24.

_____. *Mom's Brag Vlog,* accessed 5 December 2017 from http://nealey.blogspot.com.

Quirk, Adam. *video is fun of this computer website!*, 6 September 2006, https://www.youtube.com/watch?v=2DvHIxV2oQ0.

Rule, Charlene. *Dear Tesla*, 17 January 2007, http://www.scratchvideo.tv/videos/janu-ary-17th-2012.

____. *Quarterplus*, 13 April 2012, http://www.scratchvideo.tv/videos/quarter-plus.

Verdi, Michael. *Vlog Anarchy*, 19 May 2005, http://archive.org/details/MichaelVerdiVlogAn-archy.

INDEX